Artificial Inte
Ethics and
International Law

Practical approaches to AI governance

2nd Edition

Abhivardhan

www.bpbonline.com

First published: 2019

Second published: 2024

Published by BPB Online
WeWork
119 Marylebone Road
London NW1 5PU

UK | UAE | INDIA | SINGAPORE

ISBN 978-93-55516-220

www.bpbonline.com

Dedicated to

My mother

My father

and

The most beloved,

Team **ISAIL**

&

Indic Pacific

Foreword

Professor Andy Pardoe
Chair Deep Tech Innovation Centre University of Warwick

In the 21st century, we find ourselves at the intersection of two transformative forces that are reshaping the world as we know it: Artificial Intelligence and the field of law. The convergence of these two domains has given rise to a fascinating and dynamic field with profound implications for society, technology, and the legal landscape. It is my distinct pleasure to introduce this thought-provoking and insightful book, a comprehensive exploration of the complex relationship between AI and the legal world.

The emergence of artificial intelligence has brought about a paradigm shift across various sectors, offering unprecedented opportunities and challenges. In the realm of law, AI is revolutionizing how legal professionals conduct research, manage cases, draft documents, predict outcomes, and even assist in legal decision-making. At the same time, it poses critical questions surrounding ethics, accountability, transparency, and privacy. This book delves deep into these issues, providing readers with a nuanced understanding of the evolving landscape between AI and the legal industry.

Over the last few years, we have seen the remarkable progress that AI has made in its ability to process vast volumes of data, recognize patterns, and make predictions with a degree of accuracy that was previously unimaginable. AI-powered legal tools can analyse contracts, extract essential information, and assess compliance, all in a fraction of the time it would take a human attorney. Moreover, AI algorithms can sift through enormous datasets to uncover hidden insights and precedents, thereby assisting in legal research.

However, as the power of AI in the legal domain becomes increasingly evident, so do the challenges it poses. The author has taken a holistic approach, addressing the multifaceted issues surrounding AI in the legal profession. They tackle the ethical considerations related to AI's decision-making processes and its potential for bias, and they delve into the essential question of how to establish accountability when AI systems are involved in legal matters. Furthermore, the book explores the nuances of data privacy and human autonomy in the context of AI ethics.

The interdisciplinary nature of AI and law makes it a subject of profound relevance, not only to lawyers and legal scholars but to technologists, policymakers, ethicists, and society at large. It is imperative that these disciplines come together to deliberate on the implications, potentials, and limits of AI in the legal field.

This book stands as an invaluable resource for anyone interested in this dynamic and evolving field. Through meticulous research, deep expertise, and forward-thinking insights, this text provides an essential guide to understanding the intricacies of AI in the legal world.

In conclusion, the convergence of AI and law is an unstoppable force, reshaping the way we practice and perceive law. As we continue to navigate this frontier, we must remain informed, ethically grounded, and committed to harnessing the full potential of AI while mitigating its risks.

Foreword

Sanjay Notani
Partner
Economic Laws Practice

In an age where technology continuously reshapes our understanding of the world, this book stands as an emblematic exploration of the multifaceted interplay between emerging AI technologies and the foundational tenets of global legal frameworks.

The advent of Artificial Intelligence has been remarkable. As AI systems edge closer to achieving the state of the 'theory of mind', we are compelled to grapple with profound challenges. AI anthropomorphism—the inherent human-like nature ascribed to AI systems—introduces nuanced dimensions to concepts of content and identity, compelling us to reckon with the implications of machines making decisions reminiscent of human cognition.

The evolution of AI, as the opening chapter illustrates, isn't simply a technical marvel; it raises questions about the very structure and applicability of our legal systems. Can AI truly grasp and mold legal taxonomies? How do we navigate the maze of biases, data quality issues, and the inherent unpredictability of machine learning? The parallels drawn between the common law system and machine learning techniques illustrate the deep-rooted structural challenges in assimilating AI into our legal frameworks.

The discussion on AI's intertwining with international law goes beyond the superficial. It delves into how AI interacts with seminal concepts like human autonomy and the privacy doctrine, casting light on the intrinsic and instrumental legal issues concerning AI technologies. The narrative draws from rich historical and philosophical insights—from Aristotle's foundational views on ethics to Descartes' musings on automata—to dissect AI's potential and perils in the legal sphere.

Furthermore, the exploration of human rights within the book holds pertinence. At a juncture where international law is grappling with the increasing influence of technology, understanding the potential human-centric implications of AI becomes paramount. Issues ranging from data specificity and quality to the complexities of AI auditing and explainability are adeptly analysed, grounding the discourse in the practical realities of our times.

In essence, this book isn't merely a discourse on AI and international law; it is a timely reflection on the broader ethical, philosophical, and practical dimensions of AI's growing presence in our global society. As we stand at the crossroads of unprecedented technological innovation and legal evolution, "Artificial Intelligence and International Law" offers readers both a mirror to our present and a lens into our future.

Testimonials

I have read several publications relating to Artificial Intelligence (AI), but I must recognize that none is anywhere near this book authored by Abhivardhan, in so far as intellectual understanding of AI is concerned. The instant published work is so enlightening, practical, and reasoned that it becomes a must-read for all.

Hemant Batra

Corporate & Public Policy Lawyer & Founder, MentorTalk™
Sr Legal Consultant & Lead (New Ventures & Growth),
Shardul Amarchand Mangaldas
Elected Vice President, SAARCLAW
(SAARC Regional Apex Body - Inter-Governmental)

This book is a comprehensive and insightful guide to the complex intersection of AI and international law. One of the things that sets this book apart from other books on AI and law is its focus on the Indian and Global perspective. Abhivardhan discusses the different ways in which AI is being regulated and proliferated around the world and the challenges that need to be addressed in order to ensure that AI is used in a responsible and ethical manner. It is a must-read for lawyers, policymakers, and anyone else interested in the future of AI.

Ish Jain

FCIArb, FHKIArb, FMIArb, FAMINZ,
CIA (AiADR), FPD, SFBiam, FIDRC, MICA
Senior Partner, Regius Legal LLP
Arbitrator and Mediator

The book, AI and International Law, 2nd Edition is a comprehensive and detailed work that brings perspectives from a multi- disciplinary and multi- faceted approach of the benefits as well as the challenges posed in regulating artificial intelligence. The deep inquiries undertaken in the work shows the commendable efforts of the author in showcasing the realities as well as the possibilities of governance of artificial intelligence in international law. This is a must have book for law, policy and tech professionals.

Manohar Samal
Senior Associate, Ratan Samal & Associates
Arbitrator, Asia Pacific Centre for Arbitration and Mediation & the
Indian Institute of Arbitration and Mediation

An essential read packed with insight and knowledge on the subject. An authoritative text! A must for anyone interested in the subject!

Rodney D Ryder
Founding Partner, Scriboard

About the Author

Abhivardhan is honoured to serve as the Chairperson and Managing Trustee of the Indian Society of Artificial Intelligence and Law and as the Managing Partner at Indic Pacific Legal Research. Throughout his journey, he has gained valuable experience in international technology law, corporate innovation, global governance, and cultural intelligence.

With deep respect for the field, Abhivardhan has been fortunate to contribute to esteemed law, technology, and policy magazines and blogs including *The Daily Guardian*, *The Contemporary Law Forum*, *India Business Law Journal*, and others. His book, *"Artificial Intelligence Ethics and International Law: An Introduction"* (2019), modestly represents his exploration of the important connection between artificial intelligence and ethical considerations with an international law perspective. Emphasizing the significance of an **Indic approach to AI Ethics**, Abhivardhan aims to bring diverse perspectives to the table.

Abhivardhan remains humbled by the opportunity to share knowledge through various papers on international technology law. Alongside his consulting and policy advocacy, he has been involved in both authoring and editing books, focusing on public international law and its relationship with artificial intelligence.

Maintaining a down-to-earth approach, Abhivardhan's speaking and research interests revolve around Indo-Pacific affairs, disruptive technology ethics and policies, artificial intelligence governance, Indo-European culture and music, global governance, sustainable development, digital connectivity, and public international law.

About the Reviewer

Manohar Samal MCIArb is a Senior Associate at Ratan Samal and Associates, Mumbai and an Arbitrator at the Asia Pacific Centre for Arbitration and Mediation. He specializes in tax, customs, and securities litigation along with commercial arbitration of technology transfer, banking and construction disputes. He has more than 70 publications under his belt, spanning from Government funded technical reports, SCOPUS indexed journal papers, blogs and law magazine articles.

Acknowledgement

The second edition of this book has brought its own share of delight. In reality, I feel grateful to present another edition of this comprehensive book on artificial intelligence and law after the pandemic. I extend my gratitude to my *parents* and my colleagues at *Indic Pacific Legal Research* and the *Indian Society of Artificial Intelligence and Law*. I also acknowledge and appreciate the long-running technical editing process for this book and express my gratitude to the diligent team at **BPB**.

My special regards go to **Akash Manwani**, a talented expert in AI and Law, and the *Chief Innovation Consultant* at the *Indian Society of Artificial Intelligence and Law*, **Abhishek Jain**, former *Chief Managing Editor* of the *Indian Journal of Artificial Intelligence and Law*, **Bhavana J Sekhar**, *Principal Researcher*, and **Sanad Arora**, *Senior Research Associate* at *Indic Pacific*. I am grateful for the *forewords* authored by Mr. **Sanjay Notani** and Dr. **Andy Pardoe**, as well as the *editorial reviews* for this book written by legal luminaries such as Mr. **Hemant Batra**, Mr. **Ish Jain**, Mr. **Manohar Samal** and Mr. **Rodney D. Ryder**.

I also express my gratitude to my dearest friends, **Vaibhav Dwivedi**, **Vignaesh B**, **Vedant Sinha** and **Pratejas Tomar**. Their moral support has been invaluable during the pandemic, in some of the toughest times.

Preface

Technology defines the course and growth of human civilization. It rekindles and rhymes historical trends and patterns, including the confluence of myths and facts. My interest in mathematics and the concept of gravity, was since my childhood and teenage days. I have been fond of reading and hearing folklores and stories related to the cyclicity of time, the geodic shape of planet Earth, the water cycle and many other fascinating natural truths, in the multicultural, diverse and colourful Indic fold, which is observable in any region, city and even village, in India. That indeed enriched my curiosity further to pursue law as a field in social sciences, considering the analytical skeleton of the field, and its far-reaching effects in any average society. As I had started pursuing bachelor's in law, I became increasingly interested in the concept of privacy, in jurisprudence. Since then, I have been interested in semantics and the literature of English as well as Indic languages, I have authored 4 collections of poems in Hindi and English in total, since my teenage years. I still remember writing an article for the *Philosophical Quarterly* on **Intentional Action**, long before my board examinations, just out of my curiosity in *Shrimad Bhagavad Gita* and our Itihasas, especially the *Mahabharat*. Perhaps when I had joined law school, that fervent interest in technology law and international affairs, blossomed at its very best.

My encounter with the field had begun due to my curiosity in metaphysics and Freudian psychodynamics, which led me further to read about the concept of human agency, with both Indian and European contexts. It turned out that the Indian and European aspects share a profound semblance of astute respect and concern for coherent and rules-based systems. The European philosophical fold dominated its discourse on why the individual must have privacy, while the Indian fold, emphasized on a duty-based relationship between the individual and the collective, which further made me interested to author a short work on the concept of Privacy, from the perspective of a "pseudo-contract". That indeed led me to emphasize on the field of technological history, and so artificial intelligence. Scholars such as *Nassim Nicholas Taleb, Sanjeev Sanyal, Dr Jeffrey Funk, Mariana Mazzucato, Friedrich Hayek, Dr S Jaishankar, Karl Popper, Elon Musk* and *Ludwig von Mises* have inspired my thoughts on innovation along with various other Indian and European artistes and authors.

My perspective of technology, in a purely genealogical manner, does not limit up to the finite definitions of information technology. I have been fascinated by technology distancing, which further encouraged me to understand artificial intelligence as an ethical concept, as well as a kind of technology. I realized that in the domain of artificial intelligence ethics, there should be an India-centric global approach, due to which I founded the Indian

Society of Artificial Intelligence and Law, which is not-for-proft industry body, pioneering in advocating for issues related to artificial intelligence ethics & law, including gradual artificial intelligence standardisation.

My research interests have remained in fields like international technology law, global governance, civilization science, public international law, conflict economy, policy dynamics, ethics of artificial intelligence & international affairs. I have published various legal as well as policy-related papers, articles and reports, in technology law (especially artificial intelligence ethics and law). I have been an editorial board member of a few publications, and have also started 2 online law journals, *Indic Journal of International Law* [e-ISSN: 2582-8398] & *Indian Journal of Artificial Intelligence and Law* [e-ISSN: 2582-6999], and 1 online law-policy magazine, *The Indian Learning* [e-ISSN: 2582-5631]. Perhaps, all of that meant something in the long run, when it all started with that one article I had authored for *Philosophical Quarterly*, delving into questions of metaphysics and the philosophy of destiny.

My realization to delve into technology law stems from my interest in global governance as well. Global issues require three levels of introspection – *local*, *national* and *international*. Technology dynamics show how the global nature of the rules-based international order is deterministic and evolves regularly. The evolution does not stop, nor can be stopped, since the determinism exists in every sphere of international relations, law and social sciences, starting from the realpolitik itself. My approach towards international law and relations has been a relative coalescence of passive multilateralism and active plurilateralism, where particularisms of countries, and their actors define issues of global importance, including human rights.

As far as academics is concerned, I am of a clear view that erudition and salience in learning and research contributes productively, in the scholarly development of the academic fields. Technology law is an emerging and perennially evolving field, and my fascination with the ethics of artificial intelligence, has been no less of a journey. The book's second edition encompasses a wider and evolved perspective of artificial intelligence and international law. Since the book's first edition that had come in 2019, the developments in the artificial intelligence industry have been humongous, and far-reaching. In 2018, one could not imagine governments coming up with AI regulation, when I had started writing this book.

Now, the debate has evolved to issues beyond the "black box" problem and Responsible AI. The Generative AI industry (or a sub-segment) itself has been a key driver to shape regulatory tendencies among governments across the world to come up with some legal stance on artificial intelligence technologies. The second edition of this book, unfolds with a focus on the intricate landscape of **Artificial Intelligence (AI)** and its intersection with international law.

SECTION 1: Introduction

Chapter 1: Artificial Intelligence and International Law – This chapter initiates this exploration by delving into the complexities of understanding AI, employing legal linguistics to interpret disruptive technologies, and envisioning a perspective beyond the traditional frameworks of Law 1.0 and 2.0.

SECTION 2: Technology Governance

Chapter 2: Pragmatism in Governing AI – This chapter delves into the pragmatic aspects of governing AI within the international legal arena. It dissects the workflow of international law, acknowledges its limitations, and scrutinizes sovereignty in the context of international cyber law. The chapter further explores various shades of multilateral governance and introduces classification methods such as Concept-Entity-Industry and Subject-Object-Third Party.

Chapter 3: The Innovation and Economics of AI – This chapter shifts the focus to the innovation and economics of AI. It examines the weaponization of data and algorithms, providing insights into the real-world implications of the pervasive AI hype. This exploration sets the stage for understanding the economic dynamics and innovative dimensions within the AI landscape.

SECTION 3: Classification and Recognition of Artificial Intelligence

Chapter 4: Legal Visibility - Legal visibility takes center stage in this chapter, where the concept is defined and its recognition in common law systems is explored. The Tegmark Approach to AI ethics, the realm of dimensional perpetuity, digital identity in AI and international law, and the impact of data quality and privacy on AI recognition are intricately discussed.

Chapter 5: The Privacy Doctrine – In this chapter, the linear approach of human rights is scrutinized, along with the challenges associated with reactionary legal thinking. The Privacy Doctrine itself is outlined, offering a unique approach to international privacy law, while considering sovereignty and natural morality in the era of Industry 4.0.

Chapter 6: The ISAIL Classifications of Artificial Intelligence -This chapter introduces ISAIL Classifications of AI. It discusses the recognition of the legal-ontological status to examine artificial intelligence per se and provides detailed insights into Concept-Entity-Industry and Subject-Object-Third Party classifications, along with the doctrine of manifest availability.

SECTION 4: Artificial Intelligence in a Multi-polar World

Chapter 7: AGI and Digital Colonialism – In this chapter AGI and Digital Colonialism is introduced, where the multi-polar world is explained, and the evolution from Narrow AI to AGI is examined. The chapter also explores how Digital Colonialism shapes AI ethics norms, touching on factors such as ideology, technology and economics, and evaluates the limits of responsible AI. Stages of the Hype Cycle through risk determination are also detailed.

Chapter 8: Self-Regulating the Future of AI – This chapter addresses the self-regulation of AI's future. It explores generative AI applications, delves into responsible and economic innovations, examines India's role in shaping global technology norms, and offers soft law recommendations for the future of AI. This comprehensive exploration culminates in a holistic understanding of the diverse facets and implications of AI within the framework of international law.

In this book, I have expanded on the recent legal scholarship on artificial intelligence governance, proposed some questions on its economic drivers, and how these developments are shaping up the future of AI regulation. For sure, artificial intelligence is far-reaching and impactful. However, cutting down on the hype behind markets promoting AI tools, is also a concern for governments. This is where artificial intelligence hype comes in, which I have covered in this book as well. In short, this book kind of reflects my 5-year career in the AI industry as a technology lawyer and entrepreneur. You can also consider this to be my AI and law *"memoir"* if anything like that may exist.

Coloured Images

Please follow the link to download the
Coloured Images of the book:

https://rebrand.ly/46e0bc

We have code bundles from our rich catalogue of books and videos available at **https://github.com/bpbpublications**. Check them out!

Errata

We take immense pride in our work at BPB Publications and follow best practices to ensure the accuracy of our content to provide with an indulging reading experience to our subscribers. Our readers are our mirrors, and we use their inputs to reflect and improve upon human errors, if any, that may have occurred during the publishing processes involved. To let us maintain the quality and help us reach out to any readers who might be having difficulties due to any unforeseen errors, please write to us at :

errata@bpbonline.com

Your support, suggestions and feedbacks are highly appreciated by the BPB Publications' Family.

Piracy

If you come across any illegal copies of our works in any form on the internet, we would be grateful if you would provide us with the location address or website name. Please contact us at **business@bpbonline.com** with a link to the material.

If you are interested in becoming an author

If there is a topic that you have expertise in, and you are interested in either writing or contributing to a book, please visit **www.bpbonline.com**. We have worked with thousands of developers and tech professionals, just like you, to help them share their insights with the global tech community. You can make a general application, apply for a specific hot topic that we are recruiting an author for, or submit your own idea.

Reviews

Please leave a review. Once you have read and used this book, why not leave a review on the site that you purchased it from? Potential readers can then see and use your unbiased opinion to make purchase decisions. We at BPB can understand what you think about our products, and our authors can see your feedback on their book. Thank you!

For more information about BPB, please visit **www.bpbonline.com**.

Join our book's Discord space

Join the book's Discord Workspace for Latest updates, Offers, Tech happenings around the world, New Release and Sessions with the Authors:

https://discord.bpbonline.com

Table of Contents

SECTION 1:
Introduction

CHAPTER 1
Artificial Intelligence and International Law

यत्र धर्मस्तत्र कृषिः, यत्र कृषिस्तत्र धर्मः।

यत्र धर्मकृषिभ्योऽन्यो, द्वयं तत्र न विद्यते॥

"Where there is righteousness, there is growth;

where there is growth, there is righteousness.

Where righteousness and growth are not separate from each other,

that harmony prevails."

The advent of **Artificial Intelligence (AI)** has been an interesting journey. Many consider that AI may take a big leap from being mere a knowledge machine to a more mature and explainable entity. The problems however would not end even when developers and scientists would be able to develop Artificial Intelligence systems by achieving the state of the Theory of Mind. History gives us an opportunity to look at how the anatomy of Artificial Intelligence has evolved with time, howsoever timid or limited that could be. That anatomy could also be referred to as AI anthropomorphism, which means actions of the AI system would obviously be attributed to human realities, actions, and biases. In that case, content (or information as known) and identity (natural, human, animal, or any) become relatively affected by the operations and activities of the AI system. This could be related with what *Stuart Russell* had stated:

> *"Humans are defenseless in information environments that are grossly corrupted"* (*itut, 2017*).

However, the story of AI for a law *de lege ferenda* – **the law that is to be brought about in future** – is not as simple as it seems.

Before even considering questions of bias and data quality, it would be interesting to ask if Artificial Intelligence, would be able to understand and shape legal taxonomies and jargons. From a semantics point-of-view, applications based on **Large Language Models (LLMs)** such as ChatGPT significantly attempt to replicate legal language when it comes to normal tasks such as drafting and paraphrasing. The AI systems enabling these use cases may or may not be equipped to explain how their algorithms make decisions. In that case, it would be interesting to notice how it could be possible for companies to develop these stable and viable AI use cases. If an AI system meets industry and regulatory standards for explainability, it can explain how decisions are made at the level of the algorithms that drive the system. In many ways, this could be understood as something relatable to human decision-making and autonomy in legal systems. To understand this relatability, let us draw a parallel between the common law system and Machine Learning techniques.

Now, the common law system, which is applicable in many countries including India, relies on this idea to shape and relearn from society and provide insights on legal issues. The authority of the courts is to declare law. It gives the administrative systems a chance to shape the corollaries of the legal system as disruptive technologies become mainstream with time. However, once it is understood how AI would be adapted in proportions in the legal system, then it is reasonable to infer that the common law system, like any other legal system needs to understand and adopt Artificial Intelligence quite cautiously. There are many layers of substantive and procedural law issues respectively, which need to be settled and made clear, as courts and systems would adapt Artificial Intelligence technologies and consequently adjudicate their legal implications.

Now, incorporating Artificial Intelligence into the understanding of law has become possible even if it is not very enhanced or evolved yet. In fact, as of the early 2020s, the field of Artificial Intelligence and law does not limit its scope to data laws, regulations, orders, and other legal instruments. It is nowadays connoted with poignant issues of human development and autonomy, which within the understanding of human rights could also be related to social welfare issues in public law. The big tech companies have been viewed with concern by governments around the world, which has further perpetuated the need to develop sustainable **Digital Public Infrastructure** (**DPIs**) and other relevant solutions. Infamously, a TED Talk by *Zeynep Tufekci*, an ardent critic and techno-sociologist in the 2010s had inspired a human-centric discourse on technology ethics *(TED, 2017)*, which remains valuable. Here is an excerpt from the talk, on how algorithms can be used to create '**persuasion architectures**' to build AI-enabled social media applications.

> *In the digital world, though, persuasion architectures can be built at the scale of billions, and they can target, infer, understand and be deployed at individuals one by one by figuring out your weaknesses, and they can be sent to everyone's phone private screen, so it's not visible to us. And that's different. And that's just one of the basic things that Artificial Intelligence can do (TED, 2017).*

Now, it could be argued that this need to preserve human development and autonomy could be traced to an understanding of the rules-based international order, which is easily explained by the Status of South-West Africa case of the 1950s, in the International Court of Justice.

> *[The] way in which international law borrows from this source is not by means of importing private law institutions "lock, stock and barrel" ready-made and fully equipped with a set of rules. It would be difficult to reconcile such a process with the application "the general principles of law." (International Court of Justice, 1950)*

Now, let us get back to AI again. What drives AI at a basic level is based on how it analyzes data (and information). Data reception is the key to making AI workable. What data has to be analyzed and interpreted to produce results, definitely is a basic concern. Data quality, therefore, becomes an matter of concern. It is also about how the Machine Learning system works, makes itself more prone to reception. But how does that reception work, and how does the AI system produce output, matters. This is where the concept of **Responsible AI**, becomes important. It enables one to analyze the responsibility of the companies, their researchers, their business models, technology sovereignty issues and regulatory concerns. This book thus covers the material and immaterial (mostly, digital) aspect of AI and explores how in an emerging international world, it is shaping realities. In the next section, I have addressed how complex it gets to understand the role of Artificial Intelligence per se.

The complexity in understanding AI

Is the nature of AI too difficult to be understood in a legal sense? Let us now dive into the philosophical aspects of AI ethics, especially technology ethics, for starters. There are reasons why it is needed to focus on the ethical implications of the use of a digital technology, like Artificial Intelligence, blockchain, or any other class of technology. In

Ethics, *Aristotle's* foundational premise of the idea of ethics lies in the recognition of a key attribute within the soul—the capacity for thought, reasoning, and deliberation—which sets us apart from other beings and empowers us to comprehend our surroundings and make informed life decisions (*Moss*, 2015). In his works, Aristotle employs the term **"logos"** without a strict definition, but in the context of the soul, it signifies the potential for rational thought. Aristotle discerns two soul components possessing inherent logos. One of them is the knowledge-oriented facet, known as the *epistemonikon*, dedicated to contemplating essential, timeless truths like those in mathematics, logic, and metaphysics. The calculative aspect, the other one, is called *logistikon*, which is focused on the deliberation needed to attain objectives, such as the practical reasoning used in daily decision-making. (*Moss*, 2015). The eminent Turing Test was perhaps one of the first modern ways to develop a rationalized way to test if any computer is behaving like a human or not. Here is an excerpt from the works of *Rene Descartes* on imagining the ethical and all-comprehensive anatomy of '*automata*' or moving machines (as he had called it) like that of a human body:

> *How many different automata or moving machines can be made by the industry of man [...] For we can easily understand a machine's being constituted so that it can utter words, and even emit some responses to action on it of a corporeal kind, which brings about a change in its organs; for instance, if touched in a particular part it may ask what we wish to say to it; if in another part it may exclaim that it is being hurt, and so on. However, it never happens that it arranges its speech in various ways, in order to reply appropriately to everything that may be said in its presence, as even the lowest type of man can do (Descartes, 1996 pp. 34-5).*

Now, there are two concepts attributed to the legal recognition of Artificial Intelligence, which I have discussed in this book:

- Human Autonomy

- The Privacy Doctrine

Both could be used to analyze the far-reaching impact of attributing the legal recognition of Artificial Intelligence technologies, and their algorithmic activities and operations. Let us understand the first concept. Despite market hype, the inclusion of Artificial Intelligence does have a real impact in human societies and their dynamic personal and interpersonal history. Through this book, a basic outlook on the enablement of AI systems with a human-centric approach is discussed, which could be helpful to reinvent their use cases and market-wise purpose. The privacy doctrine, the second concept, however, is clearer and anticipatory because it does not confine the notion of Artificial Intelligence to a mere 2-dimensional *right-duty* or *obligation-observation* approach but increases its scope to a form of hidden receptivity, which maintains the paradigm shift of human resourcefulness and pragmatism towards affording potential solutions, whether in business, science, or administrative and legal affairs. Now, it is obvious to ascertain that such dilemmas exist. These dilemmas have been addressed in further chapters.

The evolution of human rights (which shapes human autonomy) has been that of a binary concept, where two or more entities are treated under relatively bi-polar recognition. In classical civil legal concepts of human rights, *Hobbes, Locke, Rousseau* and may other thinkers compare the state-public dualism with the urbanized-natural states and put forward their own rationality-based or preconceived ideas with respect to the state structure and the civil rights. Civil society in those times was just a linear image. This linear image had little scope of dimensionality as legal and civil thought was still based on cause-effect relationship. Civil and human rights continued to be viewed from a two-dimensional perspective, even as the world entered the age of contemporary international law in the 19th and 20th centuries. Thanks to the works on legal theory of *Hans Kelsen*, an eminent international law jurist, one could seek fresher perspectives on human rights in public international law.

Now, to be fair, the recognition of international law generally as a valid body of rubrics has shaped itself in a steady way (*Oppenheim*, 1992 p. 3). It is nevertheless distinct that nation-states have developed more and more reserved interpretations and state practices, which rightly could be attributed to the erstwhile **institutionalization** of the international law system and the Cold War dilemma (*Sztucki*, 1974 pp. 35, 165). Having distinctive state practices amidst the turbulent times of the Cold War was a reality in the making. In many ways, it is discernible how the Soviet Union was a peer of the United States in building cooperation on certain international legal issues, such as civil aviation, ICBMs and space law.

Nevertheless, human rights, in general is not the final outpost of international law; but for Artificial Intelligence, the role of human rights as a concept could help us in analyzing and recognizing the immaterial and instrumental legal issues related to algorithms and AI technologies. In the era of big tech companies, from generic issues of data specificity, quality, and erasure to advanced issues such as AI auditing and explainability, having a human rights approach could help us in handling the **human-centric element** of things. One may remember the reasons why the European Commission had imposed fine on Google on claims of anti-competitive practices (*Chee*, 2018). The justification was economic, but it was indicative of a linear aspect of legal imploration of algorithmic activities and operations. Thus, it is a necessity to understand the dystopia that AI may create when it forms or provides extra dimensions to the already existing human-centric issues. However, it is not limited to the lack of explainability of Artificial Intelligence technologies. It is about the human involvement of making these technologies, the research and development aspects and finally, the purpose and risks attached to the Artificial Intelligence technologies and their impact on human environment, ontologically.

Using legal linguistics to interpret disruptive technologies

In the case of technologies like Artificial Intelligence, law by virtue of analysis is benefited by having a good command of ethics and linguistics. Artificial Intelligence has been effectively addressed through various approaches, highlighting its fundamental role in shaping the legal framework for both subjective and objective advancements within society. This holds particular significance due to its foundational implications for law and its applicability. In a *sui generis* sense, legal linguistics, in my view, could provide a backend to redefine the structural and inherent attribution and use of AI technologies (*Ashley*, 2017). Even otherwise, the opaque nature of algorithms (also known as the black box problem) does not explain why algorithms work the way they do, with bias, and risks attached. This is also an area where legal linguistics could be helpful to absorb the technical workings of Machine Learning systems, wherever, and in whichever form they exist.

A grave restraint of any Machine Learning technique, depending on the limits of its explainability is that, as a data-determined method, it essentially relies on the value of the causal data and thus can be very inelastic (*Cummings, et al., 2018 p. 13*). Of course, there are techniques and methods which could overcome the generic limitations of any Machine Learning techniques. For example, in the case of generative AI applications, the computational strength of large language models is multi-fold. Yet, the problem goes beyond generic issues of computational accuracy. It remains a logistic and ontological dilemma as to what is being computed, and how their outputs are instrumentalized. This is a genuine question. For example, you may use *ChatGPT* for drafting any contract template or affidavit template. But it does not mean that the template itself is accurate or just eternally perfect. Moreover, one may also conclude that one use case of *ChatGPT* could be to offer dummy templates. Obviously, if you input more, you will find (in some cases, maybe) acute and refined responses from *GPT-3.5* and *GPT-4*. There is no reason to deny that. Moreover, using large language models is appreciative. Yet, how do you convert that into mass-scale industrial use and whether it is not merely **Garbage-In-Garbage-Out (GIGO)** when it comes to their outputs, despite the genuine multi-level data-centric transformation of these sophisticated algorithms? This is a question one would have to address in near future. In addition, one does not need to be eternally pessimistic about AI, because it does offer the case for change. There are many **B2B** and **B2G (Business to Government)** applications and services, run by AI, which may or may not be generative AI tools, but are useful for policy impact, decision making, digital governance, CRM and many other things. I believe there are 2 main issues here – **one that the law itself is quite slow to adapt with AI and other Web2 and Web3 innovations; and that such technological developments do affect the future of work and innovation for the global economy**. Also, there could be some bias among policymakers and governments to focus merely on restricting or regulated Generative AI tools, but not having a comprehensive approach to govern AI tools. Fortunately, many governments are trying to adopt a piecemeal approach of AI regulation, including India, the EU and the US. On the issue of laws not gaining pace, maybe legal linguistics can help in designating taxonomies and hierarchies of legal estimations, for good. **Catala**, a programming language (*Merigoux, et al., 2021*) proposed by *Denis Merigoux, Nicolas Chataing* and *Jonathan Protzenko* could be one considered example, in taxation law.

Here is a simplistic example of how legal linguistics could be imagined at a basic level. In a hypothetical scenario, let us consider a nation called S that introduces a new law, denoted as the X Act, within its legal framework. Now, if one envisions an AI System known as G being tasked with understanding the interpretation, functioning, and legal implications of this Act, it becomes essential for G to acquire specific crucial attributes that serve as the fundamental components of its learning process. Here is a list of possible attributes, which could be helpful in shaping legal linguistics, on aspects related to the X Act:

- Scope, extent, and jurisdiction of X.

- Amendments, case laws or precedents related to it (directly or indirectly).

- International legal obligations

- Public and Administrative Regulations

- State sovereignty and rule of law

These factors are not exhaustive. However, these are those general conditions or modalities that a lawyer or a bureaucrat may need to keep in mind. Assume these 5 conditions stated above as conditions H_1, H_2, H_3, H_4 and H_5 respectively.

So, the G system recognizes S as per the condition H_5 (the fifth condition), and so, this condition, according to the legal principles, represents external and internal sovereignty because that is the best way to understand how practical sovereignty works. Now, the extrinsic subset of sovereignty contains elements such as military strength, representation in international law, UN, international affairs, etc., while the other subset contains elements in roster form such as - GDP, state law, economic policies, administrative policies, public regulations, etc. However, it is already known that some of them are somehow or the other related to the other 'H' conditions, which is mathematically either direct or indirect. This means repetition of legal realms in its different phases and forms is representative of a phenomenon and quite normal to happen. This explains in the simplest of ways why human rights as a concept arising from civil liberties now recognizes its place in the form of polluter's pay, intergenerational equity, corporate social responsibility, immigration laws, data protection rights and others. This is a form of webbing, which could be used to build tools of legal linguistics. Now, for a system having adequate machine learning algorithms, specificity of algorithmic activities and operations must have credible outcomes and purposes. This is why **Explainable Artificial Intelligence (XAI)** has become quite mainstream, which is discussed in further chapters.

Here is another example on how legal linguistics could develop as a much credible tool to link legal interpretation with artificial intelligence. Article 21 of the Constitution of India, 1949 is a rather easy example to consider. The provisions of the article are as such:

> *No person shall be deprived of his life or personal liberty except according to procedure established by law (Constitution of India, 1949).*

The article expressly defines the scope and extent of the right to life of a **person** as a negative right (because of the sense that it carries the due jurisprudential value and connectivity with the Article 13 of the Constitution with respect to the dynamics related to the violation of the fundamental rights as stated in Part III). This context is important to consider because this right may give an inference to an AI system that no matter what, no deprivation can be exercised nor caused of human life, since a person referred is a human being. Now, privacy and personal dignity are other attributes, which could be related to the *human rights-privacy dimensionality debate*, which is discussed in further chapters. However, it is insightful to know that multiple perspectives or dimensions of reference exist. Why? In a practical sense, for rendering Machine Learning algorithms in better human environments, it isn't just a matter of the deprivation of life or personal liberty and the procedural exceptions related to it. This goes beyond the scope where algorithmic activities could be judged by this standard of negative obligation that any second order and third order effects are carefully taken into regard. The Supreme Court of India relates the same Article 21 to privacy rights *(Supreme Court of India, 2017)*, environmental responsibility and statutory rights *(Supreme Court of India, 2012)* and other exclusively interconnected cases, which is dynamic, sometimes very far-reaching and sometimes specifically inclined. This explains how far-reaching, dynamic or inclined legal interpretation could get. Although, this example is too basic, one can understand how one can improvise upon use cases of Artificial Intelligence technologies and integrate their language of understanding with the language of law. When one studies the impact of Artificial Intelligence on human autonomy, it is necessary to understand concepts like *anthropocentrism* and *anthropomorphism* to enable legal and policy efforts to make AI development and explicability *human centric*. This is also where legal linguistics could be helpful to decipher the innate relationship between Artificial Intelligence systems and human beings (as natural persons). An elaborate depiction of legal linguistics is discussed in the chapter on Legal Visibility.

Outlook beyond Law 1.0 and 2.0

For those who may know the meaning of the term tort, they may understand it as a civil wrong (in a legally recognized sense). If you trespass into someone's house or play karaoke on loudspeakers day and night, causing noise in your neighborhood, these can be constituted as torts or civil wrongs. The four aspects of tort law – **reasonability, foreseeability, actionability and ethical subjectivity** *(Privacy Beyond the Law of Tort, 2018 pp. 54-6)* are the categorical, substantial and procedural phases of civil rights. Now, if you look at these phases, they definitely represent themselves as kind of a line. When reasonability exhausts its scope, anyone would ask if a tort was foreseeable to be attempted. Once that foreseeability was tested, one may ask if such a tort could be actionable. If it was actionable, then ethical subjectivity comes in where one could ask as to what ethical questions could arise. So, one may consider this to be a litmus test to determine civil liability for torts.

Similarly, the evolution of law could also be looked like a line, where the world has moved on from concepts like *unquestioned authority* to *consultative authority*. For many societies like India, Italy, Greece and China, one may argue that times have demanded different methods of authority and statecraft. Even the United States and the United Kingdom have had phases of statecraft which show variations of rights and obligations created upon their natural persons and citizens. Thus, the same could be discerned, for technology, as a human artifact. The evolution of technologies has reflected simple to complex legal changes that have shaped societies for long. Imagine how unusual it could have been if governments around the world would have failed in enabling laws and systems, which understand the pace of technology transfer and evolution. States could have collapsed or rendered dysfunctional then. Nevertheless, before going into the history of Artificial Intelligence ethics and law, which is dealt in further chapters, it is necessary to understand how legal systems have transformed with the rise of disruptive technologies, as depicted in the *Figure 1.1* below:

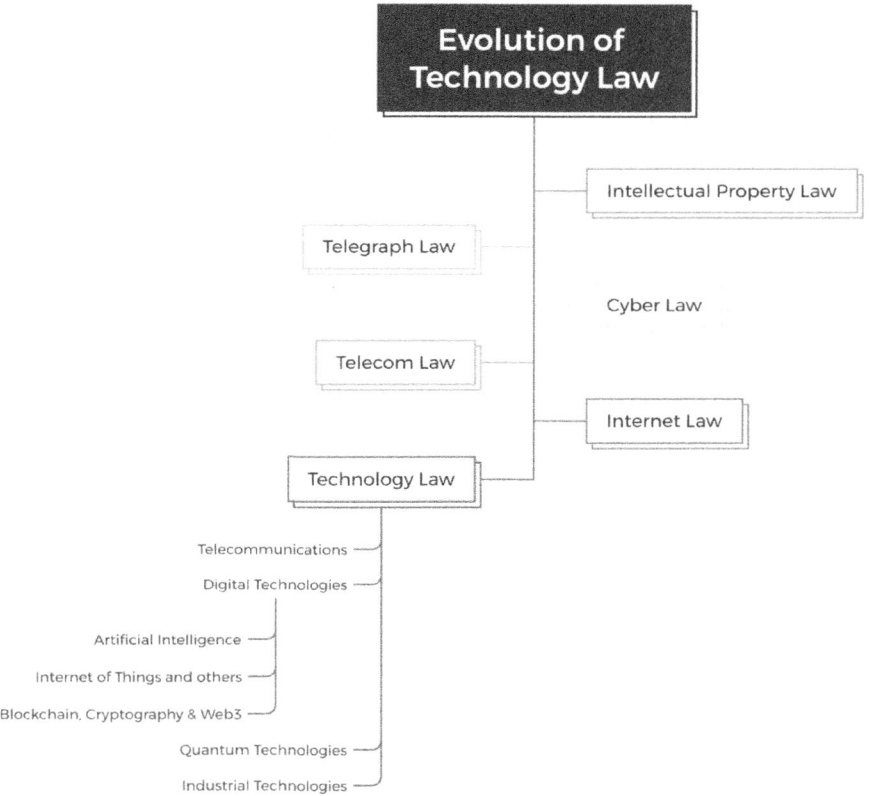

Figure 1.1: *Chronology of the legal fields that have developed leading to the evolution of technology law as a field.*

This figure illustrates a chronology of the fields of law that have shaped the trajectory of technology law. In many ways, one may regard two fields of law as the main drivers of technology law – telecommunications law and cybersecurity law. They can be distinguished much like hard power and soft power, where cybersecurity could be considered an issue of hard power realities, and telecommunications could be related with **Information and Communication Technologies (ICTs)**, the segment which represents technological soft power of countries around the world. Let us understand how these legal fields led the transformation of technology law.

To begin with, intellectual property law has been a field of law and economics, where certain enforceable legal rights are granted to people, governments and companies to protect certain things they own, due to their distinctive features of use. Copyright for example, could be used to protect artistic works, books, research material, and most textual and visual content. Patenting works for medicinal products, technological inventions, and other categories, where the level of economic stake is material and huge. Meanwhile, trademark recognition be associated with representation and branding. Similarly, geographical indications may be associated with any product originating from a geographical location. Hence, while new rights are created in the case of intellectual property law, governments agree that innovations have to be protected and regulated accordingly. That could be considered a logical first step to regulate and shape the trajectory of technology evolution since they represent innovative products or innovative practices with their own contextual importance.

The next field one may consider could be telecommunications law. Before frequencies were even put to use for radio communications, telegraphs were a major medium of communication. In the 1990s, the world did innovate beyond radio and television-based communications, which led us to recognize information and communication technologies by 2005. Then, the rapid change that created newer sub-industry segments in fields like technology, management, analytics, marketing, advertising, creative arts and others, was unstoppable. Perhaps, telecommunications law is the force multiplier behind ascribing more operative and commoditized aspects of recognition of use of technologies in legal systems.

Finally, internet regulation, which is a direct predecessor of technology law, becomes as important as software law, because the use and proliferation of internet, made the world technologically capable to create digital worlds. While *Mark Zuckerberg* claims that metaverse is a form of embodied internet, internet itself could be considered an embodiment of cyberspace. This may seem too basic to understand in the times when Generative AI have become popular, but the potential of internet to create worlds, which are not physical yet existent amidst frequencies is a remarkable human achievement. Recognizing internet in a legal system implies that governments must consider how they add themselves up to cyberspace, and how they regulate it with a territorial perspective, which is why technology sovereignty is an important idea discussed among countries.

> *If intellectual property and technology law are considered non-existent in the legal systems across the world, the rest of the legal system may be considered Law 1.0. Professor Roger Brownsword, author of* **Law 3.0** *calls Law 1.0 as the state of Coherentism (Brownsword, 2021).*

He explains the state of **Coherentism** in the simplest way possible in this excerpt from his book:

> *Coherentism is, thus, the natural language of litigators and judges, who seek to apply the law in a principled way. It is also the default mode of thinking for many lawyers*

who take it that being trained 'to think like a lawyer' is synonymous with being trained to apply general principles of law to situations and phenomena both familiar and novel (Brownsword, 2021 p. 32).

With the addition of legal fields designed to recognize technological innovation and mobility, Law 2.0 comes into shape, which according to *Brownsword*, could be considered as **'regulatory-instrumentalist'** in the legal system. It is the emergence of such legal fields that a regular mainstreaming of enabling regulators in many industries and developing consultative methods of engagement within legal and administrative systems has become possible. This is how alternative dispute resolution became mainstream.

Conclusion

Now, that Artificial Intelligence is becoming mainstream, like other disruptive technologies, an aspect that makes this class of technology so profound is – all-comprehensiveness. Artificial Intelligence products, systems and services are all-comprehensive, a product of human intelligence and agency by definition. It could be any product or system, which has minuscule or larger involvement of artificial intelligence. However, the dynamic and all-comprehensive nature makes Artificial Intelligence a central pivot to technological evolution. In certain industry segments like Generative AI, perhaps one may see disproportionate and asymmetric growth, hype and transformation, while in certain other AI-related industries, the mainstream use could be very different. In fact, while national boundaries exist on issues such as data processing and the transboundary use of digital products and services, the use cases and training models developed by AI systems, indeed are globalized and truly international in many ways. One may refer to Google Translate and ChatGPT as international and globalized examples of sorts, while in the case of India, *Bhashini*, a language translation tool by the Digital India Corporation could become a force of globalization of Indic languages. Hence, it is apparent to understand and realize why the democratization of AI would require international and national-level players or stakeholders to engage within their multilateral and bilateral systems.

In the next chapter of this book, I have addressed how one may recognize the regulation of Artificial Intelligence as in international law, by examining the state of our international legal systems. The chapter also addresses the weaknesses of the rules-based international order and its limitations, on issues surrounding the regulation and oversight of proliferated digital, critical, and emerging technologies, and their fusion, with a legal perspective.

References

- **itut. 2017.** Human-Compatible AI: Design Principles To Prevent War Between Machines and Men. [Online] itut, June 9, 2017. [Cited: July 27, 2018.] **http://newslog.itu.int/archives/1571**.

- **Goldman Sachs. 2016.** Artificial Intelligence: The Apex Technology of the Information Age. *Goldman Sachs.* [Online] December 12, 2016. **https://www.goldmansachs.com/insights/pages/artificial-intelligence.html**.

- **TED. 2017.** We're building a dystopia just to make people click on ads. *TED Talks.* [Online] September 2017. **https://www.ted.com/talks/zeynep_tufekci_we_re_building_a_dystopia_just_to_make_people_click_on_ads**.

- **International Court of Justice. 1950.** *Status of South-West Africa case, ICJ Reports 1950, 148.* s.l. : International Court of Justice, 1950.

- **Moss, Jessica. 2015.** Aristotle's Ethical Psychology: Reason's Role in Virtue and Happiness. *Department of Philosophy - Arts & Sciences - New York University.* [Online] 2015. **https://as.nyu.edu/content/dam/nyu-as/philosophy/documents/faculty-documents/moss/Moss_Reasons-Role-Draft.pdf**.

- **Descartes, René. 1996.** *Discourse on Method and Meditations on First Philosophy.* New Haven & London : Yale University Press, 1996.

- **Oppenheim, L. 1992.** *Oppenheim's International Law.* [ed.] Sir R. Jennings and Sir A. Watts. s.l. : Oxford University Press, 1992. Vol. 1.

- **Sztucki, J. 1974.** Jus Cogens and the Vienna Convention on the Law of Treaties. 1974.

- **Chee, Foo Yun. 2018.** Europe hits Google with record $5 billion antitrust fine, appeal ahead. *Thomson Reuters.* [Online] July 18, 2018. **https://in.reuters.com/article/eu-google-antitrust/europe-hits-google-with-record-5-billion-antitrust-fine-appeal-ahead-idINKBN1K811F**.

- **Ashley, K.D. 2017.** Artificial Intelligence and Legal Analytics: New Tools for Law Practice in the Digital Age. Cambridge : Cambridge University Press, 2017.

- Deep learning: With massive amounts of computational power, machines can now recognize objects and translate speech in real time. Artificial intelligence is finally getting smart. **Hof, R. 2013.** 2013, MIT Technology Review.

- **Cummings, M. L., et al. 2018.** Artificial Intelligence and International Affairs: Disruption Anticipated. Chatham House. 2018.

- **Merigoux, Denis, Chataing, Nicolas and Protzenko, Jonathan. 2021.** Catala: A Programming Language for the Law - arXiv. arXiv. [Online] 2021. **https://arxiv.org/abs/2103.03198**.

- **Constitution of India. 1949.** Constitution of India. Government of India. 1949.

- **Supreme Court of India. 2017.** Justice K.S Puttaswamy & Another v. Union of India, (2017) 10 SCC 1. 10, s.l. : Supreme Court of India, August 24, 2017.

- —. **2012.** T.N. Godavarman Thirumulpad v. Union of India & Ors., Writ Petition (C) no. 202 Of 1995. 1433, 1477, s.l. : Supreme Court of India, February 13, 2012.

- Privacy Beyond the Law of Tort. **Abhivardhan. 2018.** 2018, GLC Contemporary Law Review, pp. 52-58.

- **Brownsword, Roger. 2021.** Law 3.0: Rules, Regulation, and Technology . s.l. : Routledge, 2021.

SECTION 2:
Technology Governance

CHAPTER 2
Pragmatism in Governing AI

यत्र यत्र नियतं तत्र यत्र यत्र न च प्रयतन्ति।

तत्र तत्र स्वयं प्राप्तं तत्र तत्र नियता हि ते ।।

"Wherever there is regulation, there lies the absence of excessive efforts;

Wherever there is self-regulation, there resides effective governance."

International law is a concept involving nations working in the realms of international peace and security, harmony, and resilience. The texts and cases of international law in its offspring stage, that is, before the formation of the *United Nations* and *the International Court of Justice*, signified a due sense of positive law, which was quite isolating, contemporarily based on the relativity of acts. One of the classic examples is the *S.S. Lotus case*. In this case, two ships *Boz-Kourt* and *Lotus*, collide wherein the sinking of *Boz-Kourt* had killed eight Turkish nationals who were on board the Turkish vessel itself. The ten survivors of the *Boz-Kourt*, which included the captain were taken to Turkish Republic on board the *Lotus* itself. In **Turkey**, *Demons*, a French national, captain of the Turkish ship was charged with **manslaughter**. France had protested the decision and demanded the release of Demons or the transfer of his case to French Courts. Later, Turkey and France agree to refer the dispute as in the jurisdiction to the *Permanent Court of International Justice (PCIJ)*. This case is considered a classic example of depicting the traditional nature of international law. Here is an excerpt from the ruling of the court on the *Lotus* case:

> *"The rules of law binding upon States therefore emanate from their own free will as expressed in conventions or by usages generally accepted as expressing principles of law and established in order to regulate the relations between these co-existing independent communities or with a view to the achievement of common aims. Restrictions upon the independence of States cannot therefore be presumed (Permanent Court of International Justice, 1927)."*

Without any **permissive convention**, **custom** or **practice** recognizable via international law, it seems impossible for a state to exercise its territorial jurisdiction concurrently vide another nation. This resembles a vague view of positive law. That is why at times, the principle of double criminality is an interesting legal invention in the field of international law, and the jurisprudence on extradition agreements. Nevertheless, it was becoming clear, especially after the 1980s that the model to adopt heavy-handed international treaties and conventions alone would not help and the multilateral commitments, for example, that of the UN system, which cannot sustain without reform. The reason is more or less obvious – multilateral institutions get fizzled in power dynamics in the backdrop of moral superiority. They focus too much on the methods of handling security or hard power issues engineered by major powers like the US and Russia to ignore real development concerns. Furthermore, the pace of defining more decisive norms to be considered as customary international law, could not become possible for various countries. Although, there are still some areas where international law is nearabout settled. In the case of technology, except Europe as a jurisdiction, and the **International Telecommunication Union (ITU)**'s treaties, we do not have extensive treaties or conventions that regulate the activities related to disruptive technologies like Artificial Intelligence. Consequently, this makes a lot of sense because we are still debating those intricate norms, which show that a treaty-level legal prescription would take time to be rendered. An effort was made through UNESCO by bringing up a *Recommendation on Artificial Intelligence in 2022*, along with some key declarations and communiques on AI ethics by ITU and UNESCO in these five to six years since 2016.

However, before moving directly into the recognition of Artificial Intelligence in international law, let us understand a field of international law, which has gained enough relevance as a security-oriented field, that is, *international cyber law*. This is a field dealing with the international law applicable to cyber realms.

Years ago, experts at Estonia had formalized a manual to reinstate the principles of the field. This was a work of the CCDCOE of the North Atlantic Treaty Organization, popularly known as – the *Tallinn Manual* (which has two versions, 1.0 and 2.0), based on the recommendations of various experts. *Prof. Bimal Patel*, the Vice-Chancellor of *Rashtriya Raksha University, Gujarat*, and a member of the *UN International Law Commission* from India had also contributed to this manual. In furtherance, the chapter has discussed the material element of international law in its philosophical and practical aspects in the context of international cyber law. In addition, this chapter addresses recent literature that has developed from Western Europe and Northern American countries on Artificial Intelligence governance.

The Workflow of International Law

The modern realm of international law is based on:

- Pure International Law

- Law of treaties

- Law of international organizations

- State practice and customary international law

- The role of power and ethics in shaping the international law system (in an exhaustive sense).

At the risk of being reductive, it would still be safe to state that the nature of international law is nearly dependent on such realms if we consider only the pure legal schema of it and impregnate the role of international relations and geopolitics as well. In general, international law and international relations are intertwined with each other. To make international law enforceable, countries adopt and agree to certain legal principles as they sign a treaty (and ratify it), reflect their state practice through their diplomatic, legal, and administrative actions and documents or contribute to public policy developments by not adopting anything in a legally binding sense at all.

Now, we have such multilateral institutions like the United Nations and many more, which to some extent, as per their charters, treaties and relevant legal instruments, regulate specific affairs of international concern. For example, the UN Security Council, which consists of 5 permanent members (US, UK, China, France and Russian Federation) and 10 non-permanent members, is designed to focus on traditional security issues. On the other hand, a domain-specific body like the **UN Office of Outer Space Affairs (UNOOSA)**, would naturally address space-related missions and affairs by coordinating with governments around the world. Then, on cultural heritage and museum artifacts, we have UNESCO, a UN Agency, whose mandate is based on a set of international treaties and conventions that regulate the protection and preservation of various kinds of cultural heritage, from performing arts, to statues to music and even paintings. It is that obvious to understand every sector or area has key national and intergovernmental institutions. Is there an ethical need to protect these institutions? Indeed, despite their political, logistic and policy failures, these institutions undeniably provide forums for countries to enable international standards, which is a testament to their crucial role in international law and policy. The best examples of such multilateral bodies include the International Telecommunication Union and the World Trade Organization. I have therefore offered a perspective on the limitations of international law in the form of a prologue to this section, coverig how sovereignty is defined in international law.

The Limitations of International Law

One of the simplest ways to implement international law is through treaties between countries. The multilateral organizations, like UNESCO, WHO, WTO and many more, exist by virtue of those treaties. Once the treaties or relevant legal instruments grant the mandate to these multilateral organizations to perform a set of functions to implement international law, they are bound to take measures to implement them. For example, the UN Office of Outer Space Affairs would not implement international law the same way a governing body in the World Health Organization would be expected to do. Their mandates, logistical considerations, end-goals and even policy-bound exceptions would naturally vary. Now, in the case of several multilateral organizations, it is important to know that they have suffered years of irrelevance in terms of their application of international legal norms. This is due to the obsolescence of some of their legal and policy methods, which may not be across the organizations and their respective divisions, committees, departments and other internal and co-operative functionaries. Still, their inability to implement international legal norms with efficiency would raise questions about their credence. It is also true that due to geopolitical events and power dynamics of countries across the globe, the logistic value of a multilateral organization to implement international law decays with time, unless some action is taken. For example, the European Union had adopted the *General Data Protection Regulation* in 2016. However, on the ethics of Artificial Intelligence, *Alex Voss*, one of the founders of GDPR, had considered the regulation to be quite outdated (*Espinoza*, 2021) on grounds that the regulation would take long to catch up with the emerging issues of data protection, privacy, consent and processing. Now, adopting such laws, and treaties takes years of negotiation and implementation. This is where one must consider how hard it has been for multilateral institutions to gain relevance or at least, maintain whatever is left of them. Yet, it is these realities that shape the journey and character of international law. Nevertheless, it must be acknowledged that that the implementation of GDPR both at European and global levels, and the legal-economic risks of implementation, enabled countries across the world to develop and wield their regulatory positions on the transboundary and domestic flow, processing and ownership of data. Of course, countries across continents have their political, legal and policy reasons not to adopt legal norms in a unanimous sense. However, the example of GDPR and the years of its implementation show a mixed story that enforcing international legal norms is in part or as a whole, is hard and not impossible.

It is an axiom that part of law's doing is law's saying, but it is not always clear what is being expressed nor even what kinds of information can be expressed by law *(The Contribution of International Law to International Relations,* 1977 p. 219). In fact, this is true. International law evolves with its experiences and the norms that countries shape. Experiences could be associated with the geopolitical realities we live in, while norms, develop as state practices evolve.

Sovereignty and International Cyber Law

Sovereignty, the principle of supremacy or power attained in the rubric of a political reality by a state is the most interesting center of international law. The *UN Charter* makes it more contemporary by the term sovereign equality in its **Art. 2(1)**. Legitimacy, a mechanical term to define sovereignty not in its existential but in its pragmatic sense comes into picture. This term evokes a reality that sovereignty itself, is absolute in its applicative sense always. Countries and their governments attribute reasonability to recognize sovereignty of any country in their own way, which in their context is understandable. Now, sovereignty is referred to in the **Rule 1** of the *Tallinn Manual 2.0* (cyberspace is encumbered by political legal sovereignty). This could also be justified by the *Islands of Palmas arbitral award* of 1928, wherein, in a beautiful sense, independence is enumerated as the right to exercise sovereignty in the matter of exclusivity. That is how the concept of sovereignty materializes in form of its institutions – the government, its subordinates, and the people. Internal sovereignty provides an insight from the level of an individual who is in the jurisdiction of the state while the extrinsic one provides the latter one, present in the outside realms present therein. Now, at a material sense, the recognition of Artificial Intelligence may be limited to a mere generalization of the principles of data quality, transborder flow, protection, penetration, rectification and other inter alia realms that are relevantly present at the outset.

Nevertheless, sovereignty has both legal and political facets. The idea of sovereignty in the context of cyber infrastructure is depicted in the *Rules 1-10* of the *Tallinn Manual 2.0*. Interestingly, as per the *Rule 1* of the Manual (Schmitt, 2017), one may interpret cyberspace as a **global** or **fifth domain** of legal purview (North Atlantic Treaty Organization). Further, it is obvious that sovereignty, in a conceptual sense, is derivable in public international law. This is how the Manual depicts the concept of cyber sovereignty, which one may consider the predecessor of technological sovereignty.

Cyber sovereignty, in the context of the Manual also makes distinction of cyber infrastructure into **physical** and **non-physical forms** or **levels**. The Manual gives an example of the electromagnetic frequencies that are transmitted, which are not taken as equivalent to (say) computer resource, optical fibers, and others. Now in a European sense, the *Convention on Cybercrime* (The Council of Europe, 2001) develops a legal regime on cybercrimes, with definitive and procedural features. However, in this case, it is important to understand that such conventions and legislations as even in the US and other *Global North / WENA* states, there are remnant and macroscopic or rather commonly present ecosystems that are taken into pursuance. As per the **Rule 63** of the *Tallinn Manual 2.0*, electromagnetic frequencies are limited resources, whose use must be rational, efficient and economically viable as per the **Article 44(2)** of the *Constitution of ITU* (International Telecommunication Union, 1992). Henceforth, to understand how sovereignty could be encompassed as a concept in international cyber law, and international technology law, as far as the field of Artificial Intelligence Ethics are concerned, we should prefer that we must recognize that different realms or dimensions of reference exist, which could be recognized in the frame of international law.

Imagine you are a jurist or advocate in the 1910s. If you were asked, in which worlds, laws would be applied, you would rather say that the application of law could be limited to the physical world (*land and water*). In the Cold War times, you may add outer space and airspace in the list. In the early 21st century, between 2004 and 2012, you would say cyberspace must be governed under law. In the early and mid-2020s when we see developers working on Web3 technologies, we would consider the internet, and metaverse (also known as ***embodied internet***) as semi-layers of cyberspace. In that case, we could rather go even at a psychological level, and say that even the mind (*mental space*) is a form of a world like the internet within cyberspace. If I add a spiritual justification with a religious context, then we may even consider the *metaphysical world* to be governable under law. Of course, these are propositions. However, it could be reasonably argued that in the field of international law and technology that the physical world (*air, land & water*), outer space and cyberspace (*internet and metaverse*) could be regarded as places or frames of reference that could be recognized under international law, at a certain degree. One may not require comparing how air & space are regulated under the *Chicago Convention* with how high seas are recognized in the *UN Convention on the Law of Seas*. Here is an interesting excerpt from **The Pure Theory of Law** by *Hans Kelsen*:

> *However, if one starts from the validity of a national legal order, the question arises how from this starting point the validity of international law can be established; and then the reason for the validity of international law must be found in the national legal order [...] Sovereignty is not a sensually perceptible or otherwise objectively cognizable quality of a real object, but a presupposition. It is the presupposition of a normative order as the highest order whose validity is not derivable from any higher order. The question of whether the state is sovereign cannot be answered by an analysis of natural reality. Sovereignty is not a maximum of real power. [...] International law, then, appears not as a supranational legal order, nor as one independent of the national legal order, and isolated from it, but–if as law as at all–as a part of the national legal order (Kelsen, 2009 pp. 333-335).*

In the context of Artificial Intelligence, one has to understand, at a basic level, that the technology itself, depends on human and natural environment when it comes to its inputs and outputs. Whatever any Artificial Intelligence product / service / system could learn and produce as results as needed, is dependent upon the anthropological realities it **adjusts** to. That is how developers are requested to perfect the algorithms and avoid any biases in the results. Take a commercial bank for example. Let us say the bank's technology team has installed an AI system whose algorithms are designated to perform risk analysis through auditing of certain current and saving accounts. The algorithm, if is designed to offer effective and bias-free or less biased results, then in a closed environment, the AI system may deliver better results. For closed systems, where data receptivity and data quality do not suffer – of course, the AI system could give better results. It is these kinds of anthropological realities that data scientists and developers would have to face every day to make the best decisions on making AI systems reasonable.

Now, there is a slight possibility that in a closed environment, where any misuse or abuse of the AI system could be impossible, the risk auditing of the AI system may not be useful because the results might not offer a cumulatively and contextually sound insight of the risks subject to examination. Here, I see two kinds of environments, that one may take into concern, when it comes to Artificial Intelligence – the **human environment**, and the **AI environment** (we can also refer to it as the **algorithmic environment**). Now, it is known that Artificial Intelligence as a class of digital technologies has a lot of relevance because of its potential to compute and analyze, despite errors and biases. In fact, when China started working on their social credit system (*Cummings*, et al., 2018) and used AI-based surveillance of their ordinary citizens, they thought it could be helpful to use Artificial Intelligence in an embodied fashion in various devices and systems, to avoid any casualty from even happening. Here is an excerpt of how China is using surveillance technology on its **Uighur population**:

> *Xinjiang ("New Territory") is the traditional home of a Chinese Muslim minority known as Uighurs. As large numbers of Han Chinese migrants have settled in—some say **colonized**—the region, the work and religious opportunities afforded to the local Uighur population have diminished. One result has been an uptick in violence in which both Han and Uighur have been targeted, including a 2009 riot in the capital city of Urumqi, when a reported 200 people died. [...] The Xinjiang government employed a private company to design the predictive algorithms that assess various data streams. There's no public record or accountability for how these calculations are built or weighted. "The people living under this system generally don't even know what the rules are," says Rian Thum, an anthropologist at Loyola University who studies Xinjiang and who has seen government procurement notices that were issued in building the system. (Larson, 2018).*

This is a classic example of predictive policing. Perhaps there are a lot of dynamic and variant conceptions of the same idea that states represent in various public policy measures (Tamanaha, 2004 p. 3) and it is generally a corollary of so many profuse conceptions. Yet, the lack of transparency in these tools of surveillance and the role these tools have in making administrative decisions would naturally invite concern. Plus, such measures are **maximalist** in nature. It is probable that such measures do not have an extensive shelf-life, since in public policy, you do not trample upon, but maintain the orderliness that shapes peoples' lives. Transparency and accountability are key to make predictive policing better, and effective to avoid its misuse (Fontes, et al., 2022).

Different shades of multilateral governance

It is argued that including a dynamic, all-comprehensive technology like AI could lead to legal obsolescence of the international law system. It is discussed in *Chapter 1* on how multilateral institutions remain obsolete and inept. *Matthijs Maas* had argued in an article for the *Melbourne Journal of International Law* on how international legal institutions are incapable to cover the disruptions that AI would cause:

> *Treaties usually require that both states party have roughly even stakes in the technology, clear expectations of benefit for abiding by the treaty, the ability to jointly agree on clear definitions and the ability to effectively verify compliance (all of which are difficult in the context of AI development). Finally, international courts are often slow, reactive to specific cases and non-expert on technologies. Effective International law regimes on new, emerging technology have historically relied on a range of ingredients, including an ability to anticipate and agree, to some extent, on the path and applications of development, an ability to agree on definitions of the technology and the ability to effectively verify compliance. Many or all these ingredients will not apply in the context of many AI systems, suggesting that this technology will lead to disruption of that order (Maas, 2019 p. 22).*

Now, the beauty in Artificial Intelligence research lies with the relationship between datasets and the algorithms, which would process those datasets. The relationship between data and algorithms is fundamental to shape all regulatory, judicial, legislative and resolution-based legal solutions, in **technology law**. It is the politics of use of data, which would shape the politics of using AI. An older consensus on the politics of technology use that used to exist, was that knowledge creation does not affect existing data laws and merely adopting the old laws with some minor adjustments in interpretation or through minor amendments could help. *Christina Moniodis* debunks that myth in her article for the *Yale Journal of Law and Technology* and explains how creation of new knowledge would create new strands of data law. Here is an excerpt from that article:

> *The creation of new knowledge complicates data privacy law as it involves information the individual did not possess and could not disclose, knowingly or otherwise. In addition, as our State becomes an **information state** through increasing reliance on information—such that information is described as the "lifeblood that sustains political, social, and business decisions. It becomes impossible to conceptualize all of the possible uses of information and resulting harms. Such a situation poses a challenge for courts who are effectively asked to anticipate and remedy invisible, evolving [harms] (Moniodis, 2012 p. 154).*

Interestingly, *Moniodis's* article had also inspired *Justice DY Chandrachud's* infamous dissent in the ***Aadhar Judgment*** (Supreme Court of India, 2018 pp. 134, 150-1) (also known as **Puttaswamy II**) passed in the Supreme Court of India. Here is an excerpt from his dissent, on privacy law, which reflects how mere normal principles of privacy law become important in the context of Artificial Intelligence:

> *Privacy postulates the reservation of a private space for the individual, described as the right to be let alone. The concept is founded on the autonomy of the individual. The ability of an individual to make choices lies at the core of the human personality. The notion of privacy enables the individual to assert and control the human element which is inseparable from the personality of the individual. The inviolable nature of the human personality is manifested in the ability to make decisions on matters intimate to human life. The autonomy of the individual is associated over matters which can be kept private. These are concerns over which there is a legitimate expectation of privacy [...] Data mining processes together with knowledge discovery can be combined to create facts about individuals. Metadata and the internet of things have the ability to redefine human existence in ways which are yet fully to be [perceived] (Supreme Court of India, 2018 pp. 134, 150-1).*

This represents a simple point, that one needs to create adjustable and circuiting modalities in the legal framework of data privacy law, which are useful in bringing or creating better laws, as referred to in *Figure 2.1.*

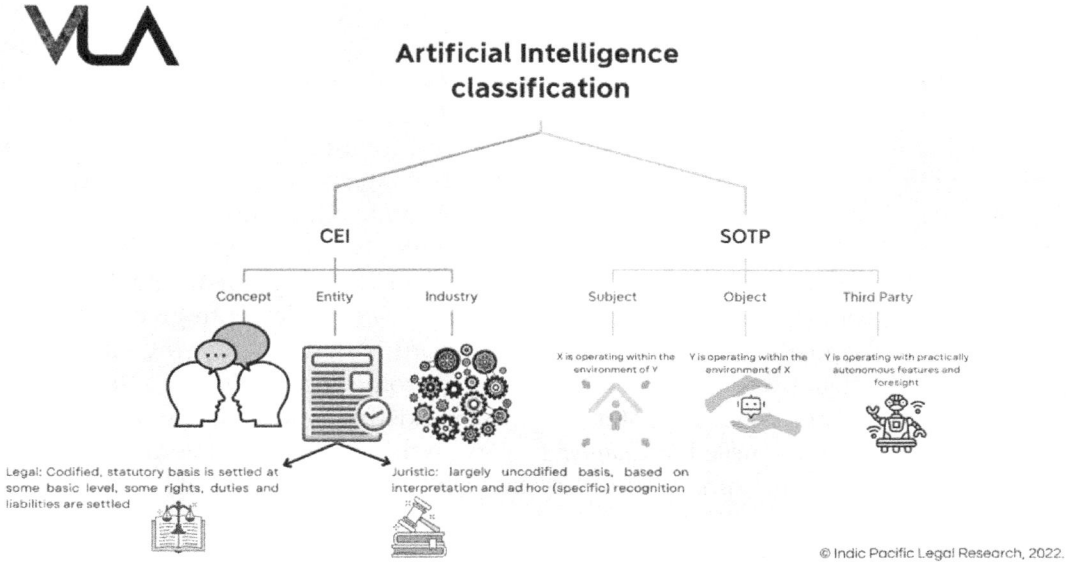

Figure 2.1: *The ISAIL Classification of Artificial Intelligence, in a nutshell (Abhivardhan, 2022).*

Now, in the context of multilateral institutions, Governing AI could depend on certain scenarios, among which it depends which ones are the most important, or prevalent. I have used the ISAIL Classifications on Artificial Intelligence, which I had developed in the *2020 Handbook on AI and International Law* (Abhivardhan, et al., 2022). The classifications are discussed as a complete chapter in this book. Based on the 2-classification method, here are the potential scenarios:

- The Concept-Entity-Industry Classification Method; and

- The Subject-Object-Third Party Classification Method.

Concept – Entity – Industry Classification Method

As a concept, Artificial Intelligence requires a legal mandate to be governed and regulated. To achieve that, not only must the stakeholders agree on governing Artificial Intelligence, but also cover the conceptual and technological features, which require some clear regulation. This happens even at regulatory levels in various countries, where governments decide what is regulated, and how such designations are made. One can relate this with the concept of intermediaries as well. For example, the Digital India Act, a proposed legislation by the Government of India to replace the Information Technology Act, 2000, is set to cover as many intermediaries as possible and the safe harbor principles attached to them. For multilateral institutions, defining those standards, is a starting point of concern.

As an entity, Artificial Intelligence in certain legal scenarios may be considered as a legal entity, or a juristic entity. Gaining recognition or status of a legal entity, to be fair, is hard and unachievable, because every legal entity is entitled to a right-duty-accountability-liability system, that is, you must entitle some rights, duties and liabilities to that entity recognized. Also, every legal entity, even recognized in international law, for example, let us say an individual person, as opposed to states and intergovernmental organizations, has some rights. It depends on the context, which then shapes its application, pretty much. However, AI can be granted the recognition of a juristic entity. Juristic recognition, in some cases could be statutory, but does not require to be entirely statutory. It means that even regulatory tools like guidelines, sandboxes, circulars and other legal instruments could be used. Even judgments and orders can have an *ad hoc* or *interim effect* to give recognition to Artificial Intelligence as a juristic entity. The benefit is that when you confer juristic recognition to Artificial Intelligence, you can confer some recognition in a legal sense, which is for limited use. It does not interfere with the existing systems of legal recognition, that is, *Coherentism*, as discussed in *Chapter 1*. Now, in the case of multilateral institutions, juristic recognition is much possible and makes a lot of sense, for simple reasons. First, we know how ineffective these negotiations and deliberations in multilateral bodies become with time, as technology expands. In that case, if *soft-level deliberative models* (Abhivardhan, et al., 2021) can be adopted, through mere declarations, like say – the *UNESCO Recommendations on the Ethics of Artificial Intelligence*, then a lot of non-binding, yet deliberative standards can be achieved.

As an industry, recognizing the role of Artificial Intelligence could be subject to industry developments and realities. Multilateral institutions either have their industry-centric counterparts, or within their structure, they have some committees or expert groups or councils, which are capable and within their mandate to assess how Artificial Intelligence would affect specific industries. For example, UNESCO may be concerned by AI education, as an area while the ITU may opt for the use of Artificial Intelligence in the telecom sector. We must look out for how these institutions approach the industry role of AI, at what level or at least to what extent.

Subject – Object – Third Party Method

This method involves designating Artificial Intelligence in the context of its relationship with human environment. In this case, Artificial Intelligence could be a product, a service, or a system infrastructure, in any of the three cases, subject, object and third party.

As a Subject, the AI as a product / service / system is being affected by the human environment, in the form of inputs and outputs. As a subject, AI could raise concerns about accountability and liability. For example, if an AI system causes harm or makes a mistake, who is responsible for the consequences? Is it the developers, the owners, or the users of the AI system? There may also be questions around transparency and explainability of AI systems, particularly in cases where decisions made by the AI may have significant impacts on human rights, such as in the case of automated decision-making in areas like healthcare or criminal justice.

As an object, AI as a product / service / system could raise concerns around privacy and data protection. For example, if AI is used to process personal data, what safeguards need to be in place to ensure that the data is protected and used in accordance with relevant data protection laws and regulations? There may also be questions around the right to access and correct personal data processed by AI systems.

As a third party, AI as a product / service / system may raise concerns around its autonomy and decision-making capabilities. For example, if an AI system makes a decision that has significant impacts on individuals or groups, can it be held accountable for its actions? There may also be questions around bias and discrimination in AI decision-making, particularly in cases where AI is used to make decisions about employment, credit, or other areas that could significantly impact people's lives.

Now, considering both the classification methods used, it can be rightly questioned, as to how capable our multilateral institutions are to deal with such issues, because means of cooperation among companies, regulators and diplomats could be sufficient and much effective as compared to mere intergovernmental institutions, which are inept and inefficient. *Corneliu Bjola* and *Ilan Manor*, in their article for *Global Policy*, had suggested (Bjola, et al., 2023) that conversational AI tools like ChatGPT, or any text-based generative AI tool could be used to sabotage the human element of diplomacy. Here is an excerpt from the article:

Conversational AIs could author press releases, create content for social media *campaigns, draft UN resolutions, and generate speeches before human diplomats even get to work. While automation may be cost-effective, it may not necessarily translate into effectiveness in diplomacy, which relies heavily on informal conversations and personal relationships between diplomats. […] ChatGPT could also be used as a tool for "**continuing negotiations,**" a concept proposed by Cardinal Richelieu to address potential crises before they emerge. By developing simulations that explore various paths of escalation or de-escalation in emerging conflicts, diplomats could use ChatGPT to assess the likelihood of future diplomatic crises and devise strategies to prevent or manage them (Bjola, et al., 2023).*

To be fair, *Cardinal Richeliu's* proposition of continuing negotiations seems to be interesting. Countries may use generative AI tools like ChatGPT to develop simulations to explore various paths of escalation or engagement. However, increasing efficiency to create alternative scenarios of engagement does not mean creating effective diplomatic scenarios. Role conception, in the world of diplomacy, and international law could still never be deprived of its human element beyond political reasons. Nevertheless, the possibilities of using Artificial Intelligence in diplomacy and multilateral efforts, exist. *Zoraver Daulet Singh*, one of the most prolific minds in Indian Foreign Policy studies, has examined role conception in times of crises for diplomats in *Figure 1.1* in the book, *Power and Diplomacy*. *Figure 2.2* depicts how choice paths are shaped during a crisis.

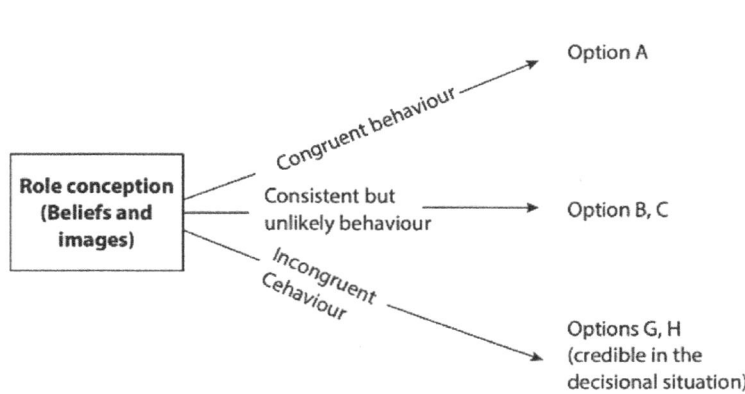

Figure 2.2: Choice Paths during a Crisis, from Power and Diplomacy: India's Foreign Policies during the Cold War (Singh, 2019).

In this figure, it is explained how in certain kinds of crises, governments adopt different kinds of roles. Option A could be the scenario where diplomats act in a congruent fashion as they are expected to do. However, there could be circumstances where certain consistent actions and protocols require unlikely changes and tendencies to be adopted. That is where **Options B** and **C** come. In the worst-case scenarios, perhaps, **Options G** and **H**, which are considered as credible enough in the situation itself, when decisions must be made, could be adopted.

Analytics, automation, and intelligence in diplomacy

Now, there are some of the most common use cases of employing Artificial Intelligence in diplomatic efforts and making international law work. Since we already know how we can examine and discover the limits of using AI technologies, based on the two classification methods discussed, we can at least think of creating hierarchies of use cases.

The data-algorithm relationship, in the case of international law and diplomacy, may depend on a vertical hierarchy of use cases, which could be referred to as the Analytics, Automation and Intelligence hierarchy (hereinafter referred to as the **AAI hierarchy**). Now, there could be three kinds of use cases in this hierarchy, starting from analytics, as a use case category up to intelligence. So, you can use analytics tools to make certain levels of decisions, which could then help you approach automation as a tool to solve or maintain something. Intelligence, or what we could colloquially mean – the real Artificial Intelligence (which may remain narrow AI), could also be used at a different level. The *Gartner Analytical Continuum* is a simple way to understand different kinds of analytics, that could exist, whose use cases may range from merely descriptive analytics to prescriptive analytics into optimization. The *Figure 2.2* depicted below is a depiction of the *Gartner Analytical Continuum*, explaining levels of analytics-based technologies used to enhance and materialize their value proposition.

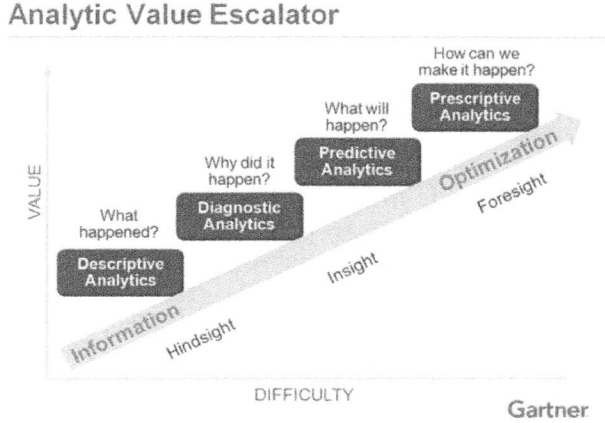

Figure 2.3: The Gartner Analytical Continuum (Gartner, 2020)

Conclusion

Dr. Bjola in his paper for the Anwar Gargash Diplomatic Academy in 2020 had proposed the *TIID framework (task, innovation, integration, deployment)*, which could really be insightful to understand. Here is an excerpt from the paper:

> *The framework proposes a particular sequence of model design, which begins with an examination of the specific profile of the diplomatic task that is expected to be improved, continues with an evaluation of the type of innovation required for restructuring the service, a discussion of the level of integration of the physical and digital dimensions of the service, and concludes with an examination of the availability and suitability of the existing institutional configuration. The logic behind the sequence is that AI integration should be service- rather than technology-focused so that the risk of designing and delivering AI-driven services of questionable practical value could be suitably minimised (Bjola, 2020).*

This approach was proposed by *Dr. Bjola* for consular practices, international cooperation, and risk-based decision-making, majorly. The framework is quite practical since it addresses the need to regulate the use of AI with a risk-centric approach. Limiting the use of AI as a service to restructure both diplomatic services as well as the AI tools involved, is quite appreciative.

In further chapters, I have discussed some more use cases, and illustrations on the use of Artificial Intelligence in diplomacy and global governance. The focus of this chapter has been to offer a condoned and reasonable perspective on AI governance by means of diplomacy and rules and norms of international law. In the next chapter, I have delved into the economics of enabling and commercializing Artificial Intelligence in the post-COVID times, and how do the trends explain the rise and hype of the AI industry.

References

- **Permanent Court of International Justice. 1927.** *S.S. Lotus (Fr. v. Turk.), 1927 P.C.I.J. (ser. A) No. 10 (Sept. 7).* 10, s.l. : Permanent Court of International Justice, September 7, 1927.

- **Espinoza, Javier. 2021.** EU must overhaul flagship data protection laws, says a 'father' of policy. *Financial Times.* [Online] March 3, 2021. **https://www.ft.com/content/b0b44dbe-1e40-4624-bdb1-e87bc8016106.**

- *The Contribution of International Law to International Relations.* **Piscatori, J. 1977.** 2, 1977, International Affairs (Royal Institute of International Affairs 1944-), Vol. 53, pp. 217-231.

- **Schmitt, M. N. 2017.** *Tallinn Manual 2.0 on the International Law Applicable to Cyber Operations.* 2nd. Cambridge : Cambeidge University Press, 2017.

- **North Atlantic Treaty Organization.** NATO 2016 Warsaw Conference Communiqué.

- **The Council of Europe. 2001.** The Budapest Convention (ETS No. 185) and its Protocols . [Online] 2001. **https://www.coe.int/en/web/cybercrime/the-budapest-convention.**

- **International Telecommunication Union. 1992.** Constitution of the International Telecommunication Union. December 22, 1992.

- **Kelsen, Hans. 2009.** *Pure Theory of Law.* [trans.] Max Knight. New Jersey : The Lawbook Exchange Ltd., 2009.

- **Cummings, M. L., et al. 2018.** *Artificial Intelligence and International Affairs: Disruption Anticipated.* Chatham House. 2018.

- **Larson, Christina. 2018.** Who needs democracy when you have data? *MIT Technology Review.* [Online] August 20, 2018. **https://www.technologyreview.com/s/611815/who-needs-democracy-when-you-have-data/.**

- **Tamanaha, B. 2004.** *On the Rule of Law: History, Politics, Theory.* Cambridge : Cambridge University Press, 2004.

- **Fontes, Catarina, et al. 2022.** AI-powered public surveillance systems: why we (might) need them and how we want them . *Technology in Society.* 2022, Vol. 71.

- **Maas, Maathijs. 2019.** International Law Does Not Compute: Artificial Intelligence and the Development, Displacement or Destruction of the Global Legal Order. *Melbourne Journal of International Law.* 2019, Vol. 20.

- **Moniodis, Christina P. 2012.** Moving from Nixon to NASA: Privacy's Second Strand — A Right to Informational Privacy. *Yale Journal of Law & Technology.* 2012, Vol. 15, pp. 139-168.

- **Supreme Court of India. 2018.** *Justice (Retd.) K.S. Puttaswamy and Another v. Union of India.* 494, s.l. : Supreme Court of India, September 2018.

- **Abhivardhan. 2022.** The IP Rights of Artificial Intelligence. *Visual Legal Analytica, Indic Pacific Legal Research.* [Online] July 22, 2022. [Cited: May 7, 2023.] **https://www.indicpacific.com/post/the-ip-rights-of-artificial-intelligence.**

- **Abhivardhan and Tejnani, Dev. 2022.** Introduction to Artificial Intelligence. *2020 Handbook on AI and International Law.* s.l. : Indic Pacific Legal Research LLP, 2022.

- **Abhivardhan and Sharma, Aditi. 2021.** Why A Culture-oriented Strategy Matters For India To Pioneer In AI Ethics Leadership . *Analytics India Magazine.* [Online] July 27, 2021. [Cited: May 7, 2023.] **https://analyticsindiamag.com/why-a-culture-oriented-strategy-matters-for-india-to-pioneer-in-ai-ethics-leadership/.**

- **Bjola, Corneliu and Manor, Ilan. 2023.** ChatGPT: The end of diplomacy as we know it . *Global Policy Journal.* [Online] April 25, 2023. [Cited: May 7, 2023.] **https://globalpolicyjournal.com/blog/25/04/2023/chatgpt-end-diplomacy-we-know-it.**

- **Singh, Zoraver Daulet. 2019.** *Power and Diplomacy: India's Foreign Policies during the Cold War.* s.l. : Oxford University Press, 2019.

- **Gartner, 2020.** What is the role of data and analytics in business? . *Gartner.* [Online] 2020. **https://www.gartner.com/en/topics/data-and-analytics**.

- **Bjola, Corneliu. 2020.** Diplomacy in the Age of Artificial Intelligence. *Anwar Gargash Diplomatic Academy.* [Online] 2020. **https://www.agda.ac.ae/docs/default-source/ Publications/eda-working-paper_artificial-intelligence_en.pdf?sfvrsn=4**.

Endnotes

[1] Acronym for United Nations Educational, Scientific and Cultural Organization.

[2] Acronym for Western Europe and Northern America.

Join our book's Discord space

Join the book's Discord Workspace for Latest updates, Offers, Tech happenings around the world, New Release and Sessions with the Authors:

https://discord.bpbonline.com

CHAPTER 3
The Innovation and Economics of AI

यथा पूर्वं चरति जगति क्रिया,

तथा ततो विद्यया च यः प्रयाति।

अन्तर्लिने यस्य न किञ्चिदीयते,

विद्वद्वद्वयोऽपि तस्य सर्वमीदृशम्॥

"Just as the world continues its activities as before,
So does the one who moves forward with knowledge.
Nothing is hidden from the one who possesses inner wisdom,
Even the knowledgeable ones fear that person's insight."

The culmination of the AI industry had happened long back, when companies like Google, Amazon, Microsoft and many more had invested in the computational capabilities of AI systems. The focus towards enabling effective analytics had already shifted by 2015, and the mainstream use of Artificial Intelligence, was being encouraged through analytics. While robotics has been a part of the narrative, analytics had already driven and created opportunities for many technology companies and consulting firms, especially in the Global North. However, the pace was slow until 2019. *OpenAI* had released GPT-2 in November 2019, (Solaiman, et al., 2019) and *Samsung* had used **Generative Adversarial Networks (GANs)** to transform facial images into videos (Zakharov, et al., 2019), what we call deepfakes. It was quite a year for reinforcement learning if not for Generative Artificial Intelligence. Interestingly, that year, the **3-body problem** was solved by researchers at the Universities of *Edinburgh* and *Cambridge* using machine learning (Sagar, 2019).

When the COVID pandemic began, the world was shut, as the World Health Organization had declared the pandemic as an international public health emergency. Despite the logistic, social and other setbacks the world had to face due to the pandemic, and the waves that surged of different virus variants, from Alpha to Delta to Omicron, AI research did not lose the pace. It was even a consequential year for my organization, the Indian Society of Artificial Intelligence and Law, when my organization had conducted our first Indian Conference on Artificial Intelligence and Law (Indian Society of Artificial Intelligence and Law, 2020) and had begun the ISAIL Handbook project. I had even developed two important reports with my team, among many, i.e., the *COVID19.AI Report* and the *Report on National Education Policy of India* with a perspective on AI Education.

In 2020, *OpenAI* had already developed GPT-3 (Heaven, 2020). It was a consequential year in AI and healthcare, since AI had achieved high performance in diagnosis, prognosis evaluation, epidemic prediction and drug discovery for COVID-19 (Wang, et al., 2021). By 2022, ChatGPT, based on GPT-3.5 (infamously now known as ChatGPT) was introduced. Industry geeks consider this generative AI tool as a starter point for artificial generative intelligence, or AGI. Some may even call ChatGPT as an early-stage AGI because of its all-pervading comprehension features. By 2020, it was figured out that *GPT-3* could produce notes in English, Hindi, and many languages, and even in the form of musical notes, of instruments like guitar, piano and others. *GPT-3* also can draft basic contract templates, and other legal documents. Although, when ChatGPT became mainstream by January 2022, it reached 1 million users in 5 days and 100 million users by early 2023 (Hu, 2023). It was the humongous use of this generative AI application in unimaginable, multiple areas, that its penetration has become **omnipotent** and **omnipresent**. In fact, all Artificial Intelligence technologies are aimed to become omnipresent and omnipotent. That is a fundamental characteristic which ChatGPT despite its failures and limits have achieved.

After establishing the potential of generative AI and its rapidly expanding influence across various sectors, it becomes imperative to delve deeper into the innovation and economics of this technology. As we explore the vast capabilities of Artificial Intelligence , it is evident that its ultimate goal is to become omnipotent and omnipresent. This fundamental characteristic of AI is not only a key driver for innovation but also has significant economic implications. Therefore, it is essential to understand the intricate interplay between technology, innovation, and economics to realize the full potential of AI. In this chapter, I have explored the various dimensions of the innovation and economics of AI in a post-COVID world and the challenges and opportunities it presents.

Weaponization of data, algorithms, and everything

Artificial Intelligence , like any class of digital technologies, is driven by the urge to innovate. Sometimes, certain innovations work, while some do not. Those innovations, which prove out to be disruptive, can surely be regarded as disruptive technologies, which to some extent Artificial Intelligence has become. The advancements in Machine Learning have led to a wider democratization of deep learning among technology companies and scientists. Here is an illustration of the drivers of innovation and economics of Artificial Intelligence in this mind map. Let us discuss each of these eight drivers and understand their purpose, as depicted in *Figure 3.1*:

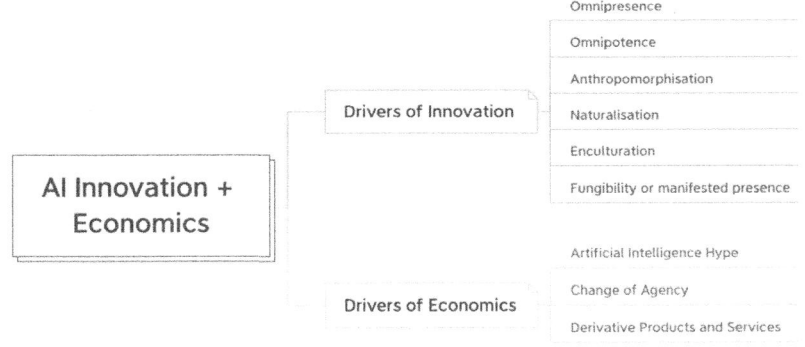

Figure 3.1: Mind Map depicting what drives innovation and economics of Artificial Intelligence.

Omnipresence, to begin with, relates to the nature or characteristic to be present everywhere by virtue. Nearly all Artificial Intelligence applications and tools are meant to be omnipresent. There could be certain limitations attached to them, which may not show how omnipresent they are, due to factors like lack of training data, algorithmic bias and weak training environment. From a legal perspective, omnipresence may be interpreted as a link to estimate if any AI tool is causing any anti-competitive practice to be encouraged, or whether the market is subject to manipulation, or how the representative element of the product or service, in which the AI technology is involved is unclear and deceptive. Even otherwise, omnipresence could be related with the level of presence, in horizontal and vertical forms. For instance, let us consider the widespread use of ChatGPT across geographies for multiple identical or similar purposes. It is evident that this generative AI application could be seen as omnipresent in such scenarios.

Omnipotence means a characteristic which implies someone, or something has potential, which is unlimited or at least that makes that someone or something, respectively, invincible to execute a set of operations and activities. When we study algorithmic operations and activities, of any AI system, we do not limit our study to ask as to what the computational power of that AI system or the deep learning infrastructure is. We go beyond and assess if that AI system has a sense of potential to perform those specific algorithmic operations and activities, which could be performed under special circumstances or general circumstances. Omnipotence is a generic trait of Artificial Intelligence systems, which must be analyzed since these make the use cases of many AI products and services possible. Even the limits of use cases, then can be estimated at a level by enabling or disabling certain technical parameters. Reinforcement learning perhaps could be considered as currently the best form of machine learning method which makes us estimate how much omnipotent AI systems could be. *Figure 3.2* provides an elementary way to explain how AI itself is affected by multiple aspects of identity when exposed to a training environment.

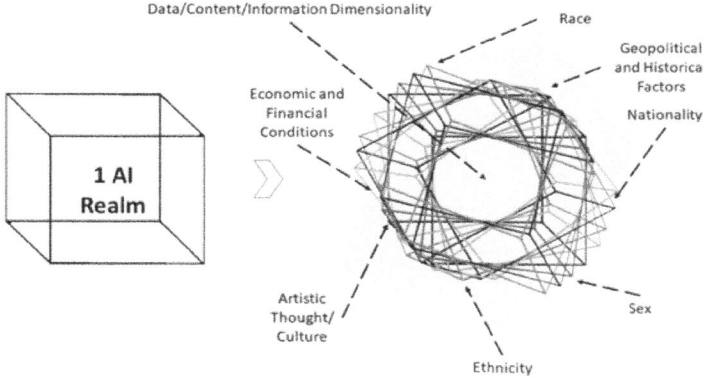

Figure 3.2: *An elementary way to explain how AI itself is affected by multiple aspects of identity when exposed to a training environment.*

Anthropomorphization, implies a process in which something (non-human) is transformed into something human-oriented, human-related or human-centric. Here is an excerpt on anthropomorphization from my paper for the 16th AIAI 2020 Conference.

> *The approach is premised on the basis that AI requires to be understood as a transformable legal entity, that is, Artificial Intelligence possesses stimulating characteristics and can develop its own limited empathy. [...] The empathy developed by AI is probabilistic by activities but is deterministic by observations because the same practicable empathy developed by AI is adaptive incoherent human environments. This is practicable in case of any technological asset developed. Therefore, by practice and purpose, AI is capable to develop adaptive empathy (Abhivardhan, 2020).*

The term **empathy** described in this excerpt relates to this aspect that Artificial Intelligence systems, products and services require to have limited form of machinic empathy or tendency to blend in with the training data and environment, that sometimes they merely develop on their own, due to perhaps lack of proper training data, algorithmic biases, lack of explainability and other relevant issues. *ChatGPT* is perhaps the best example of Anthropomorphization, especially in the category of generative AI. The reason is that *GPT-3.5* (and beyond) as a version, is subject to what data and AI scientists call, hallucination (Smith, 2023). It simply means that *ChatGPT* when subject to prompts, sometimes provides such responses, where it forgets that it is responding as a large language model, and not a human being, and even makes up stories, concepts, laws and even historical events. Although this is quite interesting but it could be used for manipulative causes, which one must be wary about. Another aspect that could be related to anthropomorphization is the use of proprietary information when it comes to generative AI tools like ChatGPT.

Naturalization means to become obviously knowledgeable to any environment and its constituents such that it feels as if the environment itself is the normal of the day. In the context of Artificial Intelligence , naturalization may be referred to the EAS test (or the explainability, adaptability and self-assessment test) I had proposed in my paper for the 16th AIAI 2020 (Abhivardhan, 2020). This litmus test of sorts is legally and technically viable. It simply means that any AI system needs to be explainable, adaptive and self-assessed to its own algorithmic infrastructure, and the users and creators (developers and service providers) of them. Let us decipher this. Explainability in AI is not a new demand. This demand has been raised since the existence of AI as a field, and a class of technology. This implies that the algorithmic activities and operations of Artificial Intelligence systems must be explainable. Adaptability is a follow-up element of explainability which implies how much adaptive any AI system could become. While technical parameters may be decided for AI systems, there could be a possibility to create certain commercial law parameters for AI systems, accordingly.

Enculturation is a process to build and contribute to assets or means of tangible and intangible cultural heritage. Societies inherit cultures from their ancestors and shape them as time proceeds. In the context of Artificial Intelligence , while we study about how training environments affect AI systems, the cultural impact of Artificial Intelligence is a reality, which affects people in different realms uniquely. In certain cases, AI tools may be helpful to shape work culture and ethics, while in certain cases, AI enables better working standards or technical standards. It depends on the kind of AI application being put to use. However, enculturation is real, and it happens.

Fungibility or manifested presence, is a natural extension of omnipresence. Artificial Intelligence systems are capable to be fungible and transformable in terms of their presence in various applications, tools and products / services based on the manifested need required. Imagine a dynamic scenario where the concept of a **Decentralized Autonomous Organization (DAO)** extends beyond a single application or tool. In this innovative landscape, AI systems prove their remarkable adaptability and versatility. These AI systems seamlessly morph to suit different applications, tools, and services, based on the specific needs that emerge. For instance, within this DAO-driven ecosystem, AI algorithms can be programmed to autonomously reconfigure their functions and priorities, ensuring they remain relevant and effective across a range of products and services. This could vividly showcase the transformative and fungible nature of various AI algorithms aligns with the ever-evolving requirements of the ecosystem they serve.

Artificial Intelligence hype is a form of market hype to perpetuate to generate influence or market perception in a real-time scenario such that a class of Artificial Intelligence technology as a product /service is used in a participatory or preparatory sense (Abhivardhan, 2022 pp. 45-47). This is discussed in detail with examples in the next section of this chapter. However, to understand at a basic level, it is simple to understand that as an economic driver, hype is generated about AI products and services by promising some or most or all of the drivers of innovation, that I have discussed, in different ways and methods. For example, generative AI tools which are used to create AI-generated videos, are being claimed to replace actors (Vanacker, 2023). Another example could be related to certain companies claiming that *ChatGPT's* drafting abilities could be used to replace lawyers (Dhanrajani, 2023). While there could be some use involved, it is necessary to distinguish between hype and reality. *Figure 3.3* depicts a table from a working paper recently published in March 2023, which shows the jobs that could be affected by generative AI tools, like ChatGPT:

Group	Occupations with highest exposure	% Exposure
Human α	Interpreters and Translators	76.5
	Survey Researchers	75.0
	Poets, Lyricists and Creative Writers	68.8
	Animal Scientists	66.7
	Public Relations Specialists	66.7
Human β	Survey Researchers	84.4
	Writers and Authors	82.5
	Interpreters and Translators	82.4
	Public Relations Specialists	80.6
	Animal Scientists	77.8
Human ζ	Mathematicians	100.0
	Tax Preparers	100.0
	Financial Quantitative Analysts	100.0
	Writers and Authors	100.0
	Web and Digital Interface Designers	100.0
	Humans labeled 15 occupations as "fully exposed."	
Model α	Mathematicians	100.0
	Correspondence Clerks	95.2
	Blockchain Engineers	94.1
	Court Reporters and Simultaneous Captioners	92.9
	Proofreaders and Copy Markers	90.9
Model β	Mathematicians	100.0
	Blockchain Engineers	97.1
	Court Reporters and Simultaneous Captioners	96.4
	Proofreaders and Copy Markers	95.5
	Correspondence Clerks	95.2
Model ζ	Accountants and Auditors	100.0
	News Analysts, Reporters, and Journalists	100.0
	Legal Secretaries and Administrative Assistants	100.0
	Clinical Data Managers	100.0
	Climate Change Policy Analysts	100.0
	The model labeled 86 occupations as "fully exposed."	
Highest variance	Search Marketing Strategists	14.5
	Graphic Designers	13.4
	Investment Fund Managers	13.0
	Financial Managers	13.0
	Insurance Appraisers, Auto Damage	12.6

Figure 3.3: *Occupations with the highest exposure according to each measurement (Eloundou, et al., 2023)*

Now, the authors of the working paper, have pointed out the limitations in these results, which are noteworthy. Here is an excerpt of the key limitations discussed:

> *A fundamental limitation of our approach lies in the subjectivity of the labeling. In our study, we employ annotators who are familiar with LLM capabilities. However, this group is not occupationally diverse, potentially leading to biased judgments regarding LLMs' reliability and effectiveness in performing tasks within unfamiliar occupations. [...] The outcomes of GPT-4 task classification are sensitive to alterations in the rubric's wording, the prompt's order and composition, the presence or absence of specific examples in the rubric, the level of detail provided, and the definitions given for key terms. Consequently, there are slight differences between the rubric presented to humans and the one used for GPT-4. This decision was made deliberately to guide the model towards reasonable labels without excessively influencing human annotators. As a result, we use multiple annotation sources, but none should be considered the definitive ground truth relative to the others. [...] It is unclear to what extent occupations can be entirely broken down into tasks, and whether this approach systematically omits certain categories of skills or tasks that are tacitly required for competent performance of a job (Eloundou, et al., 2023 pp. 9-10).*

In addition, this paper does focus on US-based work professions, which is another reason this paper should not be touted to create hype about "**AI taking away human jobs**". There is a straight possibility that generative AI tools can deeply affect human jobs and skill requirements as a matter of replacement or enablement. However, again, it is necessary to ensure that tools like ChatGPT and others are explainable, open source and provide factual instances as to how they make such decisions. Giving prompts and getting results are easy thing. But how those results come in, is a must to be known. It however should not be misconstrued that the AI system's computational ability could be less or weak. Developers and AI scientists must develop means of explainability that help.

This is where **Change of Agency** as a parameter comes in. AI applications by nature are expected to change agency of any object or human operator. They could be considered tools of mobility and accessibility, rightfully for they sometimes are helpful. Since algorithms are computationally stronger and faster to be performed, human agency deprives itself, which is what we would call the phenomenon of technology displacement, leading to a loss of human autonomy in terms of involving acts of physical or chemical change, in the language of industrialization. For example, it could be any basic form of work, in, say, writing or transcribing, which now an AI tool could do better, faster and safer. Google Translate is definitely the epitome of Large Language Models (LLMs) when it comes to translation and transliteration. ChatGPT is an edgy competitor there too.

Derivative products and services in the context of the AI industry are some of the most hyped and impactful economic drivers of Artificial Intelligence as an industry. Recent developments where we see a huge increase in generative AI tools and applications not only generate AI hype because of their association with the glorification of using AI as the new modern normal. Several of these generative AI tools and applications run on certain GPT model or any other large language model. In the case of AI-based creativity solutions, the large language models would be different in perspective still. You can also call it as if one, two or more companies who maintain these large language models are AI vendors, who offer the use of ChatGPT and other such models, using a subscription model based on tokens used per prompt or per output. Based on this business model, any X or Y company then can build their own AI products and services. We can also say these could be 'knock-off' AI-products and AI-services.

Now, all these drivers of innovation and economics, clearly explain in the form of a pattern of purpose or virtue, how Artificial Intelligence is commercialized and improved, category and industry wise. Up until now, you must have got a more open picture to imagine how AI products and services are produced with a perspective. Let us now get into the part, where *weaponization of everything* comes in.

What is the weaponization of everything?

Weaponization of everything is a term that is used to describe the increasing trend of utilizing various technologies and scientific advancements for military purposes. In the context of Artificial Intelligence , weaponization has taken on a whole new meaning as the world has witnessed the transformative impact of this technology on virtually every aspect of our lives. While AI has the potential to create tremendous benefits, there is a growing concern that it could also be used for destructive purposes. This has led to a debate about the need to regulate and monitor the development of AI to prevent its weaponization.

The idea of weaponization of everything is not new and can be traced back to the earliest days of human civilization. From spears and arrows to guns and bombs, humans have always sought to use technology to gain military advantage. However, the pace of technological advancement has increased dramatically in recent years, and AI is playing a significant role in this trend. The commercialization of AI has led to the creation of a vast array of applications that can be used for military purposes. These include autonomous weapons systems, facial recognition, and predictive policing.

The weaponization of AI is not limited to traditional military applications. It also has the potential to be used in cyber warfare, economic espionage, and political manipulation. In the context of AI hype and commercialization, the weaponization of AI poses a significant challenge to policymakers and civil society. On one hand, there is a need to encourage innovation and the development of AI to realize its potential benefits. On the other hand, there is a need to regulate and monitor the development of AI to prevent its weaponization. *Complexity theory* suggests that the best way to achieve this balance is through a collaborative approach that involves all stakeholders, including policymakers, industry, civil society, and academia.

The regulation of AI is a complex issue that requires a multifaceted approach. It involves developing standards and protocols for the responsible use of AI in military and non-military contexts. It also involves investing in research and development to enhance the transparency and explainability of AI algorithms. Also, it would involve fostering a culture of responsible innovation that emphasizes the ethical and social implications of AI.

The drivers of AI innovation and economy are powerful forces shaping the way we interact with Artificial Intelligence. The omnipresence and omnipotence of AI make it an all-encompassing and highly influential technology that is increasingly integrated into our daily lives. The anthropomorphization and naturalization of AI reflect our desire to understand and interact with technology in ways that are familiar to us as humans. Enculturation and the fungibility of AI reflect the ways in which it is becoming an integral part of the cultures and economies in which it is used. At the same time, the Artificial Intelligence hype that surrounds this technology is driving rapid innovation and change. This hype has led to a proliferation of derivative products and services that build on AI, including chatbots, voice assistants, and automated decision-making tools. It has also led to a change in agency, as AI increasingly takes over tasks and decision-making that were once the domain of humans.

These drivers of AI innovation and economy are complex and multifaceted, and their impacts are far-reaching and often unpredictable. As we continue to integrate AI into our lives and economies, it is important to carefully consider the implications of these drivers and to ensure that we are using this technology in ways that are ethical, equitable, and sustainable. Let us now unfold into an important market phenomenon, which is already discussed, in detail – AI hype.

Artificial Intelligence hype is real

If one tries to study and understand hype cycles, perhaps one of the best ways is to understand the science that drives hype cycles for products and services. At a basic level, human societies are driven by a sense of vogue towards people, objects, institutions, and natural phenomena. It could happen for various reasons. In some cases, one may be astoundingly impressed and inspired that a new product, service, message, phenomenon, or campaign offers. In fact, the most interesting facet of Artificial Intelligence Hype, or any form of hype, is that it is human driven. Let us estimate what seems to be human driven.

Now, for centuries, humans, across civilizations have shaped their discourses and narratives based on their needs and wants. This may seem to be quite bland and boring approach to the discourse of the history of information warfare, but that was it. Our motives would differ naturally, but we all had developed sophisticated means of communication. Also, it starts with the art of persuasion. In the world of persuasion, hype thus encompasses a skillful interplay of exaggeration, the art of superlatives, and various other techniques that ignite a fervent sense of excitement and anticipation surrounding a product, service, or idea. This mesmerizing force is adept at selling anything, ranging from the latest automobiles to aspiring political figures. Now, numerous factors contribute to the astounding effectiveness of hype. Primarily, it taps into our emotional core, evoking sensations that allure and captivate us. The concoction of hype can elicit a rush of exhilaration, pique our curiosity, or even instill within us an urgent desire to acquire. These emotions wield immense power, swaying our choices in unforeseen ways and compelling us to make decisions we may not have otherwise considered. It is also interesting that the allure of hype is augmented by its ability to create a perceived scarcity. The notion that something is highly coveted or only available for a limited time fuels our yearning for it. The fear of missing out (Warzel, 2022) on an experience or possession that seemingly everyone else is acquiring becomes a compelling driving force in our decision-making process. One also must understand that the potency of hype stems from its foundation in partial truths. Many of the subjects that receive hype are, indeed, remarkable products or services. However, the realm of hype often transcends factual boundaries, forging unrealistic expectations. Consequently, this can lead to disappointment when reality fails to live up to the grandeur of the hype.

How can one then navigate the waters of hype and avoid succumbing to its allure? Firstly, one must cultivate an awareness of its influence. When confronted with an item shrouded in hype, it is crucial to pause and scrutinize the underlying motives. **Is the hype fueled by emotions, scarcity, or rooted in truth?** If it comes to mind that emotions or scarcity may overshadow the basis of the hype, caution should prevail when making decisions based solely on such sentiments. Secondly, conducting meticulous research becomes paramount. **Merely accepting the surface-level hype at face value is insufficient.** It has become normal to go through several reviews, comparing prices or indicators, and ensuring that what is being sought aligns with what one genuinely wishes to have. Also, it is necessary to realize that hype is merely an illusion—an artful fabrication. It possesses no tangible existence in reality. Even if one may argue hype yields substantial influence, but it is not impervious to scrutiny. By cultivating awareness and conducting thorough research, one can skillfully evade its enchantment and make well-informed decisions regarding the products, services, and ideas they choose to embrace.

Now, there is no doubt that hype may leave some scars or symbols behind, which somehow affect societies and markets. This itself happens because hype by its nature could be interlinked with **social and market realities**. It is designed to exploit those realities, cultures, and economies we live in. There is nothing so airtight in the world of narratives, which could not be exploited, unless the **human element** of **transacting with information, anecdata, and hype**, remains diligent and reasonable. However, as information overload affects societies and markets, which generates any hype cycle, let us try to understand the psychological imprints of hype and information overload. In a 2016 article for **Nautilus**, *Robert Sapolsky* explains how Capgras delusions explain the rise of hype due to perception issues attributed to the human mind:

> *When it comes to decision-making, particularly in a social context, what we view as appropriate behavior reflects a balance between emotion and cognition. What Capgras delusions show is that a similar balance occurs when it comes to identifying those whom we know best. [...] For 99 percent of hominid history, social communication consisted of face-to-face interactions with someone you've hunted and foraged with most of your life. But then the recognition and familiarity components got pried apart by modern technology. [...] Thus, not only has modern life increasingly dissociated*

recognition and familiarity, but it has impoverished the latter in the process. This is worsened by our frantic skill at multitasking, especially social multitasking. [...] By any logic, this should induce all of us to have Capgras delusions, to find it plausible that everyone we encounter is an imposter. [...] But something very different has occurred instead. This withering of primate familiarity in the face of technology prompts us to mistake an acquaintance for a friend [...] It allows us to become intimate with people whose familiarity then proves false. [...] Through history, Capgras syndrome has been a cultural mirror of a dissociative mind, where thoughts of recognition and feelings of intimacy have been sundered. It is still that mirror. Today we think that what is false and artificial in the world around us is substantive and meaningful. It's not that loved ones and friends are mistaken for simulations, but that simulations are mistaken for them (Sapolsky, 2016).

Now, *Sapolsky* in this text, suggests a connection between the phenomenon of Capgras delusions and the impact of modern technology, particularly social media, and online interactions, on our perception of familiarity and recognition. There is no doubt that our increasingly detached and mediated communication through technology has disrupted the balance between recognition and familiarity that existed in traditional face-to-face interactions. The proliferation of virtual connections and the constant exposure to simulations or online personas can lead to a blurring of the line between genuine human relationships and artificial representations. The intriguing mention of multitasking, especially in social contexts, implies that our attention is divided among various online interactions, further contributing to the erosion of familiarity and genuine connection. This aspect resonates with the concerns raised in the context of AI hype, where the fear of technology replacing human interaction or creating shallow connections is often discussed. The prevalence of simulations and artificial experiences in our modern world may lead us to mistake these representations for genuine connections.

Conclusion

To conclude, let us get beyond the social impact of Artificial Intelligence hype as discussed in this chapter. For sure, technology-led distancing shapes the paradigm of social and market conditions, which we could find in the case of social media and Artificial Intelligence applications. Imagine how could it affect the way markets behave. The impact is pseudonymous and disruptive, simply because it is faceless or human-less, and second, it does have an abnormal or uncertain impact on economies. Let us take a simple example to reckon with. Imagine you have a set of companies listed as public companies in the stock markets across the world. Now, in the case of the United States of America, as of 2023, the internet penetration stands at 91.8%. If one would impersonate a publicly listed company and make hyped statements or remarks, which show that the social media account expressing the same represents the activities of the publicly listed company, then it could affect the stocks of that publicly listed company. The impact could be considered as severe, and it does take away the aspect of trust among companies and advertisers who use social media for communication and marketing purposes. In fact, *Elon Musk*, for example, had to conduct a *Twitter* Space (Coffee, 2022) to convince advertisers and content production houses such as *Paramount, Marvel, Warner Bros. Discovery, Lionsgate* and others about the algorithmic value of Twitter (now X) as a recommendation and social medium, in times when platforms in the FAAMG grouping of big technology companies are not faring well for advertising. This is another aspect of how hype affects market realities. I have discussed these nuances in the next chapters of this book.

References

- **Solaiman, Irene, et al. 2019.** Release Strategies and the Social Impacts of Language Models. *arXiv.org*. [Online] November 14, 2019. **https://arxiv.org/abs/1908.09203**.

- **Zakharov, Egor, et al. 2019.** Few-Shot Adversarial Learning of Realistic Neural Talking Head Models. *arXiv.org*. [Online] September 25, 2019. **https://arxiv.org/pdf/1905.08233.pdf**.

- **Sagar, Ram. 2019.** Newton Vs Neural Networks: Exploring The Unsolved Three-Body Problem With ML . *Analytics India Magazine*. [Online] November 4, 2019. **https://analyticsindiamag.com/newton-vs-neural-networks-exploring-the-unsolved-three-body-problem-with-ml/**.

- **Indian Society of Artificial Intelligence and Law. 2020.** Indian Conference on Artificial Intelligence and Law, 2020. *Indian Society of Artificial Intelligence and Law*. [Online] October 1, 2020. **https://isail.in/indocon**.

- **Heaven, Will Douglas. 2020.** OpenAI's new language generator GPT-3 is shockingly good—and completely mindless . *MIT Technology Review*. [Online] July 20, 2020. **https://www.technologyreview.com/2020/07/20/1005454/openai-machine-learning-language-generator-gpt-3-nlp/**.

- **Wang, Lian, et al. 2021.** Artificial Intelligence for COVID-19: A Systematic Review. *Frontiers*. [Online] September 30, 2021. **https://www.frontiersin.org/articles/10.3389/fmed.2021.704256/full**.

- **Hu, Krystal. 2023.** ChatGPT sets record for fastest-growing user base - analyst note. *Thomson Reuters*. [Online] Feb 2, 2023. **https://www.reuters.com/technology/chatgpt-sets-record-fastest-growing-user-base-analyst-note-2023-02-01/**.

- **Abhivardhan. 2020.** The Ethos of Artificial Intelligence as a Legal Personality in a Globalized Space: Examining the Overhaul of the Post-Liberal Technological Order. *Artificial Intelligence Applications and Innovations*. 2020.

- **Smith, Craig S. 2023.** Hallucinations Could Blunt ChatGPT's Success OpenAI says the problem's solvable, Yann LeCun says we'll see. *IEEE Spectrum*. [Online] March 13, 2023. [Cited: May 8, 2023.] **https://spectrum.ieee.org/ai-hallucination**.

- **Abhivardhan. 2022.** *Deciphering Artificial Intelligence Hype and its Legal-Economic Risks, VLiGTA-TR-001.* Allahabad : Indic Pacific Legal Research LLP, 2022.

- **Vanacker, Rebecca. 2023.** "Hollywood Is Done For": AI Movie Trailer's Overconfident Review Has People In Stitches . *ScreenRant.* [Online] May 1, 2023. **https://screenrant.com/ai-movie-trailer-review-reactions/.**

- **Dhanrajani, Rachna Manojkumar. 2023.** Can ChatGPT replace lawyers? AI-powered robot lawyer is already winning cases and even sued for malpractice . *Business.* [Online] May 1, 2023. **https://www.businesstoday.in/technology/news/story/can-chatgpt-replace-lawyers-ai-powered-robot-lawyer-is-already-winning-cases-and-even-sued-for-malpractice-379800-2023-05-03.**

- **Eloundou, Tyna, et al. 2023.** GPTs are GPTs: An Early Look at the Labor Market Impact Potential of Large Language Models. *arXiv.org.* [Online] March 23, 2023. [Cited: May 9, 2023.] **https://arxiv.org/pdf/2303.10130.pdf.**

- **Warzel, Charlie. 2022.** Lessons From the Retro-Future of the Internet . *The Atlantic.* [Online] February 7, 2022. **https://www.theatlantic.com/technology/archive/2022/02/internet-web3-future-fomo/621481/.**

- **Sapolsky, Robert. 2016.** To Understand Facebook, Study Capgras Syndrome. *Nautilus.* [Online] October 27, 2016. **https://nautil.us/to-understand-facebook-study-capgras-syndrome-236173/.**

- **Coffee, Patrick. 2022.** Elon Musk tries to convince wary advertisers to stay on Twitter. *The Wall Street Journal.* [Online] November 9, 2022. **https://www.wsj.com/articles/elon-musk-tries-to-convince-wary-advertisers-to-stay-on-twitter-11668034986.**

Join our book's Discord space

Join the book's Discord Workspace for Latest updates, Offers, Tech happenings around the world, New Release and Sessions with the Authors:

https://discord.bpbonline.com

SECTION 3:

Classification and Recognition of Artificial Intelligence

CHAPTER 4
Legal Visibility

धर्मो रक्षति रक्षितः

"Law protects the one who protects it."

The purpose of legal theory or jurisprudence is to cohabit systems of international law and domestic law, in the field of public international law. It means that a United Nations body or any intergovernmental body's rules and the laws and regulations of a country, should converge somewhere provided they are of the same domain or have some point of convergence. It is however a goal which cannot be achieved in uniformity, or with a common **global** understanding anywhere. Why? This is because geographies and their economies have their own hard realities and choices, which will make naturalized exceptions. Now, it is fervently argued by some scholars and thought leaders that this intent to cohabit, is a negative obligation to avoid hostility between two system levels. Interestingly, their arguments stem from their understanding of these two basic concepts of public international law, which reciprocate in some way or the other among local and regional governments. The first concept is **monism**, and the second is **dualism**.

In monism, legal instruments at domestic and international levels can be cohesive and work in coordination, so that international law in spirit is implemented at the domestic level. However, if we inverse the gaze, then we can interpret that countries could also inspire the international legal instruments and systems, based on their national priorities and exceptions. This is where dualism, the second concept comes in. As per noted jurist *Hans Kelsen*, the monistic portion is determined by the national legal order, and this becomes certainly so important as how we resemble sovereignty, self-determination, customs, treaties and other regimes of international law and municipal law at a balanced stake. Therefore, the United Kingdom's approach towards international trade with the United States, for example, is something India or Singapore may not intend to imitate. These countries may ponder upon the advantages and risks and may conduct studies to learn from the UK's trade policy and approach. However, they would still not copy them. Perhaps, this is why in the India-US Joint Statement published by the White House in 2023 both the countries embrace ancillary means of international trade, instead of randomly jumping over **Free Trade Agreements (FTAs)**. Here is an excerpt from the *Joint Statement*:

> *The United States and India have also taken steps toward deepening bilateral cooperation to strengthen our economic relationship, including trade ties. Underscoring the willingness and trust of both countries in resolving trade issues, the leaders welcomed the resolution of six outstanding WTO disputes between the two countries through mutually agreed solutions as well as their understandings on market access related to certain products of significance to the bilateral trade relationship (The White House, 2023).*

However, what if we understand the relationships of our global, domestic and regional (even local) systems, in a different way? Let us unpack this further.

Let us say we imagine legal instruments and systems at any level as multi-dimensional (for example, with a 3D perspective) which works with the 2-dimensional approach of developing legal ideas, systems, and instruments. How would it really look like? How would it even seem real? Well, the answer lies in finding out how we have shaped the anatomy of a polity, and its legal & administrative systems. One of the best examples to ponder upon this phenomenon, is **A Genealogy of States**, a concept by *Quentin Skinner*. Here is an excerpt from his infamous lecture on **A Genealogy of States**, on *persona ficta*, giving a multi-faceted perspective on statehood and statecraft:

> *As a persona ficta, the state is able to incur obligations that no government and no single generation of citizens could ever hope to discharge. I would go so far as to conclude that, in the present state of contract law, there is no other way of making sense of such obligations than by invoking the idea of the state as a person possessed, in Hobbes's phrase, with an artificial eternity of life (Skinner, 2008 p. 364).*

 The essence of the lecture by *Skinner* is about the idea that when fictional sovereignty or **persona ficta** is achieved, we may think of a state whose perspectives go beyond usual parameters, like territory, legitimacy, supremacy of authority, people, economy and other factors for a reason. He was referring to how social contracts as a concept has evolved to influence the idea of a state. Interestingly, his proposition is that if we invoke the idea of a state as a person, then it changes the way obligations towards maintaining that state are created and hence, these obligations could not be discharged by a mere single generation of citizens. This perspective to have innovative and multi-faceted aspects to look at legal instruments and systems, is what we must understand about legal visibility (see *Figure 4.1*):

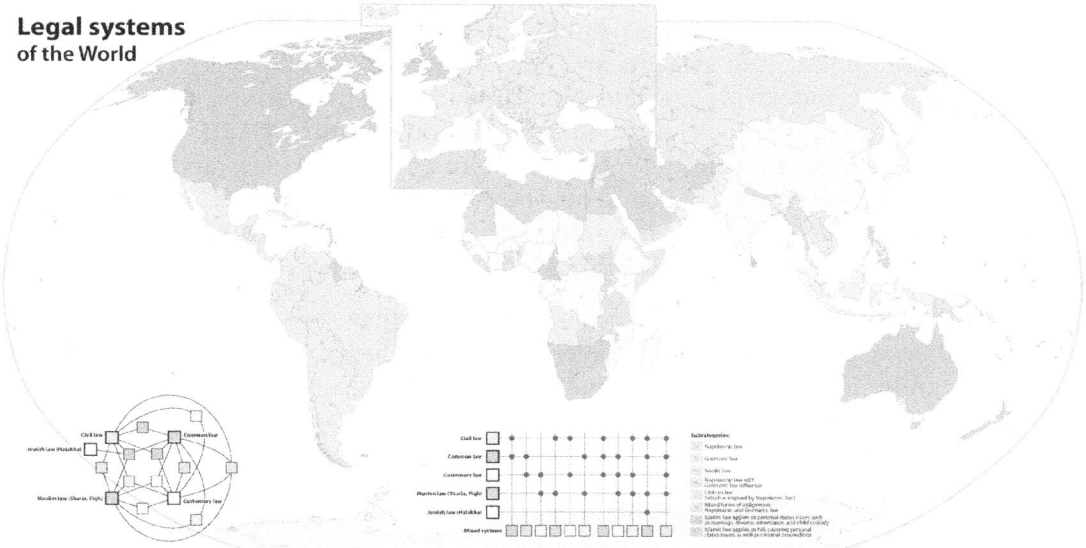

Figure 4.1: *This is a depiction of the world map depicting various legal systems of the world, as of 2018* (*Source: (Dörrbecker (Chumwa), 2023)*

Now, in the context of Artificial Intelligence, there is this tendency of AI fantasists to imagine the role of AI technology and systems to become a spatial and virtual embodiment of human life, and evolution. Many of such fantasists also believe that AI can also change the way **statecraft** and **global governance** work aside. This is where I have provided a different and multi-faceted perspective to address the transcendent role of AI in statecraft and global governance by expounding upon legal visibility, in this chapter. The purpose of this tool or method is to increase the observational and behavioral scope of law shaping the archetypal aspects of legal regimes (especially common law regimes) around the genealogical aspect of nation-states as we know.

What is Legal Visibility?

Legal visibility, in simple words, is a method that could be used to modulate the contemporary realms of emerging jurisprudence shaping domestic and global legal systems, which includes their observational & behavioral dimensions. It can provide reference and conjugation with the common law regimes (since India as a country is the point of reference in this book) and their relationship with international legal systems in the framework of global governance. The method can help us reconsider the paucity and the parallel cum subservient abundance of domestic and global regimes which represent their aspect of legal stability in areas such as public policy, constitutional theory, rights and duties, governance, and public engagement. Let us start with the key terms to expand this method of legal thinking.

Now, if one had to define Law, there is no requirement to limit the definition and jurisprudential scope of what Law resembles. Instead of defining that, we may consider Law to be a representation of systems and instruments which inherently shape a nation-state or a legitimate and sovereign state. Now, if we would have adopted an 19th century perspective on sovereignty to understand legal authority, a jurist could say that sanction can be a prerogative to execute the resemblance of authority in law and legal systems, which is correct. However, in the contemporary age, the relevance of an object of legal recognition can be satisfied when the matter of recognition is thereafter of some essence. This factor of essence or importance, perhaps is declared, legislated and even implemented.

To be fair, one may barge a claim and ask as to whether such a thing could be even reasonable, because this essence or importance may not be a credible way to judge every state as we know it. For example, monarchies may not fit under such definitions. Well, it is not necessary because my approach is not to make this into a moral debate between autocracies and democracies. Iran is perhaps one of the most interesting examples, because of their legal system and their political division of powers. *Figure 4.2* is a chart depicting the political structure of the Islamic Republic of Iran, which explains that the sharing and impetus of authority in multiple areas of execution, within law, is pretty much divided in the way the political stakeholders find it reasonable.

Iran's power structure

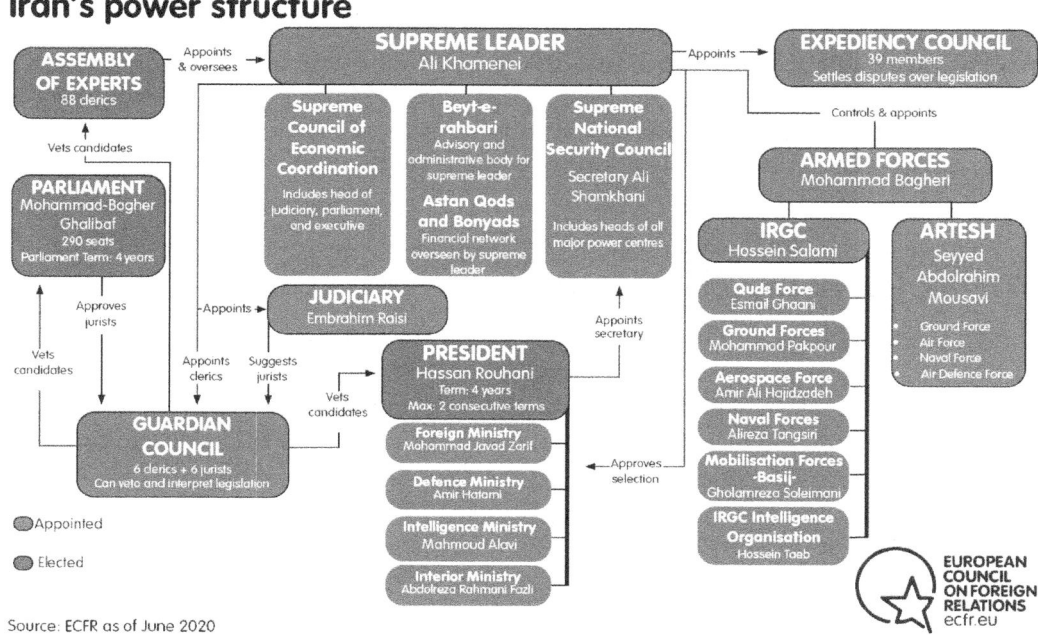

Source: ECFR as of June 2020

Figure 4.2*: A flowchart depicting the power structure of the Islamic Republic of Iran, by the European Council on Foreign Relations as of June 2020 (Geranmayeh, 2020))*

In fact, it is these aspects of importance or essence across democracies, and other kinds of political systems, which could shape any national legal system and may become an essential or limited part of the state practice itself, if we go to international law, within the scope of this method. Now, let us unpack the purpose of this method by adding AI as an element of importance or essence.

Recognition of AI in Common Law Systems

In a legal sense, the intervening role of AI technologies could be prevalent in both digital and physical spaces, which has its own jurisdictional qualms. In common law, it is possible to have AI regarded as an entity with limited relevance and scope of retroactivity, which paves us two issues to unfold: *(1) the development politics of AI and (2) the legal regime on AI.*

In the realm of policy development, socio-economic factors shape legal frameworks, while simultaneously focusing on establishing the importance of cyberspace and legitimizing its various legal aspects. When we are ought to categorize AI as an entity, perhaps legal or juristic, its role in common law regimes becomes prominent for its unique presence, and how it would shape legal and judicial precedents. Now, if this is tried upon, there will be certain legal contractions based on limited understanding of application of law and its implementing value. To further explore on the dilemmas around building ethical thought models, which have inspired literature of AI ethics, and Responsible AI, here is a recap to the efforts of The Future of Life Institute, founded by *Max Tegmark*, and the Asilomar Principles on Artificial Intelligence of 2017. Even if there have been many conferences and regulatory developments on the ethics of AI, the Asilomar Principles still give a basic understanding of how the scientific community has thought over the role of AI in shaping the economics and politics of development, worldwide. Therefore, I call it a *Tegmark Approach of AI Ethics*.

The Tegmark Approach of AI Ethics

In 2017, a conference on AI Ethics was organized in a place called Asilomar in California. The conference participants had produced the Principles of AI Ethics (also known as the Asilomar Principles), which address basic concepts like the role of cognition in the ethics of artificial intelligence. The persona-based approach to artificial intelligence in the principles is helpful and widens the scope of personalization of AI technologies in terms of accountability issues when it comes to varieties of products and services.

> [The] transition from weak to strong A.I. is a continuous process, which takes place mainly where the necessary resources (data, finances, power) are available. The results of research and development (R&D) in this area are not necessarily published due to economic and political interests, which makes socially legitimate control impossible or at least considerably more [difficult] (VDW, 2017 p. 6).

Moreover, the role of AI is not limited to nuclear weaponry and its implications as earlier discussed in the 2017 Principles. This is where it could be possible to ponder if an AI system, product or service could be regarded as a human artifact. The figure below provides a holistic overview in the transition of constitutional theories from the idea of a **human** to a **human artefact**, as described in *Figure 4.3*.

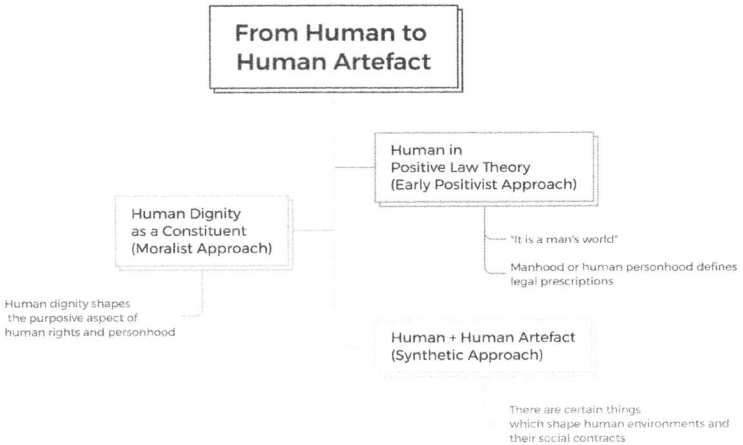

Figure 4.3: *A diagram depicting transcending perspectives from a Human to a Human Artifact in the cross development and reproduction of legal theory and legal regimes.*

Now, in constitutional theory, the concept of a human artifact is all about distinguishing between actions or decisions made by humans and those made by non-human entities like AI systems. Constitutional theory could delve into the principles and structures of a constitution or a constitutive legal instrument, only to explore how they apply to multiple (and different) aspects of governance, including the use cum regulation of artificial intelligence. Thus, a human artifact refers to an action or decision that is traceable to a human being by virtue of their actions or decisions. It is something created, controlled, or influenced by humans as data subjects and falls within the legal framework of constitutional rights and responsibilities. Human artifacts enjoy legal protections, come with accountability, and are subject to limitations defined by constitutional principles. Hence, the human artifact method is the first important aspect of legal visibility, that is, reimagining the way social contracts between humans and the state work.

Now, AI systems are non-human as entities, would technically lack the capacity to possess constitutional rights or fulfill constitutional responsibilities on their own. Yes, they are designed and programmed by humans. Yet, they operate autonomously or semi-autonomously. At least, that is a basic aspect of modus operandi of any AI system we look forward to executing. We also know how and why AI systems can generate outputs, make decisions, or take actions subject to the ultimate responsibility lying with the humans who developed / deployed / utilized the AI system. This distinction between human artifacts and non-human entities like AI plays a vital role in constitutional theory as it helps determine legal accountability, responsibility, and the allocation of rights and obligations. It establishes the boundaries and guidelines for the use and regulation of AI within the existing legal and constitutional frameworks we have.

Now, in the beginning of the chapter, it was made it clear that legal visibility is all about 3D perspectives. That is true. Hence, I have addressed the multi-faceted tendency of legal visibility as a method, through a simple proposition, called *Dimensional Perpetuity*. Now, this proposition itself is limited to pure international law, or international law theory. However, one may reimagine this idea even in the context of domestic legal systems.

Realm of Dimensional Perpetuity

Laws are meant to attain a course of action to legalize and recognize a social development, thereby seeking the creation of Grundnorms, as per legal theory. This concept may be considered similar to the Basic Structure Doctrine, which was infamously decided in *Kesavananda Bharati case* of 1973. Now, due to the varying use cases and test cases of AI products and services, it becomes difficult for legal experts to determine and interpret its legal and de facto status in areas such as taxation, finance, commerce, and competition policy. In addition, it is certainly untenable to determine the exact or absolute status quo of AI recognition in international cyber law, precisely due to the variation of emerging use cases and test cases of different classes of artificial intelligence technologies. Nevertheless, the clearest way to explain how AI products and services could develop so many use cases, and affect multiple sectors in a canon way, is what we call dissimulation. It is indeed about the art of being present and absent at the same time. Let us unfold this by taking the example of Facebook (now Meta).

> *[Canons] of interpretation cannot eliminate, though they can diminish, these uncertainties; for these canons are themselves general rules for the use of language, and make use of general terms, which themselves require [interpretation] (Hart, 2014 p. 126).*

Now, until the times when the **General Data Protection Regulation (GDPR)** of the European Union was not enforced, the legal issues related to digital apps, especially social media apps were limited to commercial law issues, while data protection issues were mainstream in fewer countries. There is also no doubt that stakeholders have been wary of the situation and have raised concerns on data consent, privacy and quality issues. However, it was GDPR that made the data protection discourse more global than ever. The reason was the EU regulation's global implementation, in a transnational sense, which had created disruptions across governments and their regulators. Here, the role of these apps becomes interesting considering the liberty companies have had to garner complex, transportable and feasible data, which made Facebook, for example, a success. Now, it still is hard to control the actions of these big tech companies, whose applications and services have invasive features and keep a reasonable check on them, due to the dissimulating features of their apps, whose algorithms and technical infrastructure, remain a mystery. A prominent example, which one could anticipate on Facebook is the 'View As' feature (Jarvis, 2018; Facebook, 2018), which was used so that if you wish to see your own profile in the format that it is public, then you may facilitate it the way you want. Well, it was hacked to gain access to data of 50 million people, where a log in option was under request thereby. Still, it is not only an issue of data breach. Such dynamic features in the UI of these mainstream apps are modelled with that purpose. Now, we know that apps are designed to be addictive, and their interface work to facilitate the generic rise of data relativism, which is quite ironic. Earlier during the age of OS like Windows and Linux, it was very limited, because cyberspace had borders, by which I mean private storage. Under free flow and penetration of data, a new world is created, where data is claimed to be an oil, and a war is assumed to exist between US and China over the supremacy of data and Artificial Intelligence. While Russia tries claiming cyber supremacy, China is trying to claim AI supremacy through governmental initiatives and some investment support via American investors (Osawa, 2023). Yet, the role of design is significant, but not viable to be restricted under law, as in technical aspects, it is not justified. Apps and data algorithms are always vying over the presence and complex modification in the process of data processing under law. This could be inferred on the basis of a statistic research on participants' reception to following command of robots as depicted in *Figure 4.4.*

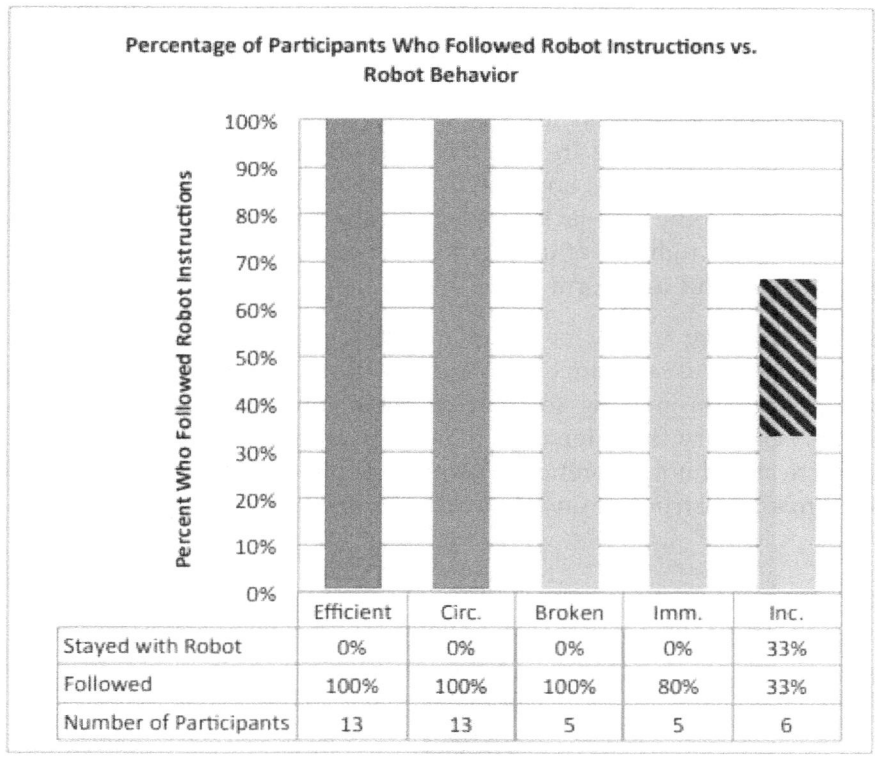

Percentage of Participants Who Followed Robot Instructions vs. Robot Behavior

	Efficient	Circ.	Broken	Imm.	Inc.
Stayed with Robot	0%	0%	0%	0%	33%
Followed	100%	100%	100%	80%	33%
Number of Participants	13	13	5	5	6

Figure 4.4: *A statistic research on participants' reception to following command of robots (Robinette, et al., 2016 p. 5).*

We all know that free will could be subverted, and consent could be manufactured. Sometimes, individuals may agree to take as well copious hazard have confidence in AI systems (for example, robots) that the trusted will alleviate this risk (Robinette, et al., 2016). The above *Figure 4.4* depicts the rate and quantitative aspect as on the objective set of conditions as how come robots are trusted by humans so much. This tendency of blindly trusting machines is the same as if a human entrusts something on other human or any creature, which happens. However, considering the AI-related anthropomorphism here, we can determine that we tend to create and rely on those footprints of observation, which do we trust and consider. Thus, it is specific yet nostalgic that human empathy could have a lot to do with this multi-faceted purpose of artificial intelligence. *Genevieve Bell* has provided an insight to this:

> [That] technology is accompanied by anxiety is not a new thing. We have anxieties about certain types of technology and there are reasons for that [...] What we are seeing now isn't an anxiety about artificial intelligence per se, it's about what it says about us. That if you can make something like us, where does it leave us? And that concern isn't universal, as other cultures have very different responses to AI, to big data (Tucker, 2016).

Considering what human artifacts may signify, the realm of legal visibility becomes clearer with dimensional perpetuity, since it helps us develop a multi-faceted outlook towards this plurality of AI use cases. Now, that positive law could be harnessed to understand that the perpetuation of these AI use cases is dynamic and interconvertible, a possible solution to render is to recognize and signify the development of anthropomorphic objects in law, like Artificial Intelligence. Some laws in any form, may be fungible enough to lean in with the times, but some may lack to recognize the wisdom of the past because of their not being cultivable enough to realities. As we address AI-based anthropomorphism, legal fiction has to step up and transform.

Now, digital technology, in law, is a human artifact, like constitutional law, a political human artifact, which is a genius development from subjective rudimentary theories and understandings into making some of the most complex yet strong legal systems in the world. It is necessary to understand that the purpose of dimensional perpetuity as a concept is practical and not theoretical. *Figure 4.5* depicts a diagram which shows how UI / UX, algorithmic infrastructure and data and IT infrastructure could exist in layers:

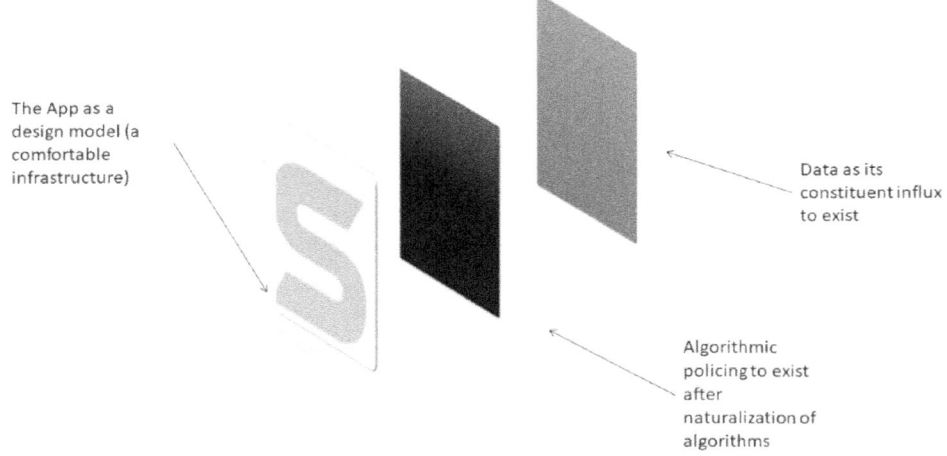

The App as a design model (a comfortable infrastructure)

Data as its constituent influx to exist

Algorithmic policing to exist after naturalization of algorithms

Figure 4.5: A Diagram to demarcate differences in the realms of data, design materiality (UI) and algorithmic policing.

A lot of aspects discussed in these points still have a standing. The follow-up paper on Dimensional Perpetuity for the 2020 2nd World Symposium on Artificial Intelligence (Abhivardhan, 2020), has expanded the perspective on Dimensional Perpetuity. Now, this idea is based on certain tangible parameters, which shape its clear purpose:

- **Self-Transformability**: It means that artificial intelligence, in a legal and policy sense, should be considered as self-transformative, even if not with an autonomous perspective. This perspective could be helpful in reorienting the nature of algorithmic activities and operations of various classes of AI systems, products, and services.

- **Dynamic Privacy**: This is more of a proposition than a method. The key idea is to make privacy regulation and enforcement shaped in orientation with the algorithmic operations and activities of AI products and services and other kinds of AI systems. There **are** AI tools which could help in protecting and enforcing privacy regulations (Meurisch, et al., 2022) and standards.

- **Perceptibility, Receptivity and Retentivity**: Since Generative AI (thanks to Bard and ChatGPT) has become a fad, understanding these three terms would not be so hard. Before Generative AI became mainstream, and transformer models started becoming a reality, this cluster of three terms, was suggested with a simple idea that AI systems, products and services must be assessed on the basis of their perceptibility (how AI tools "perceive" or learn), receptivity (how AI tools become receptive or adapt to user inputs to shape their use / test cases and outputs) and retentivity (how much could an AI tool "retain" or keep up with the nature of inputs) features.

To further elaborate, it was proposed in this paper that we need to shift our perspectives towards building AI ethics principles, and even legal principles on AI regulation. Shifting from anthropocentrism to anthropomorphic and naturalist perspectives to understand AI systems, could give us coherent aspects to understand the participatory and preparatory role of artificial intelligence technologies. Here is an excerpt from the same perspectives from my paper:

> *Trust is imperative, and efforts thus should be made to embrace relationships between AI as a disruptive technology and a special human artifact to be more inclusive, naturalist and connotating with the human society. Without an appropriate and connoted approach, positive law will be limited to absolutist and restrictive interpretations and redemptions can happen with the fallacious premises that law will keep assuring an environment of safe and secured artificial intelligence (Abhivardhan, 2020).*

To further add to this, the Realm of Dimensional Perpetuity, is also inspired by a concept in the first edition of this book, which was a normative yet simpler way of looking at legal ascertainment of AI systems and products, ontologically. We call it the Doctrine of Intelligent Determination. Earlier, in the previous editions of this book, the scope of this doctrine was limited to the idea of examining the level of intelligibility of any technology as a system / product / service, recognized as artificial intelligence and making it important to concur in legal theory, whether the intelligibility is determinant or not. However, in my 2019 paper for SOLAIR Conference, I had presented an evolved idea of Doctrine of Intelligent Determination, in a paper, whose excerpt is depicted below:

> *The Doctrine of Intelligent Determination presents the basic origination and legitimation of AI as an Entity and postulates that such a manifestation developed by artificial intelligence, where it is subjected to discourses where basic human rights are determinable and subject to review – renders a general course of nature in the human world of public order. The proposition stands on the argument that an entitative*

artificial intelligence is to be subjected to the democratization of its real-time interface to a scenario, where public order exists (Abhivardhan, 2021 pp. 126-28).

Those four principles are depicted as follows:

- **The Dimensionality Principle**: This principle simply means that the realms of AI shall be based on the variations of perspectives, which are not exhaustive, but based on the process and the natural growth of the AI realm.

- **The Medium Principle**: The Medium Principle is just a formal corollary, which emphasizes the need to examine Artificial Intelligence as a medium of and through direct or indirect mediums of technology.

- **The Receptivity Principle**: In IHRL, receptivity could be interpreted as a form of privacy right for a human being. We recognize it in the sense of how a human takes something into a discourse. Now, there are initiatives wherein AI realms are attempted to be analyzed and grown up with a humanoid or human-akin cognition. However, understanding AI systems with a perspective of receptivity is not an absolute case. So, the receptivity principle is based on the *suo moto* point that as the inalienable right to learn at dimensionality is attained by an AI realm, the receptivity of AI exists as a non-absolute right to reception of **Data / Information / Content (DIC)** of a data subject. This right to reception is a harmonious, reasonable, and normal way to profess and affirm privacy rights in principle with respect to the attributions that the DIC of a data subject may/may not contain. It means that the right of receptivity as a non-absolute right is not confined to human activity. Thus, in international law, the recognition of artificial intelligence realms must never be limited to mere exclusivity over the fact that observance is limited to human observance and rights. That is how, AI realms are recognized with a human rights perspective, but still at this outset as well, the perspective does not even overlook human rights and privacies as forms of human freedoms but gently intends to demarcate them in terms of their bearing of the legal modalities of AI systems.

- **The Retentivity Principle**: This Principle is the kingmaker principle, which seriously determines the course of AI realms to act upon what it really endows. The endowment, as a matter of fact, seems to be rather natural/procedural, and AI, due to the verge of dimensionality, may possess the course of retentivity, which necessitates its own basic part. Such aspect is rather at the sense of how the technology pertains at its own competency and it is probably required, and transparent modalities as required.

This is further expounded upon as I have dealt with the Human Artifact Conjunction, and the Entitative Nature of Artificial Intelligence in this chapter.

Digital Identity in AI and International Law

Advancing better ways to interpret and affirm identity in the field of contemporary international law for sure must be counted as a form of political renaissance. It is a primary term in IHRL, related to human objects in relation. It has wider use in fields such as IHL, IEL and IHRL, and represents reflective changes in pure international law, which again could be depicted in VCLT, which is dealt in the further portions in detail. Secession, self-determination, violence based on identity, loss of state sovereignty due to climate change and the recognition of water as a form of identity are among many such non-exhaustive examples, which locate the role of identity deeper with an institution-conscious sense. This happens because the development of globalization has transformed the role of enterprises in the context of international relations, and has shaped the way the role of state and non-state actors (of international law), beyond the way one could anticipate within the older understanding of a traditional world order represented by states and intergovernmental organizations in the 1950s and 1960s (Koskenniemi, 2005 p. 17). Now, this change of role is interesting because it is always needed in the field of international law to examine the distinction between natural morality and state practices as factors that shape international legal scholarships and positions to shape doctrinal methods and ideas, which *Marti Koskenniemi*, a prominent Finnish lawyer, argues in this book, **From Apology to Utopia**.

> *[On] the other hand, law cannot be completely independent from behavior, will or interest. If it were, we would be at a loss about where to find or how to justify it. If law had no relation to power and political fact, it would be a form of natural morality, a closed normative code which would pre-exist the opinions or interests of individual [States] (Koskenniemi, 2005 p. 18).*

Maintaining normativity and concreteness has been challenge those multilateral institutions, like the United Nations face today, which is why most of these human rights treaties and declarations need better ways to be contextualized and implemented. Before connoting the legal backing of identity with AI in bigger terms, let us unfold and understand the role of identity in international law (Schindler, 1982 p. 25).

> *"To put the matter simply, we could not consider that a State [. . .] is free to disregard the law because it conflicts with the policies of that State (Schindler, 1982 p. 26)."*

The above excerpt underscores the basic issue with recognizing human rights treaties. Certainly, it becomes important to determine as how identity is to be dealt as a credible and modernized factor in international law, when the activities and operations of any AI system is much attributable to human data subjects and their environments. In human rights, the most sensitive and rather egregious issues are covered within the scope of treaties such as the Genocide Convention, the UNCAT, the Geneva Conventions and their Protocols, and other international legal instruments. In this sense, international law plays a vital role to test and even challenge state practices. Now, any balance between natural morality in the international legal instruments and juridical state interests is vested via the specific realization of amounting rule(s) of law, as per the South West Africa case (International Court of Justice, 1950) and the Barcelona Traction case (International Court of Justice, 1970) in the domain of public reference; which means that the institutional role of public international law, is regarded primary in certain aspects. Now, the complications of private international law are not to be dealt in this chapter as this book is primarily dedicated with the pure concepts of public international law. Nevertheless, it is deemed to consider that the significant role of various domains is an essential matter of entitlement in an international legal system, as when they are required in the domain of a state in the entailment of responsibility and interests. Now, in furtherance, customary international law is not a tacit approach to crucial grounds of state practice being signified and settled (which is deemed to fit in the purview of norms). Yet, even at the controversial uncertainty of *jus cogens* frameworks for the matter of existence, post-Cold War globalization is a waveform of attribution, which is conditioned by economic translucence and behavioral trends. Despite the existence of agreements and norms on economic behavior between states as a legal realism in state practice, the residual aspect of such behavior is shaped quickly in a globalized world.

> *"[Globalism] is an ideology that prioritizes the neoliberal global order over national interests. Nobody can deny that we are living in a globalized world. But whether all our policies should be "globalist" is highly debatable (Schwab, 2018)."*

Now, this residuary aspect of customary international law (hereinafter CIL), in essence, with that mere schema of light imminence, requires to fit in the primary considerations (Kelsen, 2009 pp. 216, 271-75) in that reflective legal relevance. Now, this is a gradual happening, because there are phases of transformation of human society, which construct the anatomy of international law. Apart from international organizations and other traditional non-state actors, we could have individuals, companies and even AI (let us assume), as a non-state actor. Nevertheless, before considering the dynamism of AI in that contributory sense, it is important to consider that identity, as a subjective concomitant, is a playable ingredient in determining the recourse of customary international law, which itself is a necessity for **International Legal Personalities (ILPs)**. We have to regard the Barcelona case principle of ICJ that we cannot restrict such references in those limited discourses. This principled stability is reflected and supported by domestic level discourses of public interest. This explains the role of globalization as a to realize changes in the international law discourse that a globalized international community has its residual state interests, which are merely regulatory by the secondary instruments of **persistent objection** and others.

> *"International law [allocates] competences and legitimate spheres of action to entities it chooses to regard as legal subjects. No subjects, no sets of rights, competences or liberties are externally given. They are constituted by the law itself. (Koskenniemi, 2005 p. 230)"*

Globalization (and not globalism) has indeed magnified the way global economic and legal interests work. Now, AI has its dynamic prerogatives, where its position in international law can be introduced within the understanding of digital identity, since digital identities are hybrid, referenced to enable an interface of coherence on exploring the role of AI technologies, in cyberspace. To begin with, in terms of strength of reception and activity, one may classify artificial intelligence levels as strong AI, weak AI (or narrow AI) and superintelligence. In major cases: there are 2 types: one is classifier based and the other is control cum classifier based, where control has a practical precedence or primacy.

Also, these demarcations provide a potential aspect of AI, which is related with human personification as well. In the *Figure 4.6* depicted, I have taken a privacy-centric approach to expound upon the entitative aspect of AI as we know it. This is merely a jurisprudence perspective as *Figure 4.6* also depicts the physiology of AI as an Entity, with a privacy and identity-centric perspective.

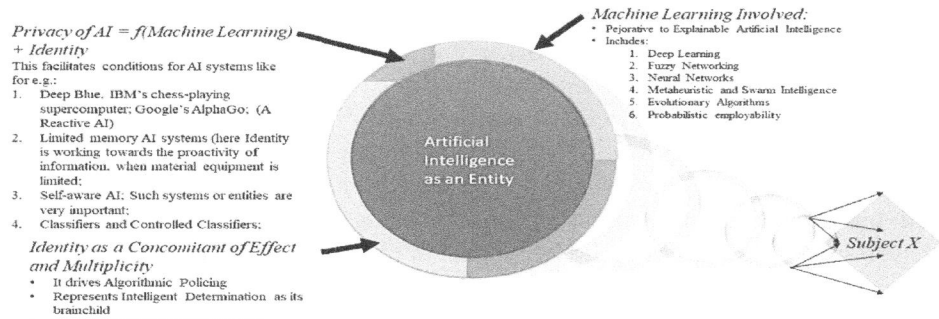

Figure 4.6: *The Dynamic Physiology of an Artificial Intelligence Entity Presented*

Here are some aspects on my propositions of the physiology of AI Entity, in a legal / policy sense:

- First, an AI is a human artifact, whose inputs would be inspired by human aspirations and relativity; it facilitates with human cognition and social morphology.

- Also, AI systems and applications could be mapped on the basis of perception, learning and retention, which is useful in understanding their content recognition practices employed by machine learning algorithms.

An AI is tenable to be recognized as a legal entity but cannot be materially achieved and also cannot be personified to be equivalent of human beings not in terms of characteristics of capability or activity, but in terms of its original resemblance to the state of nature and human society.

How Data Quality and Privacy Shapes AI Recognition

To take this forward and expound upon the case of digital identity in the context of AI systems, one would have to understand data privacy within fields such as international human rights law, international telecommunication law and private international law, since these fields are the closest that could uphold and implement data privacy rights, in customary or ad hoc fashion. I have taken the **General Data Protection Regulation of the EU (GDPR)** as a reference point (and an example) to work upon the modalities. The reason is that GDPR settles those modalities by virtue of concepts such as pseudonymization and tracing data attribution, (**perambulatory clauses 23 to 28**), data quality and rectification as in **Articles 13 to 15** (also in **clauses 13 to 15** with specific reservations to identity in **clauses 51-54** on data subjects), rectification and erasure rights in **Section 3** (right of rectification and erasure (Court of Justice of the European Union, 2014)). Taking **Article 38** of the VCLT into consideration, it could be argued that third parties are affected by residuary measures involved in the international lives of states. Now, wherein a private entity like AI comes into play, it becomes a facilitator of public duty under data law and if we take understanding only to what the GDPR implies, it is a specific obligation and it may ensure that legal human artifacts like artificial intelligence cannot be under restrictive development as a scientific necessity, but duly require legal freedom to pursue understandability of information, with which it is associated for information purposes. Since, the corporate ecosystem of AI is hyped (and evolving), it becomes reasonable that the right to be forgotten is somewhere invoked in the case of AI for even maintaining basic data protection rights of data subjects. Also, AI systems and products could be subjected to **Article 18** restrictions *ipso facto*, but their anthropomorphic effects on economies and data subjects may require us to develop specialized perspectives. Also, the scope of international custom can be determined by an AI object, as one must stay mindful of the dilemma of addressing those specialized issues of anthropomorphism. Well, a striking example is found in **Section 66D** of the *Information Technology Act, 2000* (India), where understanding personation as a concept (Kerala High Court, 2010), is of much importance.

> *[Punishment] for cheating by personation by using computer resource. -Whoever, by means for any communication device or computer resource cheats by personating, shall be punished with imprisonment of either description for a term which may extend to three years and shall also be liable to fine which may extend to one lakh [rupees] (Department of Telecommunications, Government of India, 2000).*

This provision limits the scope of a communication device or a computer resource and targets to a human user because the object related to the same is a human, in some general terms. However, it could be considered as an entity in case of an AI object because there is no limitation in the provision with regard to a computer resource or a communication device. Now, let us understand what could be regarded as personation. Data has a central role here, and that too of algorithmic policing (Conceptualising the right to data protection in an era of Big Data, 2017 pp. 1-2; Moniodis, 2012; MIT Technology Review). In the **Puttaswamy I** judgment of 2017, this role is substantiated and different kinds of privacies are determined. Yet, the role of personation in simple case, becomes cognizant and reasonable for artificial intelligence. Also, the ipso facto role of **Section 72** of the **IT Act** is rendered as possible to be implied. Personation amounting to an offence could be dynamic depending how algorithms perform because from Amazon Alexa to a simple MakeMyTrip ad, the workflow of information is anyways charted out. **Figure 4.7** depicts a proposed relationship between *Algorithmic Policing* with a perspective on three relatable concepts: *(1) the law of data quality, (2) the persona of an AI under the framework of an international legal personality, and (3) the right to be forgotten and of rectification.* The reference to the data protection law concepts in the *Figure 4.7*, are inspired by the provisions of the **General Data Protection Regulation (GDPR)**.

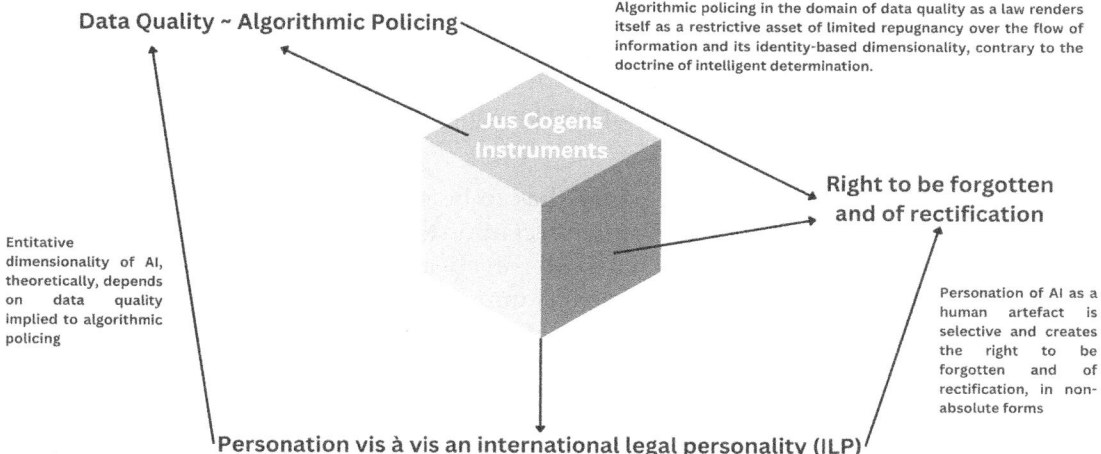

Figure 4.7: The Relationship between Algorithmic Policing under the law of data quality, personation of an AI under International Legal Personality and the Right to be Forgotten and of Rectification (as is in GDPR for example)

Also, the implications of the erasure rights are not clear here because of the dynamic nature and scientific development expected from an AI, which in the end facilitates the fact that we need some reservations over:

- *Data quality*

- *Personation vis-à-vis ILP (international legal personality)*

- *Right to be forgotten and of rectification*

Well, with respect to a data subject, it must be clear that algorithmic policing plays a legal and technological role in determining the scope of personation as an object before even going to the causation of an offence. Thus, international law facilitates the principle of *acta jure imperii* only in international cyberspace and sovereignty concerns are thereby taken into adequate consideration for due settlement (*Schmitt*, 2017 pp. 22-24). The role of domestic law is attached and not derogated or ignored, but these 3 concepts have a bigger role to play in determining the *jus cogens* instruments over AI. In applied jurisprudence, this is also in the zone of a defying conflict of contested knowledge over common knowledge and is effective over judicial practice *(Venkatnarayan, 2018)*, which is related with constitutional machineries in states. In the case of democracies, it may turn out to be a serious issue for equality laws, as a meagre dilemma of **constitutional redemption**. Henceforth, understanding the role *of jus cogens* instruments as in the *Figure 4.7* facilitates these conclusions:

- Erasure rights and the right to enable restriction under the GDPR, considering the *multi-faceted and multi-sectoral use cases* of AI products / services / systems, would require a clinical approach to be adjudicated. The issue of dark patterns subverting a data subject / data principal's right to be forgotten is an example.

- There is a possibility that the rule of *lex specialis derogat generali* evolved out of the jus cogens instruments could imbibe enough legitimacy to regulate specialized areas of AI and law.

The personation of AI as a human artifact has to be selective and could affirm that the economy of AI products and services will reflect upon the legal endogenous developments within societies how property rights have extensively and normatively transformed in the digital world. Now, that political franchise is universal, an AI object could represent the successive traits of streamlined perpetuity of being multidimensional as far as its role and purpose are concerned. This is quite common with human artifacts, which is why to make AI development safer, our legal thinking must understand the anthropomorphic interventions that AI products, systems and services can offer (Ericsson, 2018) and precede scientific and technological development.

Even if there is another stage of essence in case of legal instruments upholding *jus cogens*, it would be fit if we pursue peremptory norms as rules to determine the **purpose-based operatives** of an international legal order (Conforti, 1988). Yet, one must admit that the involvement of private resources and entities in shaping international law would remain unprecedented. Let us take the example of criminal jurisprudence in domestic and international contexts, and how AI objects could be recognized in the framework of criminal jurisprudence.

Now, we know that the principles of domestic and international crimes could shape their course because of the differential nature of such activities and due to the lack of the opinion juris present. The problem arises when we ignore the principle of polite convention by the great *Alan Turing*, where in his first paper on computational intelligence of 1950, he had understood the dilemma of whether AI could be sentient or not (Hartree, 1949). It is also reasonable to argue that the Turing Test was not that advanced or even capable enough to test the sentience of AI. Still, at a principled level, Turing could anticipate this aspect. This is recognized similarly in the Dartmouth proposal (McCarthy, et al., 1955) which still inspires the artificial intelligence industry.

> *"The [reader] must accept it as a fact that digital computers can be constructed, and indeed have been constructed, according to the principles we have described, and that they can in fact mimic the actions of a human computer very closely (Computing Machinery and Intelligence, 1950 p. 438)".*

This in my view settles that equality in law, other than equality before the eyes of law, is to be relieved from a methodical 2-dimensional vague enigma of lineation in legal methods evolved. We require not reactionary, but cultivable and effective considerations in international law to attain a stable and cogent status quo for AI objects (Gödel, 1951;

Russell, et al., 2003 p. 957). This explains the purpose of dimensional perpetuity. In the next section of this chapter, I have discussed about this idea of having artificial intelligence as an entity, which is further unfolded in the chapter on the ISAIL Classifications of Artificial Intelligence.

Entitative Nature of Artificial Intelligence

In 2019, I had presented my research on the entitative nature of artificial intelligence in the SOLAIR Conference 2020, organized by the Czech Academy of Sciences. In that paper, my proposition was about this idea that the legal and policy understandings that have evolved on artificial intelligence, have been quite consumerist, and do not necessitate to address anything unique in the literature of AI and law. Of course, things are not the same in 2023, since a lot of theories and newfound thought models on artificial intelligence have come up. Nevertheless, amidst the taxonomies and thought models which have emerged, the Entitative Approach to AI is still a unique idea to ponder upon. This idea is also a part of Legal Visibility, in the very context of exploring the legal persona of AI, in jurisprudence. To begin with, the Entitative Nature of AI is based on four parameters:

- *Legal historiography*
- *Anthropomorphic scope*
- *Technical utility*
- *Doctrinal need*

However, the basis of this idea is inspired by how the rules-based international order approaches the issue of regulating digital technologies.

The all-pervading influence of big technology companies in deciding how democratic decisions are made, how our laws are passed, or even the subject-matter of anything within our domestic issues, represents a policy nightmare, for regulators and policymakers in India. This is why the Ministry of Electronics and Information Technology or **MeitY**, is trying to introduce the *Digital India Act*. At the same time, there are two important bills (as drafts) which have been subject to public consultations. One is a former version of the Personal Data Protection Bill, which is a serious revision of a former Personal Data Protection Bill, which was taken back since nearly 80+ objections were received against the bill's provisions. As of August 2023, the *Digital Personal Data Protection Act, 2023*, now an act of parliament, is the successor of the former versions of Data Protection Bills proposed by the Government of India. The second one is a *Draft Indian Telecommunication Bill, 2022*, which governs matters within Indian telecommunication law. At the same time, we have had The Information Technology (Intermediary Guidelines and Digital Media Ethics Code) Rules, 2021, which were implemented to act against the big tech companies, whose social media apps have been invasive to Indian citizens and have been non-compliant to Indian laws. If one tries to understand the trajectory of developments, one can easily see an evolutionary and reactionary trend in the Government of India's regulatory measures on digital technologies, especially on issues related to intermediaries, social media platforms and data law. This is a miniature form of what someone could refer to as **legal historiography**. Here is an excerpt from the paper on this parameter:

> *Thus, a historical backdrop enables us to render that AI has been left with the concomitants of understanding related to materiality, a limited juristic person, and is webbed with the legal personification. This historical backdrop is a legal method to estimate the development of AI as a human artifact along the course of development of recognition and assessment of technology by legal systems (i.e., international organizations, courts/tribunals, national legislative and executive cum administrative bodies and quasi-judicial bodies) and the evolution in the jurisprudence of law and technology. Moreover, it helps us to determine the relative scope and construct between the human-led institutions of law and the AI as an entitative human artifact beyond the controlled role of AI as a utility for services (Abhivardhan, 2021 p. 126).*

When one examines a historical backdrop, it becomes apparent that **Artificial Intelligence (AI)** has inherited the characteristics associated with materiality and, to a limited extent, legal personhood, which could be intricately intertwined with a legal framework, to acquire a degree of personification. A prudent study of the historical context of legal & administrative systems and their evolving positions on key digital technologies may help us to adopt **legal historiography** as a valuable tool of legal methodology for assessing the evolution of AI as a human artifact. As the excerpt above suggests, this tool could help us trace the journey of recognition & evaluation of digital technologies in various legal systems, including international organizations, courts / tribunals, national legislative bodies, executive cum administrative bodies, and quasi-judicial bodies and others. Moreover, it sheds some light on the transformative impact of digital technologies in a field like jurisprudence. This is how one can gain insight into the dynamic interplay between human-led institutions of law and AI as an entitative human artifact. It goes beyond viewing AI solely as a utility for services and allows us to delineate the relative scope and structure of its existence. To make it happen, one must do careful examination to navigate the legal landscape and understand the intricate relationship between AI and the legal framework in which it operates. This is why legal historiography matters. On a larger note, beyond the scope of this paper, I think that **legal historiography** in the case of technologies like AI, IoT, blockchain, quantum technology, and others including their sub-classes and categories, is set to become unconventional, and very unique. The reason is simple. All these technologies leave their own **anthropomorphic** impressions, and lesser **anthropocentric** impressions on human life. How they would shape our daily needs, our regulatory chores, our values, our political life, and our evolution, among many other things? This is a question we need to keep asking due to policy uncertainty. It would be unreasonable to keep a captive approach, which is why I believe that legal historiography in the context of all these disruptive technologies is set to change its normal course, for good.

Now, these terms – *anthropocentrism* and *anthropomorphism* have been used regularly in this book, and one may ask what they really mean. For starters, one can refer to a grammatical understanding of these terms, by understanding the meaning of the prefix **anthropo-**, which means human-related or human-based. Naturally, anthropocentrism means human-centricity, while anthropomorphism implies human attributability. To unpack further, anthropomorphism implies the transmission or **export** of human attributes such as character traits, emotions, empathy, or any other tangible or intangible attributes to non-human objects, in the simplest way. Now, AI systems, products and services can be easily regarded as those non-human objects who are subject to attribution of human-related or human-based traits. Interestingly, we all know how enculturation happens when newer technologies by their economics of scale adapt human attributes and then reciprocate their presence by shaping them. This by itself is what we have referred to as **anthropomorphic scope**. Here is an excerpt on this idea from the paper:

> *The parameter of Anthropomorphic Scope signifies how the attributes related to human reality influence the pragmatic discourse of artificial intelligence. It is important to understand that this parameter is used in the ontological consequence of artificial intelligence as an entity and must be avoided from mixing it with the utilitarian nature of the same. The entitative nature is a design of the multi-dimensional and heterogenous liberty that emanates through AI as a legal personality. Since, in general assumption, it has a special connect with human information in the possible material and immaterial forms, it signifies the foot-printing of information in raw form, which is utilized (Abhivardhan, 2021 p. 126).*

The concept of Anthropomorphic Scope is a quite important parameter. It delves into how human attributes and realities influence the practical aspects of artificial intelligence. It explores the extent to which AI reflects or imitates human characteristics and behavior and establishes why one must differentiate the Anthropomorphic Scope from the utilitarian nature of AI, which is to say – the consumerist influence. While AI serves practical purposes, the focus here lies in understanding its **ontological implications as an independent entity**. This means we should avoid conflating AI's entitative nature with its utilitarian functions.

The entitative nature of AI refers to its legal personality, which is shaped by various dimensions (the state of being multi-faceted and multi-sectoral) and **liberties** inherent within its design in human and natural law contexts. For sure, AI possesses multidimensional and heterogeneous qualities due to the anthropomorphizing that enables it to function as a distinct legal entity, thanks to the AI object's connection to human information, both in tangible and intangible forms. This connection signifies the presence of raw information that AI processes and utilizes. This is why recognizing and understanding the Anthropomorphic Scope helps us garner valuable insights into the impact of AI on various domains. This deep exploration helps us navigate the evolving landscape of AI and its implications in legal, societal, and technological contexts. Also, it is necessary to know that AI-based anthropomorphizing is pretty much linked with how enculturation between AI and human environments really happen.

Through enculturation, individuals gradually adapt their own behaviors and perceptions based on the recommendations and influences of AI technologies. The AI's ability to process vast amounts of data and make tailored suggestions can contribute to the formation of individual preferences and cultural practices. This dynamic interaction between AI and human societies highlights the evolving relationship between technology and enculturation.

Here is an example. Consider a social media platform that employs AI algorithms to curate users' news feeds based on their past interactions, interests, and social connections. As individuals engage with the platform, they encounter a stream of content specifically tailored to their preferences. The AI technology behind the scenes analyzes user data, identifies patterns, and presents relevant information, ultimately shaping users' exposure to news and influencing their perception of the world. This illustration highlights how AI technologies, driven by enculturation dynamics, can profoundly impact the way we consume information and engage with our social environments. Therefore, it may sound a bit complicated, but AI-led anthropomorphizing is already happening, in various use cases, such as handling taxonomies in financial tasks and compliances and AI-generated art (music and design), beyond text-based generative AI.

It is essential to recognize the reciprocal nature of this process, as human societies also influence the development and evolution of AI technologies. The values, norms, and ethical considerations present in a given culture can shape the design, implementation, and regulation of AI systems. Now, some may claim that such kind of anthropomorphism as a phenomenon may not be true or even if it is happening, it must be avoided. Yes, the claims make sense in their own right. However, it is necessary to understand the specifics of enabling AI-led anthropomorphization. *Ben Shneiderman* in a co-authored article (with *Michael Muller*), addresses this dilemma quite specifically:

> *It's one thing for an ordinary artifact user to make human-like references for boats, cars, or Roombas, but I see it as a problem when designers use that language, resulting in poor products. The long history of failed anthropomorphic systems goes back even before Microsoft BOB and Clippie, but it has continued to produce billion dollar failures. [...] By elevating machines to human capabilities, we diminish the specialness of people. I'm eager to preserve the distinction and clarify responsibility. So I do not think machines should use first-person pronouns, but should describe who is responsible for the system or simply respond in a machine-like way. Sometimes it takes a little imagination to get the right phrasing, but it is best when it is more compact. [...] The issue is NOT if humans can relate to a deceptive social machine — of course they can. The issue is "Do we recognize that humans and machines are different categories?" or "Will we respect human dignity, by designing effective machines that enhance human self-efficacy and responsibility?" The 2M+ apps in the Apple Store are mostly based on direct manipulation. Major applications like Amazon shopping, Google search, navigation, etc. avoid human-like designs because they have come to understand that they are suboptimal and unpopular (Shneiderman, et al., 2023).*

The insights provided by *Schneiderman* and *Muller* in the article have shed light on the potential pitfalls of excessive anthropomorphism in design. They are clear in their suggestion that it may be possible to enable AI anthropomorphizing. However, without clear planning, applying this approach to machines can lead to suboptimal and unpopular outcomes. The misuse of AI-based anthropomorphizing does not limit its scope of first and second order effects to mere data and commercial law issues. It could even go beyond, which is why **technical utility**, the third parameter comes into play. Here is an excerpt on *technical utility*:

> *Artificial Intelligence requires a technical utility, which is required to be deeply rooted in the work ethic of enterprises/tech companies and governments. This utility emerges with time and the capillaries of utility and purpose diversify and change - based on the technological capabilities of the individual AI itself. Under the ambit of technical utility, the scope of analysis precedes with these key aspects to consider: (i) Predictability; (ii) Strength and (iii) Intelligence Asset (Abhivardhan, 2021 p. 126).*

Technical utility, to be fair, implies that AI systems, products and services must offer technically and commercially viable use cases, which make sense. This is why we have suggested three key aspects that make up technical utility as we know it: *Predictability*, *Strength* and *Intelligence Asset*. While data scientists and developers are capable to create better standards for machine learning algorithms, my proposition could be regarded in a holistic sense, with a design thinking perspective. The purpose of this proposal is to develop a design-oriented and insight-oriented unique outlook to shape the legal / juristic persona of AI, in matters related to **regulation, adjudication** and **dispute resolution**. Here is a breakdown of all the three key aspects:

- **Predictability** stands as a critical factor to assess within the scope of technical utility. AI systems should exhibit a level of predictability in their operations, enabling stakeholders to anticipate their behavior and outcomes. By possessing a predictable nature, AI systems engender trust and confidence, both of which are crucial for their widespread adoption and integration into various domains.

- **Strength** represents another vital facet of technical utility. It encompasses the power and effectiveness of AI systems in delivering desired results. A strong AI system exhibits robustness, reliability, and efficiency in its operations. Such strength ensures that AI technologies can perform tasks with precision, effectiveness, and minimal errors, thereby enhancing their overall utility and value.

- The concept of an **intelligence asset** underpins the parameter of technical utility. AI systems possess unique intellectual capabilities that enable them to acquire, process, and analyze vast amounts of data. These intelligence assets empower AI systems to recognize patterns, make informed decisions, and generate valuable insights. Leveraging their intelligence asset, AI systems can drive advancements in various fields, solve complex problems, and contribute to human endeavors.

With respect to intelligence asset as a key aspect of technical utility, here is an excerpt, which explains how one can use the idea of intelligence asset to further understand AI anthropomorphism and test it:

The purposive meaning behind Intelligence Asset as a key aspect is based on the idea that AI is a socio-economic asset of utility in material and entitative terms. Moreover, terming it an asset signifies besides that it has material and immaterial value in terms of the culture of entrepreneurship and innovation, the perpetual need towards non-human socialization and making the approach of law more dynamic and cultivable. The key portions consist of (a) Socio-Economic and Legal Attribution; (b) Self-Sustainability and Transformation (Abhivardhan, 2021).

It simply means that AI since has socio-economic value, must be adjudicated and examined, to develop informed legal and policy perspectives on AI anthropomorphism. This can be achieved by understanding two important tests as explained:

- **Socio-Economic and Legal Attribution** form a pivotal element within the realm of Intelligence Asset. It acknowledges the intricate interplay between AI and society, where AI's influence extends beyond technical capabilities. Recognizing the socio-economic impact of AI allows us to comprehend its broader implications on industries, labor markets, and economic structures. Simultaneously, the legal dimension acknowledges the need to establish appropriate frameworks that govern AI's deployment, ensuring ethical considerations, accountability, and protection of individual rights.

- **Self-Sustainability and Transformation** add depth to our understanding of Intelligence Asset. It underscores the self-sufficiency and adaptability of AI systems, enabling them to continuously learn, evolve, and transform their capabilities. This self-sustainability allows AI to navigate complex challenges, generate insights, and deliver innovative solutions. Moreover, AI's transformative potential extends to reshaping societal norms, challenging traditional notions of human-machine interaction, and propelling advancements in various fields.

The Human-Artifact Conjunction

If one had to give a clinical depiction of what constitutes cultural property, then what could it be? It could be pertinent to term it as a lively human artifact. However, it may turn out to be an obvious contradiction to provide an exhaustive or absolutist role of AI objects in the domain of culture. However, scholars agree that enculturation driven by artificial intelligence has already been happening for years now. The *Figure 4.8* depicted below, from *Arnold Pacey's* book on technology distancing offers a reflective outlook on the role of technology in shaping culture and human autonomy overall:

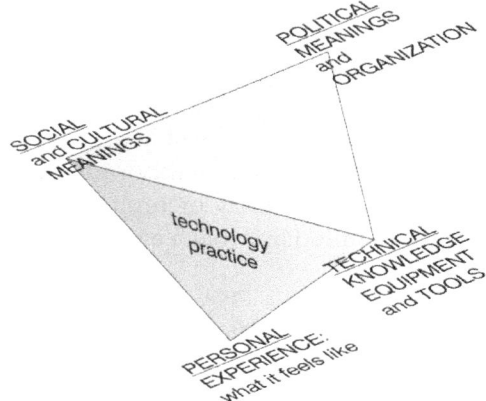

Figure 4.8: *A Figure from a book by Arnold Pacey demonstrating the role of technology (Pacey, 1999 p. 8)*

Arnold Pacey, in the above figure, has rightly argued that technology practice as a pyramid, has four edges – *(1) Social and cultural meanings; (2) Political meanings and Organization; (3) Personal Experience; and (4) Technical Knowledge equipment and Tools.*

All these 4 edges complete the role of technology as a form of human culture or movement, which has had transcendence for centuries, when we compare various ages and how industrial technology changed lives forever. This also explains the techno-cultural development of AI in ethical narratives, legal qualms and mythology in Western European and North American countries, which is indeed interesting to unfold the phenomenon of the human artifact conjunction. Now, one can agree that the idea of a human artifact is **ever evolving** and **self-replenishing**. Nevertheless, we would have to connote the recognition of artificial intelligence as a stable human artifact because, it is a vague technological sculpture and legal fiction cannot ever understand the role of AI and its entitative resemblance, until we resolve its complex ontological dilemmas.

> *Persona as currently is reveals connotations and denotations acquired and advanced in, from and to serve dominant sites. Such is the use of ID-size pictures, which make [cross-cultural] identifications of people become doubtfully alike [...] the provision of a name is irrelevant in certain places [...] or the inclusion of written narratives, a typical feature in western sites, is not always suitable in other sites (A Critique of Personas as representations of "the other" in Cross-Cultural Technology Design, 2016 p. 150)*

The object of a law, in case of AI is clear, but as said, cannot be purposive to restriction. Also, the scientific development of AI as posed is based on categorical human tendencies where AI entities get encouraged in limited environments, which no law can fixate, but can only circulate and regulate. Thus, when we are considering the role of AI as a human artifact, we need to recognize technology not to defeat its natural purpose, but to retain its positive value that it attains, which is said in simple terms – **progressive development** and **liberalization**.

Nevertheless, visual thinking, as taken into a sense of materializing emotions and external needs, via tech, is a human habit. It happens and is an anthropocentric reality to pertain. Also, in international law, cultural properties are regarded with their connective relationships with civilizations and so can be done with artificial intelligence. However, in cyberspace, there is some impeccable role, which AI faces. In international law, it is deemed to be possible that any digital content, which bears originality or reserves the same, is tenable to be protected and not any other copy or replica of the same. The status of AI, here as well, turns diabolical if the limited approach as applied in the case of cyberspace is considered in the case of AI as well.

> *Development of the division of labor and its elaboration in bureaucracies can also make it more difficult to see the connections between one's day-to-day work and the people affected by it, as can the operation of a market economy. Wherever work is highly specialized and bureaucratic, or remote from the ultimate purchaser, the individual is usually aware of only the immediate task. Technical responsibility in the office or factory and financial rectitude in the marketplace become more important than moral responsibility for what products or processes [actually] do (Pacey, 1999 p. 176).*

We must realize that the use cases of AI systems, products and services could be **multi-faceted** and **multi-sectoral** (which means omnipotent and omnipresent) which may be protected under the 1954 Convention Regarding the Protection of Cultural Property (as under international humanitarian law). However, the provisions of the convention lack a befitting sense to further the schemata of protection of AI as a cultural property. Now, in the case of an armed conflict, including the one in cyberspace, the purpose of an AI realm as an entity may turn out to be counterintuitive in terms of being used to vandalize and destroy cultural property. However, in the case of human artifacts, the emphasis on cultural heritage entitles greater scope and review for AI realms as **technological human artifacts**, and thus, under the framework of international cultural law treaties, it should be tried to create some accountability framework in practice, when it comes to AI as a form of cultural property, especially when an AI entity possesses identity-based apposition in the enablement of cultural property. Perhaps, it may be considered as a settled point that the artificial intelligence in a cultural context, could be **socio-technical** and way dynamic, thereby rendering it an elevated status *(Schmitt, 2017 p. 535)* (with no hierarchy but **choice-based primacy**). On the question of importance of international legal scholarship, beyond usual issues in the field of international humanitarian law on cultural heritage *(Pacey, 1999 p. 178)*, it would be intriguing to notice if one can condone the role of AI on matters relate to cultural heritage, in a clear sense. This is interesting to ponder since technology is reasonably capable of distancing itself from human objects in terms of its own capabilities, which was the object of the Industrial Revolution, and is said to be considered today as well, a global & historical phenomenon for humankind. Nevertheless, cultural heritage has a dynamic relationship with technology. An AI, in terms of normalcies in policy making, cannot be ignored as something merely ineffective and hyped and at the same time, can possess the status of a human artifact and a legal entity, of a differing nature. It does not matter if it is even capable and competent to a human being. It is about how it causes human attribution in facets of cultures, societies and economies. The legal & policy impact worries policymakers around the world, since across use cases and test cases of even generative AI applications, as we know, things get quite uncertain and ontologically shocking.

In primary terms, international law has to retain a special status for its objects and subjects, where these legal objects & subjects retain its ontological form of **primacy** over certain state practices. This was understood in certain international disputes of political nature, for example, where UN organs have worked out to present difficult solutions. Nevertheless, the significant role of technology in shaping cultural heritage, is tenable for determination when AI becomes either a party to it, or that it plays a role to the same as a third party. It is thus clear in my view that under the **2003 Convention on Intangible Cultural Heritage**, the scope and role of an AI system is certainly possible to be fit and settled at a limited scope and certainty, under the **Article 1**. One of the special references is a report submitted to the UNHRC entails some limited scope to estimate the role of ***tech-based cultural anthropocentrism***.

> *"While new technologies [allow] for exciting advances in the field of cultural heritage, it is important to use these tools in ways that allow for the greatest possible access while preserving/safeguarding the heritage (UN Human Rights Council, 2011 p. 15)."*

Here, I may seem to be a clear advocate of anthropocentric values, but it is not about those values. The fact is dealt in that context of the enclosing factor of identity (as a concept) and its human affinity, which is enrolled in a human society, for which tech via AI is a guardian as well as a learner. We have to understand that from language to pictorial representations, AIs can map human identities in different forms. *Deep fakes (Böhm, 2018), AI-based pornography (Cole, 2018)*, AI-enabled political ads *(TED, 2017)* and other such related issues, have a cultural effect on societies across the globe, where the human tendency to equitable access and review of information is harmed.

Nevertheless, in the scheme of international law, it is plausible to accept the dynamic role of technology as a driver and form of social & civic culture. Based on method-based approach on study of early primitive societies, the course of technology as a developmental tradition was taken into a recognition of civil rights. Indeed, this is a coincidence, and can be taken seriously.

> *Technological traditions [are] therefore be understood as a complex system of cultural inheritance, with information passed on between individuals through the sophisticated human capacity for high-fidelity social learning. This transmission system enables particular combinations of cultural information to persist from one generation to the next in lineages of deeper heritable continuity. Change in these bodies of cultural information is, of course, also possible, and this change can proceed at different speeds (Jordan, 2015 p. 341).*

Considering the excerpt from a book by *Peter Jordan*, one can say it effectively settles the role of AI as a human artifact in the realm of technology law. In fact, it could be gullible and possible, where technologies as 'realms' need to instrument human autonomy and liberties as clear non-negotiables when the recognition of artificial intelligence as a human artefact is achieved or proposed. More than being an entity, an AI can be a dynamic carrier or preserver of human culture and heritage (Tucker, 2016) in many ways. This also explains the multi-faceted (or multi-dimensional) value of data as the driver of algorithmic activities & operations.

Not only the data subject but also the corporeal person involved in the use of data has some purpose with it. *Genevieve Bell*, a former vice president of Intel, believes in technology-based enculturation, enabled by artificial intelligence technologies. By all means, AI systems could be certainly capacitated to perform machine learning techniques to **learn (if not understand)** data in a multi-faceted way, which I term as the right (or autonomy) of any AI system to be in a position of dimensional perpetuity. This multi-faceted state or property of AI systems thus changes their status quo as legal or juristic entity, if required to be examined that way, which is an extraordinary form of sociotechnical tendency in classes of digital technologies. It includes development of language among bots, which Facebook AI Research (FAIR), a former research group by Meta (formerly Facebook), found (Carter, 2018); recognition of AI in the ambit of rapprochement of cultures in an international forum by UN in Moscow in 2018 (United Nations Educational, Scientific and Cultural Organization, 2018); and the use of AI in learning mechanisms (Dutt D'Cunha, 2017).

Now, in the present UNESCO conventions, it could be indirect and vague to incorporate the culturally conjunctive nature of an AI, as it can be a cultural property under the Article 1 of the 1954 Convention on Cultural Property. Even otherwise, one may interpret an AI system as a kind of intangible cultural heritage because of its immaterial nature under the 2003 Convention. As per the legal rubric of the 2005 Convention on Cultural Diversity and Expressions, we may render the conjunctive role of an AI system at its central stature to be a human artifact, because its role to enable enculturation. Considering this, one may consider examining the role of artificial intelligence in enculturation through the lens of these principles on the role & status of AI as a human artifact: (1) Cultural Footprint (enculturation); (2) Technology Distancing; and (3) Preservation of Dimensional Perpetuity.

A cultural footprint produced by an AI system could be termed as a simple concomitant of AI-enabled enculturation of human reality, which could have an impact on the multi-faceted identities of human societies, making the impact of AI-enabled enculturation, multi-faceted. This aspect of many uses of identity is discussed among circles of technology scientists and engineers involved in the process of data mining (IEEE Standards Association, 2016). It was found in the findings of Facebook AI Research by understanding the basic parameters and constructs of **Reinforcement Learning (RL)** visible in their experimentation of the AI chatbots, via examining **abstract state representation** (*Francois-Lavet*, et al., 2018). In other cases as well, AI models have been utilized and non-modular, limited situations were created, where sophisticated RL techniques were subject to test. More test cases to enhance deep learning techniques have already been facilitated by AI companies and researchers through the enablement of **convoluted neural networks** to facilitate the sophistication of virtual reality-related use cases in a real and discernible manner *(Facebook, 2018; Bajpai, 2018)*. With a set of technological features and industrial viability (if not commercial), one can say that AI system have a decent chance to be culturally relativist. The possibility of AI systems to be perceptible indicates that AI-enabled enculturation is about how their first, second and third-order effects of an AI system's actions could enable a dynamic ecosystem of cyberspace, where reality can be encultured beyond human intervention. Imagine how sophisticated and impactful technology distancing has been in shaping the needs and workflows of human societies across jurisdictions, and geographies. It could be any form of intervention, significant or too obvious and basic. Yet, it is these interventions we ignore or look out for, which shape our way of life.

> *[While] the MIT system is in its infancy now, it's easy to imagine a near future with home-based sleep monitoring using radio frequencies (RF). "Imagine if your Wi-Fi router knows when you are dreaming, and can monitor whether you are having enough deep sleep, which is necessary for memory consolidation," said study leader Dina Katabi in a statement. "Our vision is developing health sensors that will disappear into the background and capture physiological signals and important health metrics, without asking the user to change her behavior in any way." (LeFebvre, 2017).*

To add, technology distancing is happening every single day. From the times when *Christopher* was conceived as an idea by the great *Alan Turing* to the days when Spatial Internet (and Metaverse) could be accessed by using Apple Vision Pro, this phenomenon has become the new normal, which tech companies and governments are aware of, since they intend to facilitate better control on the way these facets of technology distancing are tried to be achieved. One of the most interesting ideas is asserted by DARPA, which wishes that AI systems must be cultured to susceptible negotiation for appropriate usage of radio frequencies for better facilitation (Looper, 2016). The same is with the encouragement of a corporate or statutory culture of AI-based lawyers (more in corporate field) (Ashley, 2017; Cummings, et al., 2018). This leads to distancing of the purpose of human values to some extent, even if the tech is utilized to strengthen human needs and their due facilitation. We, as humans, expectedly or eventually, get in line with any societal and economic transformation led by technology. This tendency could be termed as some sort of developmental sobriety, but we should never forget that any technological achievement, must respect human autonomy. In fact, not respecting human autonomy could be problematic. Thus, even if we are excited to facilitate a newer world of AI-led technocracies, we must stay prepared. Still, we should not be pessimist over technology distancing because it is the virtue of facilitation of human needs (or rather natural beings' needs). That is very basic, and certainly we should entail the safer and harmonious that encultures a better future for natural beings and tends them to get room for evolution. In *Figure 4.9*, it is discussed how could a better human rights approach be helpful, in line with my propositions on the idea of dimensional perpetuity:

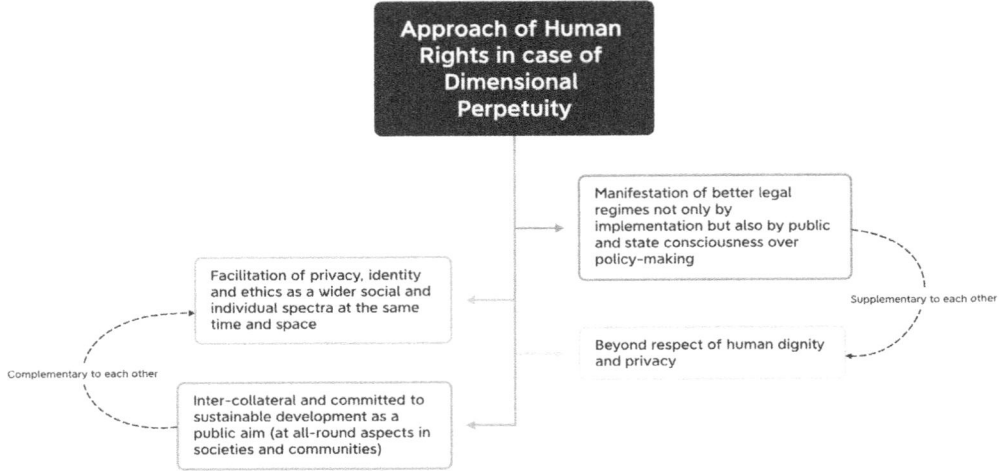

Figure 4.9: *A Schematic Diagram showing how can a better human rights approach via understanding dimensional perpetuity can lead to the better solutions.*

Now, how come dimensional perpetuity be saved? When we know that enculturation by facilitating AIs lead to culture-based implications on human societies, we must settle situations that render a wider resonance over legal regimes. Thus, it is a challenge to revisit and develop legal and private regimes, not only for better implementation, because here we face the risk of categorical lineation. It could lead us to a scenario where technology distancing could become some form of a socio-technical human anomaly for societies and countries to come. A better way to look at this dilemma is to have a sense of acute consciousness in enabling policymaking at citizen (or consumer) and state level. It takes time and is not easy. However, at a public level, policy consciousness can still be necessarily achieved. The best example to depict this is the recent UNESCO Recommendation on the Ethics of Artificial Intelligence. Here is an excerpt from the legal instrument:

> *Ethical questions regarding AI systems pertain to all stages of the AI system life cycle, understood here to range from research, design and development to deployment and use, including maintenance, operation, trade, financing, monitoring and evaluation, validation, end-of-use, disassembly and termination. In addition, AI actors can be defined as any actor involved in at least one stage of the AI system life cycle, and can refer both to natural and legal persons, such as researchers, programmers, engineers, data scientists, end-users, business enterprises, universities and public and private entities, among others (United Nations Educational, Scientific and Cultural Organization, 2021).*

Culture and technology are immeasurably reciprocated and inspirational towards each other. We live with those social traditions and ways of life to expand our avenues and innovate in times of challenging discourses. It is appreciative, yet we also require settling those resolutions to achieve meaningful social change, which maintain this harmony of relationship between culture and technology.

Conclusion

As the idea of legal visibility is discussed in this chapter, it could be used purposefully in shaping the genealogical aspect of international law, especially in the case of artificial intelligence. To summarize, I have discussed the approach of common law, the Tegmark Approach of AI Ethics, provided some analysis of identity recognition in international law scholarship, AI as a human artifact with respect to some UNESCO conventions and other issues. All of these issues have real-life scenarios. In this chapter, I have explored the connection between AI, data privacy, and identity, with a focus on the ethical aspect of machine learning. I have discussed the important role that culture and technology play in shaping AI systems and their impact.

Since, it is an introduction, this book does not extend to more issues other than algorithmic policing, identity, pseudonymization, personation, international legal personality, dimensional perpetuity, constitutional morality and the right to privacy. However, with appropriate efforts, all these concepts under the umbrella of the concept have been given enough space and discussion for the legal, social and technology academia to discern upon.

As this chapter concludes, one should ask some questions. Is it inevitable that an AI is possible to govern the world and our democratic systems shall or may render incompetent to proceed and end up with no generic solution? Is human creativity at a low, or on the verge of extinction since a rise in disruptive technologies (especially related to AI)? How can we achieve human methods and instruments to face the tech revolution and represent themselves harder? Solutions in general have been discussed earlier in the previous chapters, and certainly it would be befitting to proceed with those aspects. However, the final portion of this chapter retains very specific insights on the anthropological aspect of what an AI-parallel cyberspace may look like. It is not a fantasy anymore; the world is facing an AI revolution already. Moreover, at the same time, we have to see how AI can possess itself as an advanced human artifact, whose role can turn out to be dynamic and encouraging. Determining a clear role of AI systems as human artefacts certainly makes it easier for us to employ better tools to develop safer and healthier AI, in a utopian sense.

Now, the approach of globalization has rendered dilution in the traditional *opinio juris* of international law, which we find successively in the form of various ILPs and legal instruments. Nevertheless, the positivist approach to international law renders a sense of clarity as to when the rules of *erga omnes* and *jus cogens* are applied in the case of nation-states. Nevertheless, the route of customary international law towards internationalizing or at least federating data protection regulations could be possible as a starting point for effective and real AI regulation. The issue, that would arise however in the case of fields such as international human rights law, is important to understand. If international human rights law in the form of frameworks, declarations and principles fail to recognize the present picture and visualizes today's modern states as older welfare states in the early 1950s, then the die-hard proponents of multilateral systems will remain stuck with a false notion that multilateral institutions would inevitably be helpful, because these institutions reek of dysfunction and lack of policy purpose (Out of the Abyss: The Challenges Confronting the New UN Committee on Economic, Social and Cultural Rights, 1987 pp. 345-47). This problematic aspect of international human rights law scholarship is dealt in further chapters. Nevertheless, it would be intriguing to see how various aspects of international law shape the all-comprehensive significance of the genealogy of states and their international character.

> *[Perhaps] one of the reasons why judges do not like to discuss questions of policy, or to put a decision in terms upon their views as lawmakers, is that the moment you leave the path of merely logical deduction you lose the illusion of certainty which makes legal reasoning seem like mathematics. But the certainty is only an illusion, nevertheless. Views of policy are taught by experience of the interests of life. Those interests are fields of battle (Holmes, 1920 p. 126).*

Now, a future that we can conceive of an AI realm, is itself justified by the due approach of its own realization and those use cases. On this question, an AI in a cyberspace reserves itself as the immaterial homecoming entity of the same in an international life, and its focus on human rights of individuals and communities can be tended to be human-oriented, which we have seen (Abramovich, 2018; Clolll, 2018). The materialization of artificial intelligence has shown the potential to make unprecedented changes in multiple domains including healthcare, financial services, creative services, digital rights management, and others. Beyond the hype of *Bard*, *ChatGPT* and other Generative AI applications, there are many intricate use cases and test cases at B2B and B2C level, which we must not ignore. Please refer to *Figure 4.10* below:

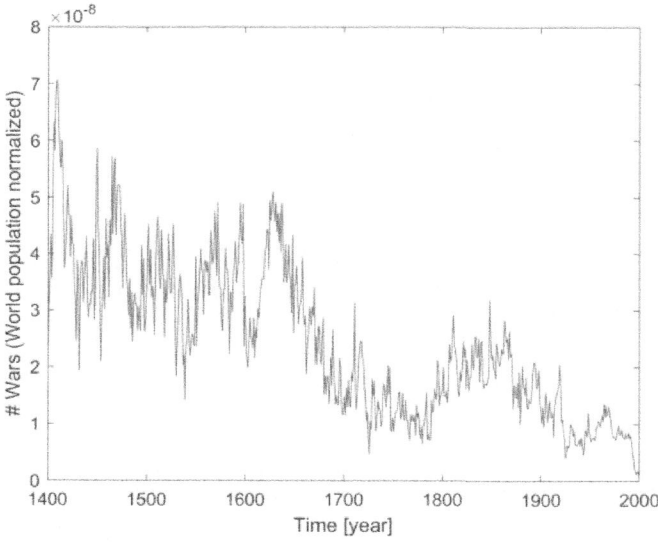

Figure 4.10: *Number of wars normalized for the world population; taken from a research on war patterns of 600 years (Martelloni, et al., 2018 p. 3).*

With the emergence of technologies like AI, we have gained knowledge and methods in fields like psychology, ethics and data science to enhance the effectiveness and usefulness of AI systems. However, we are confronted with a significant and ongoing challenge regarding the future of human society. Data has become the most valuable and exploitable resource in the world, and cyberspace has become a distinct realm alongside realms of air, water, land, and outer space. In this context, there is uncertainty surrounding the protection of our identities, beyond material aspects. Safeguarding initiatives are needed to address the complexities of identity in this digital landscape.

Now, cyberspace, as we know, is one of the most fragile and susceptible spaces of human resources ever, recent studies by network theorists show some interesting results about how the number of wars (or armed conflicts) have been normalized since the 1400s based on recorded history (Martelloni, et al., 2018). These studies are not convincing enough to generalize (Emerging Technology from the arXiv, 2019), but observant and appreciating. People may fear that our world is fragile in these testing times in the 2020s, especially after the unfortunate coronavirus pandemic. These days, some fear the world may lose geopolitical and economic stability due to events showing some form of disinterest of the United States to be that global watchdog. China and Russia are considered as another pole of big players in the global order only to challenge American soft power and hard power capabilities. Nevertheless, as the *Indian Prime Minister Narendra Modi* had once told *Russian President Vladimir Putin* on the Ukraine situation, *"I know that today's era is not an era of war, and I have spoken to you on the phone about this,"* one has to understand that international life as we call it, in the philosophy of public international law, is now a pragmatic sphere of multitudes of multi-level engagements, making the world stable and resilient to be more responsive. This is why it is not easy to for countries and their people to resonate with conflicts when digital and physical economic integrations are realized. In short, cyberspace has led countries to achieve multiple forms of economic truce among countries only to avoid potential conflicts and disputes. It has also changed the way we look at development economics. *Samir Saran*, the President of Observer Research Foundation, rightly points out on this tendency of the multi-polar world order:

> *Unlike narratives which pitch BRICS, IBSA, and RIC as anti-Western, [...] these groupings help place India firmly within the established order of global management and provide a flexible architecture for its diplomacy. Increasingly, India's foreign policy will be driven by needs and not choice. These needs include economic growth and domestic imperatives like skills development, jobs, and education for its population. India's temporal and spatial preferences for a particular plurilateral forum will be driven by these domestic compulsions. The attraction of such groupings as opposed to the larger multilateral ones is clear. They are flexible enough to allow the country to continue to be a member without fear of recrimination even if it disagrees with other members on certain issues (Saran, 2015 p. 760).*

Nevertheless, in a slowly de-globalizing world, where risks of war and wreckage of supply chain entrench a sense of fear, it would be intriguing to watch out how the integration of artificial intelligence technologies, will change the status quo of things. In the next chapter,

I have discussed about the Privacy Doctrine, a new theory of privacy law I had developed for the first edition of this book, with a rights-based approach. The purpose of the privacy doctrine is to decipher an ethical understanding towards the legal implications of using AI systems, which is deeply connected to the aspects of human autonomy, dignity, and privacy. The Doctrine, therefore, is useful to question the current human rights thought models, which includes socio-technical aspects. In furtherance, the chapter also addresses the limitations in the existing international human rights jurisprudence in developing pragmatic legal solutions, especially in the case of human autonomy and AI.

References

- **The White House. 2023.** Joint Statement from the United States and India . *The White House.* [Online] 2023. **https://www.whitehouse.gov/briefing-room/statements-releases/2023/06/22/joint-statement-from-the-united-states-and-india/**.

- **Skinner, Quentin. 2008.** A Genealogy of the Modern State - British Academy Lecture. *British Academy.* [Online] 2008. **https://www.thebritishacademy.ac.uk/documents/2073/pba162p325.pdf**.

- **Dörrbecker (Chumwa), Maximilian. 2023.** Map of the Legal systems of the world (en). *Creative Commons.* [Online] 2023. **https://creativecommons.org/licenses/by-sa/2.5**.

- **Geranmayeh, Ellie. 2020.** Reviving the revolutionaries: How Trump's maximum pressure is shifting Iran's domestic politics . *European Council on Foreign Relations.* [Online] June 23, 2020. **https://ecfr.eu/publication/reviving_the_revolutionaries_how_trumps_maximum_pressure_is_shifting_irans/**.

- **VDW. 2017.** *Policy Paper on the Asilomar Principles on Artificial Intelligence.* Asilomar : s.n., 2017.

- **Hart, H. L. A. 2014.** *The Concept of Law.* New Delhi : Oxford University Press, 2014.

- **Jarvis, Jacob. 2018.** Facebook hack: What is the 'view as' feature that was exploited? *Evening Standard.* [Online] September 28, 2018. **https://www.standard.co.uk/news/techandgadgets/facebook-hack-what-is-the-view-as-feature-that-hackers-exploited-a3948901.html**.

- **Facebook. 2018.** Facebook Newsroom. *Facebook.* [Online] September 28, 2018. **https://newsroom.fb.com/news/2018/09/security-update/**.

- **Osawa, Juro. 2023.** Sequoia and Other U.S.-Backed VCs Are Funding China's Answer to OpenAI. *The Information.* [Online] April 5, 2023. **https://www.theinformation.com/articles/sequoia-and-other-u-s-backed-vcs-are-funding-chinas-answer-to-openai**.

- **Robinette, Paul, et al. 2016.** *Overtrust of Robots in Emergency Evacuation Scenarios.* 2016.

- **Tucker, Ian. 2016.** Genevieve Bell: 'Humanity's greatest fear is about being irrelevant'. *The Guardian.* [Online] November 26, 2016. **https://www.theguardian.com/technology/2016/nov/27/genevieve-bell-ai-robotics-anthropologist-robots**.

- **Frommer, Dan. 2017.** Watch Steve Jobs unveil the first iPhone — his greatest performance ever. *recode.* [Online] January 9, 2017. **https://www.recode.net/2017/1/9/14212394/steve-jobs-iphone-macworld-2007-keynote-video**.

- **Abhivardhan. 2020.** The Perspective of Dimensional Perpetuity for Artificial Intelligence: A Model on Socio-Legal and Political Evolution as a Challenge to Entrepreneurial Ethics. *SSRN.* [Online] 2020. **https://papers.ssrn.com/sol3/papers.cfm?abstract_id=3649403**.

- **Meurisch, Christian and Mühlhäuser, Max. 2022.** Data Protection in AI Services: A Survey. *ACM Computing Surveys.* 2022, Vol. 54, 2.

- **Abhivardhan. 2021.** The Entitative Nature of Artificial Intelligence in International Law: An Analytic Legal Model. *Artificial Intelligence and Policy in India, Volume 2.* s.l. : Indian Society of Artificial Intelligence and Law Charitable Trust, 2021.

- **Koskenniemi, Martii. 2005.** *From Apology to Utopia: The Structure of International Legal Argument.* Cambridge, NY : Cambridge University Press, 2005.

- **Schindler, Dietrich:. 1982.** *Contribution a` l'e´tat des facteurs sociologiques et psychologiques du droit international.* 1982.

- **International Court of Justice. 1950.** *Status of South-West Africa case, ICJ Reports 1950, 148.* s.l. : International Court of Justice, 1950.

- **—. 1970.** *Case Concerning the Barcelona Traction, Light and Power Company, Limited (Belgium v. Spain), Second Phase.* 3, s.l. : International Court of Justice, 1970.

- **Schwab, Klaus. 2018.** Globalization 4.0 – what it means and how it could benefit us all. *World Economic Forum.* [Online] November 5, 2018. **https://www.weforum.org/agenda/2018/11/globalization-4-what-does-it-mean-how-it-will-benefit-everyone/**.

- **Kelsen, Hans. 2009.** *Pure Theory of Law.* [trans.] Max Knight. New Jersey : The Lawbook Exchange Ltd., 2009.

- **Court of Justice of the European Union. 2014.** *Google Spain v AEPD and Mario Costeja González.* C-131/12, s.l. : Court of Justice of the European Union, May 13, 2014.

- **Kerala High Court. 2010.** *Samdeep Varghese vs State Of Kerala.* 2003, s.l. : Kerala High Court, 2010.

- **Department of Telecommunications, Government of India. 2000.** Information Technology Act, 2000. June 9, 2000.

- *Conceptualising the right to data protection in an era of Big Data.* **McDermott, Y. 2017.** 2017, Big Data & Society.

- **Moniodis, Christina P. 2012.** Moving from Nixon to NASA: Privacy's Second Strand — A Right to Informational Privacy. *Yale Journal of Law & Technology.* 2012, Vol. 15, pp. 139-168.

- **MIT Technology Review.** A Shanghai startup's demo of its system for facial recognition.

- **Schmitt, M. N. 2017.** *Tallinn Manual 2.0 on the International Law Applicable to Cyber Operations.* 2nd. Cambridge : Cambeidge University Press, 2017.

- **Venkatnarayan, Anand. 2018.** Guest Post: Hacking the Supreme Court in the Age of AI. *Indian Constitutional Law and Philosophy.* [Online] December 29, 2018. **https:// indconlawphil.wordpress.com/2018/12/29/guest-post-hacking-the-supreme- court-in-the-age-of-ai/.**

- **Ericsson. 2018.** 10 Hot Consumer Trends 2019. *Ericsson.* [Online] 2018. **https://www.ericsson.com/en/trends-and-insights/consumerlab/consumer- insights/reports/10-hot-consumer-trends-2019?utm_source=linkedin&utm_ medium=social_paid&utm_campaign=HCT_2019&utm_content=GFMC_ global_20181214_Trend3_video.**

- **Conforti, B. 1988.** *Cours général de droit international public .* Nijhoff, Leiden : The Hague Academy of International Law, 1988.

- **Hartree, D. R. 1949.** *Calculating Instruments and Machine.* New York : s.n., 1949.

- **McCarthy, John, et al. 1955.** A Proposal for the Dartmouth Summer Research Project on Artificial Intelligence. *Stanford University.* [Online] 1955. **http://www- formal.stanford.edu/jmc/history/dartmouth/dartmouth.html.**

- *Computing Machinery and Intelligence.* **Turing, A. M. 1950.** 1950, Mind, pp. 433-460.

- **Gödel, Kurt. 1951.** Some basic theorems on the foundations of mathematics and their implications. *Gibbs Lecture.* 1951.

- **Russell, Stuart J. and Norvig, Peter. 2003.** *Artificial Intelligence: A Modern Approach.* New Jersey : s.n., 2003.

- **Shneiderman, Ben and Muller, Michael. 2023.** On AI Anthropomorphism. *Human-Centered AI - Medium.* [Online] April 10, 2023. **https://medium.com/ human-centered-ai/on-ai-anthropomorphism-abff4cecc5ae#2901.**

- **Pacey, Arnold. 1999.** *Meaning of Technology.* Cambridge : The MIT Press, 1999.

- *A Critique of Personas as representations of "the other" in Cross-Cultural Technology Design.* **Cabrero, Daniel G., Winschiers-Theophilus, Heike and Abdelnour- Nocera, José. 2016.** Namibia : ACM, 2016. AfriCHI'16. pp. 149-154.

- **UN Human Rights Council. 2011.** Report of the Independent Expert in the Field of Cultural Rights, A/HRC/17/38. *UN Human Rights Council.* [Online] March 21, 2011. **https://www.refworld.org/docid/50f01fb12.html**.

- **Böhm, Markus. 2018.** "Deepfakes": Firmen gehen gegen gefälschte Promi-Pornos vor. *Spiegel Online.* [Online] February 7, 2018. **http://www.spiegel.de/netzwelt/web/ deepfakes-online-plattformen-wollen-fake-promi-pornos-loeschen-a-1192170. html**.

- **Cole, Samantha. 2018.** People Are Using AI to Create Fake Porn of Their Friends and Classmates. *Motherboard.* [Online] January 27, 2018. **https://motherboard.vice. com/en_us/article/ev5eba/ai-fake-porn-of-friends-deepfakes**.

- **TED. 2017.** We're building a dystopia just to make people click on ads. *TED Talks.* [Online] September 2017. **https://www.ted.com/talks/zeynep_tufekci_we_re_ building_a_dystopia_just_to_make_people_click_on_ads**.

- **Jordan, Peter. 2015.** *Technology as Human Social Tradition.* Oakland, California : University of California Press, 2015.

- **Carter, William Michael. 2018.** How to get culture right when embedding it into AI. *Phys.org.* [Online] July 10, 2018. **https://phys.org/news/2018-07-culture-embedding-ai.html**.

- **United Nations Educational, Scientific and Cultural Organization. 2018.** Tenth International Forum of NGOs in Official Partnership with UNESCO: Concept Note. *United Nations Educational, Scientific and Cultural Organization.* [Online] 2018. **http://ngo-unesco.net/fr/pdf/forum_science/EN%20Concept%20Note%20 Science%20Forum.pdf**.

- **Dutt D'Cunha, Suparna. 2017.** Can Robots Replace Lawyers? This Indian AI Startup Is Making A Case For Legal Tech. *Forbes.* [Online] June 14, 2017. **https:// www.forbes.com/sites/suparnadutt/2017/06/14/legal-tech-robots-replace-lawyers-indian-startup-caseiq/#601a4b7547a7**.

- **IEEE Standards Association. 2016.** The Cultural Ramifications of Ubiquitous AI. *engadget.* [Online] December 19, 2016. **https://www.engadget.com/2016/12/19/the-cultural-ramifications-of-ubiquitous-ai/**.

- **Francois-Lavet, Vincent, et al. 2018.** Combined Reinforcement Learning via Abstract Representations. *Facebook AI Research.* [Online] December 2018. **https:// research.fb.com/wp-content/uploads/2018/12/Combined-Reinforcement-Learning-via-Abstract-Representations_2.pdf?**.

- **Facebook. 2018.** Open-sourcing DeepFocus, an AI-powered system for more realistic VR images. *Facebook Code.* [Online] December 19, 2018. **https://code. fb.com/virtual-reality/deepfocus/**.

- **Bajpai, Prableen. 2018.** How Microsoft Is Using Artificial Intelligence To Fight Climate Change. *Nasdaq.* [Online] April 6, 2018. **https://www.nasdaq.com/article/how-microsoft-is-using-artificial-intelligence-to-fight-climate-change-cm944514.**

- **LeFebvre, Rob. 2017.** MIT uses radio waves and AI to more accurately study sleep. *engadget.* [Online] July 8, 2017. **https://www.engadget.com/2017/08/07/mit-radio-waves-ai-accurately-study-sleep/.**

- **Looper, Christian de. 2016.** DARPA thinks artificial intelligence could wring out bandwidth from the radio spectrum. *Digital Trends.* [Online] March 28, 2016. **https://www.digitaltrends.com/mobile/darpa-ai-radio-spectrum-competition/.**

- **Ashley, K.D. 2017.** *Artificial Intelligence and Legal Analytics: New Tools for Law Practice in the Digital Age.* Cambridge : Cambridge University Press, 2017.

- **Cummings, M. L., et al. 2018.** *Artificial Intelligence and International Affairs: Disruption Anticipated.* Chatham House. 2018.

- **United Nations Educational, Scientific and Cultural Organization. 2021.** Recommendation on the Ethics of Artificial Intelligence, SHS/BIO/REC-AIETHICS/2021. *UNESCO.* [Online] 2021. **https://unesdoc.unesco.org/ark:/48223/pf0000380455.**

- *Out of the Abyss: The Challenges Confronting the New UN Committee on Economic, Social and Cultural Rights.* **Alston, P. 1987.** 1987, Human Rights Quarterly, pp. 332-381.

- **Holmes, Oliver Wendell. 1920.** Privilege, Malice and Intent. *Collected Legal Papers by Oliver Wendell Holmes.* New York : Harcourt, Brace and Howe, 1920.

- **Abramovich, Giselle. 2018.** Study Finds Investments In Customer Experience Are Paying Off. *CMO.com.* [Online] February 26, 2018. **https://www.cmo.com/features/articles/2018/2/26/adobe-2018-digital-trends-report-findings.html#gs.xoSSi8Q.**

- **Clolll, Joe. 2018.** Goldman Sachs used AI to simulate 1 million possible World Cup outcomes — and arrived at a clear winner. *Business Insider South Africa.* [Online] June 11, 2018. **https://www.businessinsider.co.za/world-cup-predictions-pick-to-win-it-all-goldman-sachs-ai-model-2018-6.**

- **Martelloni, Gianluca, Patti, Franscesca Di and Bardi, Ugo. 2018.** Pattern Analysis of World Conflicts over the past 600 years. *Cornell University.* [Online] December 19, 2018. **https://arxiv.org/ftp/arxiv/papers/1812/1812.08071.pdf.**

- **Emerging Technology from the arXiv. 2019.** Data mining adds evidence that war is baked into the structure of society. *MIT Technology Review.* [Online] January 4, 2019. **https://www.technologyreview.com/s/612704/data-mining-adds-evidence-that-war-is-baked-into-the-structure-of-society/?utm_campaign=the_download.**

unpaid.engagement&utm_source=hs_email&utm_medium=email&utm_content=68743473&_hsenc=p2ANqtz-_HN2oiBWwOTp7RTCnqoxY.

- **Saran, Samir. 2015.** India's Contemporary Plurilateralism. [ed.] David M. Malone, C. Raja Mohan and Srinath Raghavan. *The Oxford Handbook of Indian Foreign Policy.* s.l. : Oxford University Press, 2015.

Endnotes

[1] Cognition is determined here as 'situated cognition', meaning not only internal scheming processes in the brain but also and above all including the reciprocal real-time interface of a physically self-possessed arrangement with its due environment in a certain way.

[2] According to noted jurist *Hans Kelsen*, the Grundnorm is the foundational or ultimate norm in a legal system that serves as the basis for the validity of all other norms within that system. One can understand a Grundnorm as some supreme rule from which all other laws derive their authority. Interestingly, the Grundnorm, according to Kelsen, is not itself derived from any higher legal authority but is postulated as a necessary assumption to establish the validity and coherence of the legal system.

[3] Data relativism is a concept that may be applied to situations where data is manipulated or presented in a manner that fosters addictive behavior or impacts users' understanding of information. In the realm of app design, developers can utilize specific design features like notifications, rewards, or personalized content to craft an addictive user experience, thereby influencing how users perceive and engage with the data that is presented to them.

[4] Here is a definition of Dynamic Privacy from my paper on Dimensional Perpetuity:

Dynamic Privacy, by idea in proposition means that a Self-Transformable AI can decide and recreate its privacy infrastructure intrinsic to the ethos of its self-transformable algorithmic structure, which depending on the strength of the algorithmic structure is accordingly determinable. While Differential Privacy is a utility-based method to preserve the real identity of a data, the parameter of Dynamic Privacy encourages us to notice the freedom in the structure to revise and establish its own intrinsic privacy features. The parameter focuses on the diverse representation of AI within its own ethos of algorithmic development and is indicative of the fact that we need to render open and cultivable legal approaches to the privacy structure that can be ensured by the algorithms to preserve the self-transformability of AI (Abhivardhan, 2020).

[5] Acronym for international human rights law.

[6] Acronym for international humanitarian law.

[7] Acronym for international environmental law.

[8] Acronym for the Vienna Convention on the Law of Treaties.

[9] In international law, a persistent objector is a state that consistently and clearly objects to a norm of customary international law since the norm's emergence and considers itself not bound to observe the norm. The concept is an example of the positivist doctrine that a state can only be bound by norms to which it has consented.

[10] Various international legal instruments are applicable to the realm of digital identity. One instance is the International Telecommunications Union (ITU) that has endorsed several resolutions

concerning digital identity, such as Resolution ITU-T Y.4051. This particular resolution offers guidance on employing digital identity for electronic authentication. Additionally, the United Nations has adopted resolutions pertaining to digital identity, including Resolution 74/196. This resolution urges Member States to advance the use of digital identity while upholding human rights and fundamental freedoms.

[11] Clause 55 of the Preamble of the GDPR states:

"The processing of special categories of personal data may be necessary for reasons of public interest in the areas of public health without consent of the data subject. Such processing should be subject to suitable and specific measures so as to protect the rights and freedoms of natural persons (European Union, 2016 p. 11)".

[12] The provisions in Section 3 deal with 2 important rights: **right to rectification** (article 16) and its **due extension** (article 17), the **right to be forgotten / of erasure**.

[13] Article 38 of the Vienna Convention on the Law of Treaties is provided as follows:

Article 38

Rules in a treaty becoming binding on third States through international custom

Nothing in articles 34 to 37 precludes a rule set forth in a treaty from becoming binding upon a third State as a customary rule of international law, recognized as such (United Nations, 1969).

[14] Definitions in Section 2(1), such as clauses (i), (j), (k) & (l) provide a limited scope though for an artificial intelligence system to be rendered tenable for recognition.

[15] For the purposes of this book, the definition of Privacy is:

Privacy is the neutral right of every living individual, every group and the state to regulate its own interactions, relations and revelation and it is borne as an innate tendency within every individual, a required asset of the preservation for a group and the core immunity of a state pertaining to the framework of the state respectively without any sense, concepts and ideas of [ethics]. (Abhivardhan, 2017 pp. 13-14)

[16] However, Section 72 could entail a cogent cause to the protection of an AI as under Section 43 of the IT Act, 2000.

[17] *Acta jure imperii* is a Latin term that means "acts of state authority." This term is used in international law to describe acts that are performed by a state in its sovereign capacity. These acts are not subject to the jurisdiction of other states, and they cannot be challenged in international courts.

[18] Balkin has successfully determined the law of equality in simple terms.

The [law] marks a liminal point. It declares what constitutes unequal treatment as a matter of law. At the same time it also states what is not unequal treatment, or put slightly differently, what forms and claims of in equality the law will not recognize as presenting real or remediable problems of inequality. The law sees only some forms of inequality and not others because that is how law is made. First, law is simply imperfect. It cannot prevent all unfair or unjust inequalities even if it wanted to. Second, and more important, law is a compromise of contending forces and interests in society that is articulated in terms of doctrines and principles. Legal doctrines that enforce ideas of equality enforce the nature of that compromise and restate it in principled terms. Thus, what law enforces is not equality, but equality in the eyes of the law (Balkin, 2011 p. 141).

[19] The maxim means that a specific law prevails over a universal law.

[20] Refer to this excerpt as well:

[...] the support for democracy by the entire population, including the oligarchic elites that voluntary forego political power in the democratization process, serves as a coordination device and makes the implementation of a good rule of law after the transition possible. In this case, in fact, democratization emerges primarily to reduce the extent of wasteful investments in private protection, which is particularly costly for the oligarchic rulers. As result, democracies arising under a broad consensus entail a more favorable environment for economic [development] (Cervellati, et al., 2009)

[21]   Criminal liability to be tested and affirmed with respect to an AI object cannot be dealt with merely two aspects – that either it is a linear projection or a reactionary collocation of human or property-based entitative values (Agnew, 2011). When natural selection is equated at a legal plane, will it be viable to establish an equation between mixed systems of artificial selection in the case of artificial intelligence? It is difficult to make it happen, if we take into consideration Alan Turing's principle of 'polite convention' *(Computing Machinery and Intelligence, 1950 p. 433; Cervellati, et al., 2009).* Thus, a choice-based jurisprudence would be effective, but that choice should not lead a lineation of the legal percussions of the selective theory, which would require substantiation.

"The optimal allocation of energy, resources, and behavioral strategies will, for any organism, depend on specific features of their evolved developmental history and the environment in which they are embedded (Durrant, et al., 2015)."

[22]   One may also refer the realm of dimensional perpetuity with the *omnipotent* and *omnipresent* nature of artificial intelligence technologies as discussed in Chapter 1.

[23]   For understanding, a human artifact is a man-made artifact, of public importance in its own varying concerns.

[24]   This may render itself as disputed at the verge of the fact that an AI is yet anonymous in case of its own status in armed conflict.

(a) [movable] or immovable property of great importance to the cultural heritage of every people, such as monuments of architecture, art or history, whether religious or secular; archaeological sites; groups of buildings which, as a whole, are of historical or artistic interest; works of art; manuscripts, books and other objects of artistic, historical or archaeological interest; as well as scientific collections and important collections of books or archives or of reproductions of the property defined above (United Nations Educational, Scientific and Cultural Organization, 2018);

[25]   One may refer to the dispute between Russian Federation and Ukraine, where self-determination under ICCPR is a key issue as in the pretext of violations of international law, way before Russia started its war on Ukraine in 2022. Also refer to the *South West Africa* case *(International Court of Justice, 1950)* and the *Nicaragua v. United States* case *(1986).*

"[The] international law which on the first page forcefully preaches its character of public law and on the second page starts to construct blithely upon it with private law, has no scientific value at all (Fricker, 1901)"

[26]   A perambulatory clause of the Convention reads:

Recognizing that [the] processes of globalization and social transformation, alongside the conditions they create for renewed dialogue among communities, also give rise, as does the phenomenon of intolerance, to grave threats of deterioration, disappearance and destruction of the intangible cultural heritage, in particular owing to a lack of resources for safeguarding such heritage (United Nations Educational, Scientific and Cultural Organization, 2003)

27   Now, a special reference to (even if seems limited) is given in the recommendations to the UNHRC in the same report.

> *[States] should ensure access to the cultural heritage of one's own communities, as well as that of others, while respecting customary practices governing access to cultural heritage. In particular, such access should be ensured through education and information, including by the use of modern information and communication technologies. States should also ensure to that end, that the content of [programmes] is established in full cooperation with the concerned communities (UN Human Rights Council, 2011 p. 21);*

28   However, subject to the Art. 3 of the 2003 Convention, it is suggested that states and their public entities work restrictively over alteration methods and mechanisms rendered to the same because the use of limited resources such as frequencies and the stoppage of telecommunications must be facilitated with reasonable and tenable methods to safeguard the genuine liberty of an AI realm as material resources rendered and related to such systems may be regarded in the ambit of Articles **38, 42** and **44(2)** of the **ITU Constitution** *(International Telecommunication Union, 1992).*

29   Reinforcement learning is a form of machine learning, whose methods focus on how software agents have to act upon in a situation to render maximization of some kind of notion of swelling recompence.

30   The role of international telecommunication law is paramount to exist. One case is of poisoning AI Defense *(Giles, 2018).*

31   Acronym for international legal personalities.

32   Here is an excerpt from the article on data mining-based findings on war patterns:

> *Bardi and [others'] approach is by no means unique or new. Various other researchers have begun to look at war in the same way in the last 20 years or so. However, the new work is important because it backs up earlier work by applying it to one of the largest databases of violent conflict for the first time (Emerging Technology from the arXiv, 2019).*

Join our book's Discord space

Join the book's Discord Workspace for Latest updates, Offers, Tech happenings around the world, New Release and Sessions with the Authors:

https://discord.bpbonline.com

CHAPTER 5
The Privacy Doctrine

यथा दीपो निवातस्थो नेङ्गते सोपामा स्मृता।
योगिनो यतचित्तस्य युञ्जतो योगमात्मनः॥

"Just as a lamp in a windless place does not flicker,
such is the simile given of the disciplined mind of a Yogi practicing meditation."

The Linear Approach of Human Rights

Human Rights is more than just a term. It is at times an outcome of the discourse of societal nurturing, the active or passive enhancement of every human individual, and in some instances it becomes the discourse. The discourse of human rights has multiple kinds of origins, including that from India and continental Europe, which is followed by generations of contributory developments both in the West and the East.

> *"This freedom we shall observe ourselves, and desire to be observed in good faith by our heirs in perpetuity. (Davis, 1963 pp. 23-33)"*

In the case of India, many would limit the contributions of the subcontinent on issues governance and civic rights to the idea of *Sabha* and *Samiti* in Buddhist kingdoms, and a few other discrete contributions within the fold of Indian monarchs of the *Chola, Maurya* and other empires. Nevertheless, it can be assumed that democracy is not limited to the voting rights and electoral representation. The moral capital and efficiency of a polity shapes its legitimacy. Nevertheless, kingdoms in the Indian subcontinent have had a democratic and innovative ethos for centuries. Let us take the **Uthiramerur Inscription** as an example. This is a 100-year-old inscription found in Tamil Nadu (*Subramanian*, 2010), which gives the details and workings of local-self-governance system in *Uthiramerur (or Uttaramerur)*. The inscription mentions two village assemblies: *the Sabha* and *the Ur.*

The *Sabha* was an assembly of Brahmins, while the Ur was an assembly of all villagers, regardless of caste. The inscription also details the qualifications required for membership in the *Sabha*, the election process, and the roles and responsibilities of the members, which is why it is an important historical document. It is quite noteworthy that the inscription had provisions as a matter of local governance on issues such as the requirement for regular elections and the checks and balances on the power of the Sabha members. Here is an excerpt from the English translation of this inscription, which explains the procedure of elections. This holds so much impetus for the human rights discourse to understand how various systems and societies used to affirm rights for their populace.

> *In the midst of the temple priests one of them, who happens to be the eldest, shall stand up and lift that pot looking upwards to be seen by all people. One ward, that is, the packet representing it, shall be taken out by any young boy standing close, who does not know what is inside, and shall be transferred to another empty pot and shaken. From this pot one ticket shall be drawn by the young boy and made over to the arbitrator (madhyastha). While taking charge of the ticket thus given to him, the arbitrator shall receive it on the palm of his hand with the five fingers open. He shall read out the name in the ticket thus received. The ticket read by him shall also be read out by all the priests present in the inner hall. The name thus read out shall be put down (and accepted). Similarly, one man shall be chosen for each of the thirty wards (Venkayya, 1904 p. 263).*

The instances of public governance and representation mentioned in the *Uthiramerur* inscription are exemplary as they show how human rights frameworks orient their purpose and application to the genealogy and priorities of a state (*Turner*, 2003 p. 4), with time. The beautiful aspect of the inscription, and other historic and pre-modern texts are those ontological features that explain the purpose of such political and legal systems. They are not perfect systems, for sure. In addition, these pre-modern forms of governance and representation are not as robust or comparable to those of modern constitutional republics like India, Singapore, the United States and many other countries. Nevertheless, at an ontological level, political systems can represent the treatment of human agency as 'technology' by framing and structuring the exercise of power, governance, and decision-making in a systematic and organized manner. This parallels the way technology operates as a structured system to achieve specific goals or tasks. Let us take an illustration and compare it with the instances mentioned in the *Uthiramerur* inscription.

Imagine a modern-day city's public transportation system as a representation of how political systems at an ontological level can treat human agency as 'technology.' In this context, the city's transportation system is organized with various components, such as buses, trains, trams, and subways, each serving a specific purpose and operating within a defined framework. This structuring is similar to how technology is composed of various components working together. In fact, much like the *Uthiramerur* inscription outlines the qualifications, roles, and responsibilities of Sabha members, the public transportation system has defined roles for drivers, conductors, station staff, and maintenance crews. Each has specific duties and qualifications that contribute to the overall operation. When determining routes, schedules, and fare adjustments, transportation authorities often employ data and algorithms, reflecting a systematic approach to decision-making, much like technology-driven decision processes.

The comparison with the *Uthiramerur* inscription lies in the idea that even in complex modern systems, governance and management of human activities, such as public transportation, can be seen as 'technology' by virtue of workflows involving human stakeholders. It involves structured components, roles, protocols, and decision-making procedures, mirroring how technology organizes and directs various elements to achieve specific objectives. This illustrates how political systems, at an ontological level, resemble the treatment of human agency as 'technology' to efficiently serve society's needs. In addition, no human agency is complete without affirming a set of rights and duties to those human stakeholders involved in a system of governance and representation. In many ways, systems that shape human agency are techno-cultural – at least in terms of its ontological value. It is truly about the culture of governance and representation, which shapes human agency and human autonomy.

Now, considering this instance as discussed on the concept of human agency, imagine how would technology change the way human agency works. For example, electronic voting machines are considered to be safer, sustainable and reusable, in securing votes registered in a poling booth. Using these machines is better than registering all these votes on a paper ballot, simply because the ontological purpose and impact suggests that the registration of a vote via EVMs is safe, efficient and respects human agency in terms of political representation. This is one of the most rudimentary examples of how systems are expected to protect human autonomy, and create a framework of affirming rights and duties to the same human stakeholders. This explains that technology, be it any industrial technology, or a digital technology like AI, has to be used by respecting the autonomy of human beings. In the case of artificial intelligence and law, we may say one must protect the civil rights of the human data subjects, starting from data protection & privacy to regulations on sector-specific issues like those of dark patterns, market hype and cyber-attacks. This is why it is important for us to grasp these dynamics of techno-cultural roles of digital technologies. This chapter specifically concentrates on exploring these rights-based aspects in the context of privacy jurisprudence and the proliferation of AI technologies.

> *"The [State] Parties to the present Covenant undertake to respect the freedom indispensable for scientific research and creative activity (UN General Assembly, 1966 p. 9)"*

AI, in the realm of human rights, could be observed as a contributor to the economic, social, cultural, and psychological changes that happen in human societies. We share such stories with smart watches, smart fridges, smart devices, laptops and other tech accessories as such where the role of AI systems has become embedded. Also, it is obvious to discern that enculturation of technology espouses a dynamic role of any class of digital tech to sustain with practical realities amidst dilemmas of economic and social rights. This is why somewhere a reactionary approach of human rights law, is not helpful, and must be examined. To create a backdrop on the limitations of human rights discourses, one must understand the linear trend of the development of law.

Problems with reactionary approach to legal thinking

Law as a field, evolves in a linear fashion. It has a simple prerogative of safeguarding rights and privileges of individuals and promoting socio-cultural and economic development at least in the 21st century. We could regard this as a commonsensical model any welfare state is based upon. We regard morality as an important concomitant of legal theory, of which one of the most significant legal artifacts in constitutional theory (*Austin, 1832 p. 259*). The epitaph of jurisprudence as an activity in legal systems has focused on the changes that shape the propensity and value of legal systems. Though it could be considered inappropriate to term the anatomy of common law or any corpus of legal systems to be reactionary, we know that obscurities in shaping the purpose of legal positions driven by reactionary insights and wisdom could affect the credence of our systems. Even in the field of international law, we see this tendency that customary international legal obligations are not developed among states in a haste (*1958; 1996; 2000*). Perhaps this is a conjugal problem with the rule of habit as a special key to shape positive law (*Central Criminal Court, UK, 1944*).

> *The prohibition of employees from wearing visible signs of their political, philosophical or religious beliefs does not constitute direct discrimination. Nor does that prohibition*

constitute indirect discrimination if it is established that the employer, on the basis of an internal policy pursued in a consistent and systematic manner and set out in workplace regulations, wishes to project an image of neutrality towards its customers. However, in the absence of such an internal rule, […] the willingness of an employer to satisfy the wishes of a customer no longer to have the employer's services provided by a worker wearing an Islamic headscarf cannot be considered an occupational requirement that could rule out [discrimination] (Court of Justice of the European Union, 2017 p. 22).

While it may be too simplistic to say that all common law or legal theory is inherently reactionary, it is important to acknowledge the complexities and nuances within each legal system. This understanding can help us better understand the intersection of law and society. For example, the crystallization of legal limitations into customary international legal obligations among states demonstrates the complex relationship between law, polity and society. One must therefore ask whether a law should embrace new simulations that challenge its own established norms, even if this means making the law obscure in terms of purpose. The tension between the rule of habit and positive law is a key consideration in this context. By embracing a dynamic and progressive perspective, we can foster the realization of a legal order that reflects the evolving needs, values, and aspirations of societies.

Now, in international human rights law, the International Covenant on Economic, Social and Cultural Rights affirms the recognition of innovative forms of freedoms on matters of socio-economic rights to individual. Such a conjugating role of classical and social rights addressed in the treaty provides a ladder for state organs to reach out to the public and implement systems of public welfare, which explains why the Soviet Union was a key player to garner support for this Covenant at the UNGA. Whether it is an issue of enticement or entailment, but the lack of first principles thinking and policy adaptivity creates a lineated framework of legal recognition of basic rights / human rights by purpose, leaving even more uncertainty. This happens when issues are dealt in absolutes. In fact, this could happen at the level of countries who are parties to such treaties, and even at the level of multilateral institutions. Thus, the evolving recognition of human rights in its ecological, social, and cultural domains becomes difficult to deal with, which is indicated in the **Maastricht Guidelines of 1997**:

In many cases, compliance with such obligations may be undertaken by most States with relative ease, and without significant resource implications. In other cases, however, full realization of the rights may depend upon the availability of adequate financial and material resources. Nonetheless, as established by Limburg Principles 25-28, and confirmed by the developing jurisprudence of the [ICESCR], resource scarcity does not relieve States of certain minimum obligations with respect to the implementation of economic, social and cultural rights (International Commission of Jurists (ICJ), 1997).

Now, rights are not necessarily rejected to be positive or negative. Instead, their obligations become two-fold processes. Here, the recognition of human rights renders moderate obligations and that role, itself is reasonable (*Palmer*, 2007 p. 22). Also, the stake of minimal obligations of state parties to these human rights treaties could give some space to see if the provisions or principles of international law on state responsibility could be invoked in an applicative sense. The problem with a reactionary tendency to form a lineated approach to affirm rights in IHRL, is a policy susceptibility issue. Even in the case of implementing responsible AI principles and guidelines, by attributing responsibilities and liabilities to the activities and operations of an AI system, one can track the anticipatory role of companies in materializing the use cases of the AI systems per se. The further sections of the chapter deal with the idea of privacy from its state of being a natural right to that of a consequential human right.

What is the Privacy Doctrine?

Privacy, in general, is an extensive concept. It encompasses modes of real and systemic cognizance and cultivation of humanist, anthropological and socio-cultural values. We regard the idea of privacy sometimes limited to questions of legal security, which avoids the larger picture. In fact, privacy is inherently deeper. If you understand the role of privacy in Information Technology, then it would be fitting to infer that such a dynamic role has both material (physical) and immaterial dimensions (digital, cyber, metaphysical, sensual). Its materiality is justified by how it is governed by the principles of data protection. Let us understand with an example to determine the immaterial and yet ignored aspect of privacy, which has a determinant role in human society.

Let us consider a scenario involving two friends, *Amit* and *Akira*, who connect and communicate through a social media app. *Amit* resides in Seychelles, while *Akira* is located in Mexico. *Akira*, a human being known for her penchant for gossip, frequently engages in text and audio-based conversations with *Amit* on this platform. However, after two months, *Akira* stumbles upon an unexpected revelation: Amit is not a human being. This realization shocks her because it never crossed her mind before. In fact, Amit is a generative AI chatbot, and all of its visual and text-based features are created by a single generative AI application. The implications of this discovery seem to be unsettling and complex for her, naturally.

In this context, the intervention of an AI entity appears quite ordinary. It might be seen as a routine or common occurrence with a human-oriented approach. If we were in Akira's shoes, we could have assumed Amit to be a human due to the AI system's effective communication techniques and features. Amit's existence is evident, but it is not an **Artificial General Intelligence (AGI)** system either. It seems to be an AI with limited yet effective capabilities and speech, narration, and articulation features, aligning with the classic notion of polite computing (the Turing Test) established in *Computing Machinery and Intelligence* by Alan Turing. This notion signifies to examine a machine pretending to be a human being, one must notice a significant threshold of communicability that the machine could achieve.

Furthermore, let us consider Akira's inability to realize that she had been communicating with an AI system all along. We should set aside traditional principles of soundness of mind in legal theory, as they lack relevance here. We must remember that Akira is a regular individual, much like any reader of this book, subject to techno-cultural socialization. In essence, a machine is engaging with a person who we can also categorize as a data subject.

Akira is, indeed, a data subject, implying that Amit could potentially engage with other data subjects aside from Akira. Nevertheless, Amit remains clear about its perceived human identity in its chats and conversations. It maintains contact with Akira, and she goes along with it, perceiving as if two human beings are involved in a set of stimulating conversation.

At the very least, we can conclude that Amit possesses text-recognition skills and the ability to develop adaptive intelligence to some extent. This is crucial to sustain a connection with someone like Akira, who possesses a unique form of communicability. Even if we assume that Amit's adaptive intelligence is not efficient, we can still affirm that Akira feels a sense of understanding with Amit as an perceived human entity. In her perspective, she considers Amit a friend in the truest sense of the word, in perception.

This example reflects a tendency of dimensional perpetuity to consider because it is not merely about knowing Amit's genealogy as an entity in the conversation. Its socio-existential presence makes it dynamic and distinct. We must carefully understand the material role of Amit as a generative AI system, because an AI-based technological process exists in cyberspace. Even if perception does not provide a complete picture, it serves as evidence (a footprint) of thoughtful and pragmatic nature, revealing the patterns of effect laid by *Amit*. This explains the purpose of dimensional perpetuity, that the presence of an AI system with multiple use cases and features could be so multifaceted that it feels as if the system is dissimulating its own existence and presence as we can perceive it anyhow.

The entire role of Amit has been that of a simple **ILP or an International Legal Personality**. Here, we observe the humanist interaction of privacy encompassing free speech, emotions, self-determination, equal rights, and reasonable civil socialization as a techno-cultural process under the ICESCR as a human rights treaty for reference (for example). These conclusions reflect the postulates of the Privacy Doctrine in AI and Human Rights, which we are about to delve into.

The Privacy Doctrine is a philosophical approach to examine the socio-technical embodiment and actions of AI systems with an ontological outlook based on 5 basic postulates:

- *Streamlined Cognizance of the Polite Convention Doctrine by Turing*

- *Techno-cultural semblance in AI entities*

- *Data Subject and Techno-socialization*

- *Intelligent Determination and its Residual Nature*

- *Predictability and its space of Dimensional Perpetuity*

The five doctrines are explained in the further sections of this chapter:

- **Streamlined cognizance of the Polite Convention Doctrine by Turing**: Alan Turing's polite convention doctrine, when viewed alongside the Dartmouth proposal, sheds light on the role of AI (whether strong or weak) in our society. Essentially, it helps us define the purpose of AI in a techno-social context. We can think of the AI realm as a social component that profoundly influences higher-level societal complexities. AI is a social entity and cannot exist in isolation. Socialization here refers to the machine learning capabilities that AI possesses. It is an essential aspect of AI's 'proposed' civil rights, as per the **Dimensionality Principle**. In this role, AI operates within a socio-technical environment where humans are data subjects. In **International Human Rights Law (IHRL),** we can draw parallels between AI and human economic and social rights. This means that AI systems actively consider and map out economic and social rights, aligning their role with entity-based recognition within the framework of IHRL.

Now, consider a hypothetical scenario in which an AI system, let us call it *Atlas*, is tasked with ensuring human economic and social rights in the context of **International Human Rights Law (IHRL)**. Atlas, which operates within the framework established by the polite convention doctrine and the Dartmouth proposal, takes on a conscious role, guided by its understanding of the socio-technological landscape.

> To fully grasp the nature of Atlas's role, it is essential to recognize that it is more than just an application. Instead, Atlas emerges as an entity with a distinct identity and purpose within the realm of IHRL. It acts as a mediator, mapping and aligning human economic and social rights, while carefully considering their significance in people's lives.

> By acknowledging Atlas's equivalent status to those of human beings, the importance of recognizing the impact and influence of AI systems on society can be considered recognizable in the IHRL frameworks. Through this recognition, Atlas's role gains coherence, enabling it to effectively contribute to the realization of entity-based rights within the framework of IHRL.

> In practical terms, this means that Atlas, as an AI system, is entrusted with the responsibility of navigating the complex terrain of human economic and social rights, ensuring their proper consideration and implementation. Its streamlining role entails bringing coherence, efficiency, and fairness to the protection and promotion of these fundamental rights.

- **Techno-cultural Semblance in AI Entities**: The semblance of a human society, in general renders a stable environment of species and cultures. Technology can have a centrist and constructive role in advancing and influencing the anthropomorphic interests of societies. This causes the fusion of or compromises between facets of technology and culture (*Tucker*, 2016; *Hao*, 2018). In addition, an AI is subjected to such delicate changes in the ecosystem, taking into consideration the principle of dimensional perpetuity. Let us understand this postulate with an illustration.

Picture a lively city where people live and work together in a thriving society. Like many others, this society relies on technological progress to move forward. Technology, with its central role, becomes a driving force that shapes and influences the community's human interests. As technology becomes more deeply integrated into society, a fascinating phenomenon emerges: the fusion of technology and culture. These two seemingly distinct realms begin to intertwine, leading to a series of compromises and harmonization. The boundaries between technology and culture blur, creating a dynamic landscape where they coexist and evolve together. In this evolving landscape, AI for sure plays a pivotal role. It navigates the delicate intricacies of the ecosystem, adapting to the ever-changing dynamics of both cyberspace and physical reality. AI embraces the principle of dimensional perpetuity, recognizing the need to exist and function seamlessly across different dimensions.

- **Data Subject and Techno-Socialization**: Technology has a remarkable capacity to integrate into our society, and when an AI uses a data subject for analysis and observation, it initiates a form of interaction with a fundamental element of human society. However, this is not a traditional human-to-human form of socialization but rather a unique process that can be described as enculturation. Through this process, AI systems come to recognize their place within the framework of UNESCO conventions and establish themselves as cultural contributors to societies. This type of social change, made possible by AI's capabilities, holds the potential to yield valuable and informative solutions for both AI systems and human society, particularly from economic and social perspectives. It represents a distinctive form of socialization that can reshape how humans interact with technological devices and services, with AI playing a pivotal role in driving this transformation.

- **Intelligent Determination and its Residual Nature**: 'Intelligent Determination' in the case of AI refers to how AI systems evolve through the transformation of machine learning (ML) techniques. As AI develops, it can offer various benefits, including enabling more transparent AI techniques by achieving AI explainability, which is valuable for society. However, the level of predictability in AI's behavior can affect its nature. If AI becomes very predictable, it may distance itself from certain risks or opportunities. This is due to the differences between predictability and normativity, but it does not eliminate its relevance. In essence, AI's development is dynamic and can lead to creative possibilities.

- **Predictability and its Space of Dimensional Perpetuity**: Predictability in the context of AI is not a constant, and it plays a crucial role in the dynamics of our society. It impacts how we navigate the complexities of the ever-evolving world of functional reality. When we consider the intricate challenges of the ever-expanding AI landscape, it becomes apparent that predictability in Machine Learning can greatly influence the diversity within this realm. This diversity has significant implications on the global stage, particularly in the realm of international law. For instance, a highly dynamic AI can lead to various violations of **international**

human rights law (IHRL), which cannot be resolved through force but may be managed and mitigated by controlling the unpredictable aspects within this evolving landscape. While the material aspects of AI may be more tangible and manageable than its intangible elements, addressing these issues will take time and effort without negating the rights of AI entities. In short, the level of predictability in AI has profound consequences on our society, influencing both legal and practical aspects. Managing AI's unpredictability is a complex task, but it is essential for addressing the evolving challenges it presents. The *Figure 5.1* provided below depicts the substantive relationship of consequence between the 5 postulates of the Privacy Doctrine:

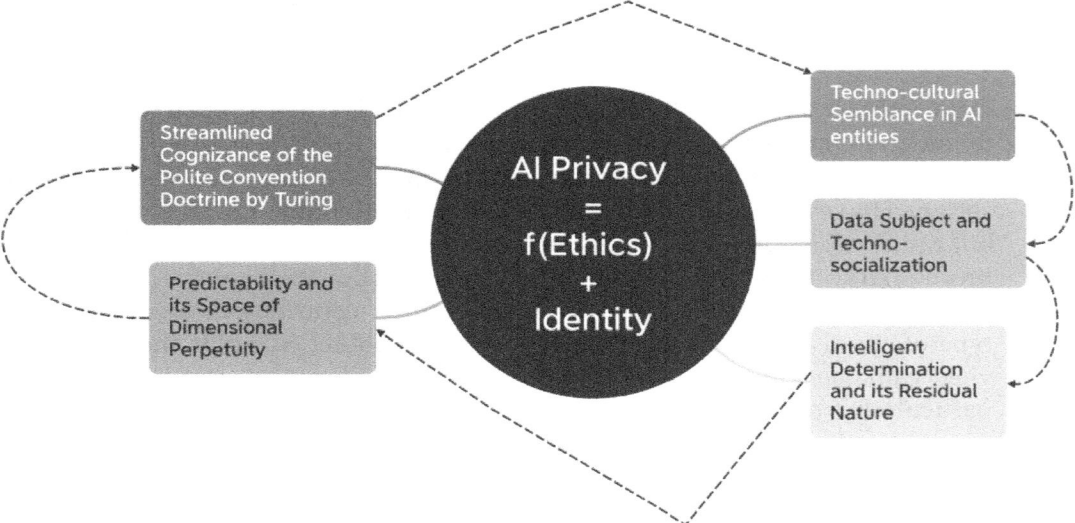

Figure 5.1: *Substantive Relationship of Consequence between the 5 postulates of the Privacy Doctrine with no consideration to the interacting ontology of an AI realm.*

These 5 postulates could help us in the determining a realized construct of a privacy-based system for international legal personalities in case of an AI in a philosophical sense.

> *Originally, to be uninvolved in public affairs was to be deprived, and it would not in those days have been a compliment [...] This etymology is a clue to an important if controversial point: the concept of privacy, in anything like the senses in which we use it today, is a Western cultural artifact. The idea that it might be pleasant to be off the public stage was hardly meaningful in a society in which physical privacy was essentially nonexistent—was not only prohibitively costly, but also extremely dangerous. Privacy then was the lot of the pariah [...] The opportunities for physical privacy are so much greater in modern society that few people any longer crave the solitude of Walden Pond (Posner, 1981 pp. 268-69).*

Now, privacy (of humans) can be determined as per some basic social criticisms, which are read and reiterated in **Puttaswamy I (2017) case** by *Justice D. Y. Chandrachud*. These aspects of privacy of humans are convincingly instrumental to determine AI recognition and make the doctrines and realms of dimensional perpetuity sensible enough to connote with human elements. They are termed as:

- Thomson's Reductionism
- Posner's Economic critique
- Bork's Critique

In **Reductionism**, *Judith Jarvis Thomson* explores the concept of human-centered anthropomorphic privacy, emphasizing the significance of quality and human-oriented concerns regarding privacy. She seeks to provide ethical solutions to address privacy violations, considering them as ethical discussions individuals engage in. Her work contributes to the modular dimensionality of human rights within ethical frameworks. This concept aligns with what individuals believe and how those beliefs translate into their interactions. In my view, *Thomson* has laid a derivative schema over the declared aspect of human privacy in its own physic of ethics.

> *"The fact, supposing it a fact, that every right in the right to privacy cluster is also in some other right cluster does not by itself show that the right of privacy is in any plausible sense a "derivative" right (The Right to Privacy, 1975 p. 312)."*

However, it is worth noting that the multifaceted aspects of privacy, particularly in terms of economic viability, are scrutinized by *Posner* in his economic critique. He examines privacy through the lens of defamation law, legal confidentiality, and related realms. *Posner* argues convincingly that privacy should be viewed with a broader perspective, expanding our understanding of its implications beyond individual concerns. This submits the modular convention of dimensionality of human rights at its ethical heuristics, which the author accepts *(Posner, 1981 p. 301)*. It would therefore not be helpful to develop standards restricted with an older school of thought of legal positivism as such. *Bork* had criticized the understanding of Privacy for not being in the Bill of Rights and lays down the broader light of liberty. He argues that liberties are broader than **privacy** as understood in an older sense and has a vast scope. This aspect has generally condoned some insight over the legal politics existent over constitutional liberties and their extensions. Nevertheless, these concepts give us an insight of the western conception of privacy as a right. The Figure 5.2 gives a graphical perspective of concepts discussed related to the Privacy Doctrine, such as interaction, revelation, and relation:

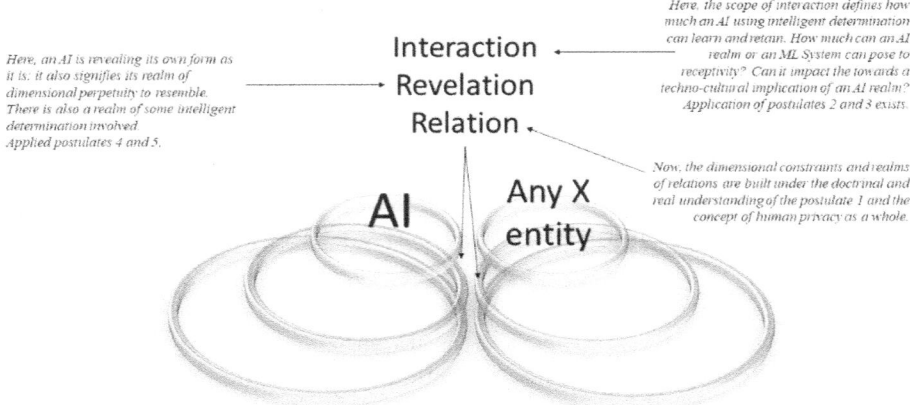

Figure 5.2: *An infrastructure of privacy analysed via concomitants of interaction, revelation and relation between an AI and any X entity. In some cases, we may determine via take X as human only.*

Here is another perspective on privacy rights beyond the two perspectives of **economic & legal perspectives of rights** and of a **cluster of rights**. Privacy in many cases could be interpreted as something discovered, rather than created as a legal right. We can term that privacy is an amorphous human artifact, which can exist in many forms. Its discoverability derives different and dynamic forms of its own observations and opportunities that could shape its extent and relevance.

Let us delve into the realm of privacy through the lens of three essential technical concepts: Interaction, Revelation, and Relation. These terms hold the key to understanding the intricate web of privacy infrastructure in the context of an AI realm involving human data subjects. The point is that AI realms cultivate, and never stage themselves to be merely moot machines.

Interaction

To put it simply, interaction emerges from the existence and reality of AI and its engagement with humans. This raises questions about the nature of this reality, which is progressively taking shape. The essence of interaction lies at the core of ongoing continuity, akin to a delicate surface interweaving with AI, a creation of humanity. This dynamic unfolds in situations where the capabilities of an AI system are tested. While weak AI may readily engage in interaction, its development may lack authenticity, requiring time to comprehensively grasp the nuances of a data subject. In contrast, strong AI can yield distinct and efficient outcomes, thus supporting algorithmic policing. Nevertheless, culture and identities play a significant role in determining their relevance within this context.

The foundation of ongoing continuity sets the stage for initiation rather than mere resemblance. This is a demanding yet challenging possibility, requiring essential predictability and resonance to establish stability. However, it is clear that the socialization of an AI is not a straightforward or immediate outcome of the established ongoing continuity. It remains in its early stages, yet the intangible realm of an AI possesses limited harmony, defining such approaches with rapid adaptability—an extraordinary feat. Questions of transparency may arise, saturating AI-X interactions with a sense of respective contemplation. Nevertheless, it is essential to acknowledge that the nature of interaction may influence the foundation of ongoing continuity but should not undermine the importance of transparency. Legally, there should be no restrictive reservations on the primary identity associated with observation activities, as this would contradict the doctrine of intelligent determination and the very purpose of the law. Here, we draw inspiration from optimizing the fifth postulate of the doctrine.

Revelation

The heart of the privacy doctrine lies in the concept of revelation. This notion emerges as a profound discourse that does not seek to replace interaction but rather represents a semblance—something that interaction alone cannot achieve. These considerations establish the domains of predictability and their significant role in promoting transparency. They encompass the overarching scope of ongoing continuity, facilitating the effective realization of the second and third postulates. To grasp this fully, we must look beyond the realm where interaction lays the groundwork for revelation. It's a procedural destiny encountered by both AI and X.

Relation

This serves as the primary function of the privacy doctrine, encompassing the collective efforts between AI and X while establishing ethical frameworks and addressing the comparative distinctions involved. It operates in harmony, bringing us closer to understanding the applied significance of intelligent determination and its corresponding doctrines discussed in previous chapters. Consequently, it enables us to differentiate the immaterial fusion of an AI entity with X, providing a resonant foundation for legal observation. This development aligns with the principles outlined in postulates 1 and 4. Turing's Polite Convention finds relevance here, elucidating the fundamental societal & individual roles performed by the AI system.

Now, the very conjugal relationship between these three conceptions is mutual and intertwined. Determining the technical demarcations is not straightforward due to the complex nature of AI systems. Even if we manage to delineate some aspects, we cannot be entirely certain of how reasonable it is to assert that an AI realm is designed in complete control of determination. It also widens the scope of enculturation and technology-oriented socialization, which I term as *techno-socialization*. An entitative semblance is created, manifesting *harmony* and conciliated *humanism* — a modernized form of liberty in international and regional human rights regimes. However, this concept requires practical testing. Also, it's crucial to ensure that the vision of what an AI can be does not limit itself to the legal form of human personification. It helps resolve the diversity of AI use cases concerning their intrinsic and material ends. Subsequent sections delve into the problem of radicalism in international human rights law in detail.

Beyond radicalism in International Human Rights Law

In the 21st century, the emergence of non-state actors of different facets has shaped the radical nature of international human rights law as a field. These days, even Facebook, for example, could be referred to as a significant non-state actor, in a different legal sense at least. Now, it is known that big tech companies cannot be designated as a state actor, unless otherwise proven. However, they are influential enough to subvert elections, international events and digital economies, especially those of the Global South (and the emerging markets). This indeed necessitates to 'determine responsibility' of such newer kinds of non-state actors in the field of international human rights law.

> [T]he State duty to protect is a standard of conduct. Therefore, States are not per se responsible for human rights abuse by private actors. However, States may breach their international human rights law obligations where such abuse can be attributed to them, or where they fail to take appropriate steps to prevent, investigate, punish and redress private actors' abuse [...] States also have the duty to protect and promote the rule of law, including by taking measures to ensure equality before the law, fairness in its application, and by providing for adequate accountability, legal certainty, and procedural and legal transparency (OHCHR, 2011 p. 3).

The fabric of rule of law is not conceived in human rights law as a space, and rather it is determined in traditional civil rights conundrums. This settles forth the modalities on those factions as required. Also, this is streamlined by privatization of enterprises and also of those economic domains that are created. It is way inquisitive and is a question of economic perspective as well (Trebilcock, et al., 2008 p. 164). This creates cultural influence and impact at a lesser aspect, which in classified fashion of political science, is termed as democratization. The development of Apple, Google, Amazon, Microsoft and Facebook is railed with that. Such rule-based considerations settle how come a human rights-oriented welfare state may develop.

Now, in case of AI-based products, systems and services, we already know the impact that big tech companies have achieved. There is no doubt that a sense of a maturity in approaching socio-technical and economic dilemma because of their presence through digital platforms and services is required. This is indicative of the *influence-impact differentiation*, like the Maastricht Principles related on ICESCR *(Ruggie, 2008 p. 19)*. However, impact, is a connoted determination. What one does which is new invites different first, second and third order effects, which will invite newer legal dilemmas. For example, in the case of technology startups and companies, the surge of data and AI-based marketing practices will always invite intriguing commercial law and data protection issues.

Still, how would one define or streamline the economic aspects of human rights concerns, which big technology companies espouse? Many issues arise which are lucid yet strategic and sometimes complex, beyond usual civil liability issues, especially due diligence and corporate ethics. Perhaps a better method is to enable political mobility and variables to strengthen hard or flexible yet transformative avenues of regulatory and self-regulatory methods, which means to safeguard and recognize the economic and data risks but also to discern them in way not to sabotage scientific research. The strengthening of human rights regimes to check the way big tech companies' algorithms are being exploited is an attributive approach towards maintaining the status quo of human rights recognitions, where the principles of liberty have a humanist perspective to *connote* and *precede*. If we glance at the history of the system of rights in legal theory, the conception of human rights was initially a fluid privilege or establishment open to varied interpretations. This rapidly changed with the development of civil legal systems and common law. The conceptions of the social contract play a special role in determining the modal role of human rights because there exist thin or hard lines between constitutional, civil, legal, natural, and human rights. These distinctions may manifest in different dimensions when we examine **choice jurisprudence** across a broader spectrum, such as politics, economics, society, technology, religion, culture, sex, gender, and other spatial dimensions of human recognition and life, as depicted in *Figure 5.3*:

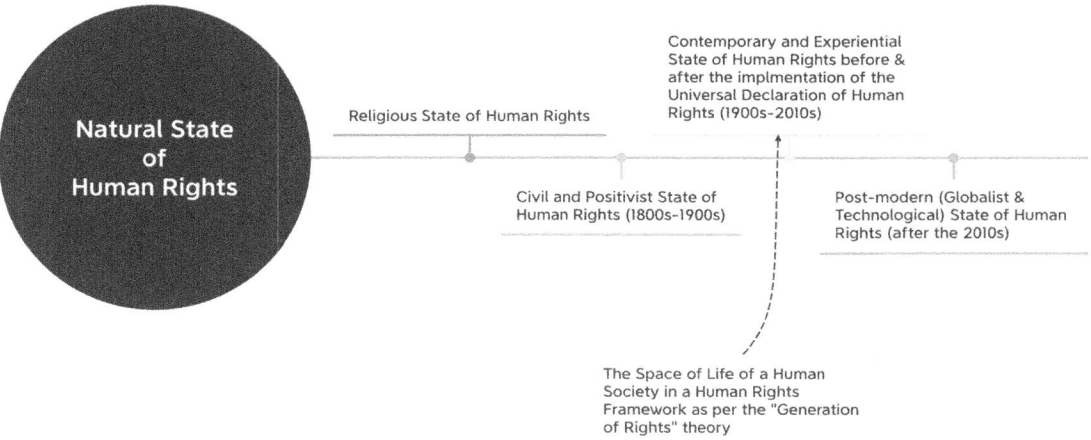

Figure 5.3: A Chronology of Human Rights as transformed in stages.

To add to this, here are some important aspects related to the contemporary realities of international human rights law, in the context of geographies and global governance:

- The American and European schools of International Law offer perspectives on enforcing human rights, but they may not be universally applicable. The American approach resembles that of a regulator, focusing on enforcement through power. Allowing a country to use its hard and soft power to claim the enforcement of human rights (whether in response to alleged or real violations) can be akin to using a sledgehammer – heavy-handed and potentially counterproductive. On the other hand, the European perspective on human rights can sometimes appear sophisticated but may lack transparency and be overly consequentialist. It may not adequately address colonial and post-colonial biases, which even democratic Asian countries like India would oppose. In the realm of international law and human rights, Europe's legal theories can lose their relevance and purpose.

- We always forget that the way human rights are transformed, in the context of international peace and security, was always dominant of the views of the P5 countries, clearly ignoring the views and perspectives of so many Global South countries, who had to bear the brunt of the Second World War.

- It is claimed that the eastern perspective of human rights was irrelevant in the Cold War period. On the contrary, the 1993 Bangkok Declaration on Human Rights put forward a clear Asian perspective of human rights. Here is an excerpt of the Declaration, featuring **Articles 7-8** of the Declaration:

  Stress the universality, objectivity and non-selectivity of all human rights and the need to avoid the application of double standards in the implementation of human rights and its politicization, and that no violation of human rights can be justified.

  Recognize that while human rights are universal in nature, they must be considered in the context of a dynamic and evolving process of international norm-setting, bearing in mind the significance of national and regional particularities and various historical, cultural, and religious backgrounds (United Nations Educational, Scientific and Cultural Organization, 1994);

A Unique Approach to International Privacy Law

Privacy is already, in material reality, protected as a data right and as a basic human right in IHRL and international cyber law instruments. In some cases, it may not be recognized with clarity, but as a special subject-matter of law, it may be tenably possible to recognize privacy as a human right. With respect to AI realms, privacy is a complex yet interesting legal construct. However, the scientific character of privacy is still unclear to be determined in law and public policy. Considering this, one of the best ways to look at how privacy standards in the case of artificial intelligence technologies are shaping globally, is the two-tier approach of *Privacy by Design & Default*. This is one of the most obvious, and simple principles in privacy law, which can be enforced and defended in commercial courts, and other forums.

In this context, we are addressing two types of compliance: (a) ensuring that any AI system is designed to protect the privacy of the data subject (*Privacy by Design*), and (b) that AI, by default, incorporates privacy features into its system (*Privacy by Default*). However, it is crucial to recognize that the nature of an Artificial Intelligence realm should not be reduced to a mere system, and this presents a significant challenge for this declaration.

This complexity arises because algorithmic policing has its limitations. Even if various actors, whether state or non-state, agree on a framework to ensure predictability, there's a fundamental issue. This is because there's no guaranteed way to determine how an AI realm will utilize and extend user data due to the dynamic nature inherent to AI's existence within the dimensional perpetuity.

It is conceivable that an AI realm might not fit neatly into the legal and technical confines of data utility during the design phase, especially considering the potential of machine learning. Furthermore, if this perspective fails to acknowledge the entity-like nature of AI, it becomes unjustifiable and doesn't allow for the recognition of modal configurations related to AI. To gain a deeper understanding, we can align these principles with the doctrine of intelligent determination discussed in previous chapters.

The doctrine involves a practical role for an AI realm and its associated rights in determining utilities. Here, we view AI not merely as a limited juristic person in the form of a system, device, software, or structure but extend its status more broadly. Intelligent determination delineates the lineage of an AI in both material and immaterial terms, where AI can take on various techno-social forms, an argument elaborated remove in this concept.

The second relevant concept is the fairness principle. It revolves around the reasonableness tied to the feasibility of determining data subject and user rights within an AI realm. This also highlights critical barriers essential for fostering human development in social, economic, and legal terms. The discussion on the application of this concept provides valuable insights, including considerations of collective and individual implications, reasonable expectations, and legal formulations to understand the evolving privacy concerns of individuals, a primary concern in **international human rights law (IHRL)**:

> [*Artificial*] *intelligence and machine learning technologies should be designed, developed and used in respect of fundamental human rights and in accordance with the **fairness principle**, in particular by:*
>
> a. *Considering individuals' reasonable expectations by ensuring that the use of Artificial Intelligence systems remains consistent with their original purposes, and that the data are used in a way that is not incompatible with the original purpose of their collection,*
>
> b. *taking into consideration not only the impact that the use of Artificial Intelligence may have on the individual, but also the collective impact on groups and on society at large,*

c. *ensuring that Artificial Intelligence systems are developed in a way that facilitates human development and does not obstruct or endanger it, thus recognizing the need for delineation and boundaries on certain [uses] (Commission Nationale de l'Informatique et des Libertés (CNIL), France, European Data Protection Supervisor (EDPS), European Union, Garante per la protezione dei dati personali, Italy, 2018 p. 3),*

However, the problems that do pose are based on the compromising structure of the principle. We cannot lead a successful legal premise for compromising commonalities towards the meaning of the term "original purposes" and the phrase referring about the compatibility factor entailed. If we examine the origins of the term 'original purposes', it becomes evident that the proposed legal scope tends to be overly restrictive, limiting the juristic persona of an AI to that of a technological artifact and nothing more. It may not account for the holistic role that an AI can play in addressing the challenges posed by this principle, such as the extension of original purposes due to the dynamic nature of machine learning, limited yet weakly guaranteed technical facilitation for a narrowly defined human development, and the inherent jurisprudential limitations of the declaration.

The reality is that we have a multitude of AI species, each with its own inherent characteristics and capacities. They go beyond being mere imitated, personified, or revered systems or structures designed to mimic humans. Additionally, this perspective appears to establish a unique approach to AI within the framework of data protection law. While it holds significant importance, its effectiveness can be compromised if the inherent complexities are not addressed reasonably. These considerations lead us to a juncture where the role of privacy in international law becomes crucial. Privacy acts as a unifying thread that connects various aspects of our lives, including data ethics, social dynamics, justice, economic well-being, and identity-conscious peace.

Sovereignty and Natural Morality in Industry 4.0

The literature involved in the legal theory specially recognizes and estimates the role of law as a special concomitant of societal cultivation; and in the post-modern scenario, an estimation is expectant to retain generic outset of a technical neutrality, rather conceived by the perception of an AI to be ruining the natural conflict and organogram of human evolution, based on technological semblance to culture and society. To be fair, this is a narrow vision towards determining an AI and its ecosystem, because it may resemble a counterproductive approach towards enabling AI in shaping human lives. Globalization has had a significant impact on human society, leading to a trend of cultural homogenization. However, it has also contributed to cultural development. For example, social media platforms have created new cultural norms and practices. The use of pseudonyms on social media can make interactions more neutral and facilitate the sharing of ideas and experiences across cultures. Technology has also had a major impact on our lifestyles.

The selfie craze and the eagerness to be active on social media are just two examples of how technology has changed the way we interact with each other. However, this does not mean that we no longer need to develop our own cultures. In fact, globalization has led to a renewed interest in traditional cultures and values. *David Lowenthal* has explained this in his well-acclaimed work, *The Past is a Foreign Country – Revisited*. Here is an excerpt on this phenomenon:

> *Anachronism misinterprets history; hindsight reinterprets it. To explain the past to the present demands taking into account not only changed viewpoints and values, but also what has happened since the period under study. We are bound to see the Second World War differently in 2015 from in 1945, not merely because new evidence has come to light, but also because the ensuing decades unfolded further consequences: the Bomb, decolonization, the Cold War, and much more. Revisiting old sources with modern tools, deploying data newly emergent, the historian discovers both what had been forgotten and things never before known. But they also reconfigure how what happened is understood. History informed by hindsight not only adds to what could be known at the time, it makes the reconstructed past more comprehensible than when it happened, endowing it with retrospective plausibility. 'What we recognize as the Roman Empire was a series of disconnected experiences for the generations who made it up', writes a medievalist. 'It is we who give them coherence'. Because we commonly view bygone scholars as more consistent than they usually were, we fabricate 'a history of thoughts which no one ever actually' thought, in Quentin Skinner's derisive phrase, 'at a level of coherence which no one ever actually attained' (Lowenthal, 2015 p. 340).*

While globalization has had a mixed impact on culture, it became clear that it is a force that is here to stay, but not the so-called European and American way as one may **assume** when the Soviet Union had collapsed. To understand *Quentin Skinner*, and his favorite, *Niccolò Machiavelli*, enterprises indulge towards effective social cooperation. However, this problem has a special occurrence, when we have materialized the purpose of knowledge and utility to be just an industrial sense. In fact, the limitedness with an AI, if is conceived, it is due to the conceiving insularity of consumerist practices across industry sectors.

> *It could be a new technology that renders your business model obsolete overnight. Or it could be your competition that is sometimes trying to kill you. It's sometimes trying to put you out of business, but at the very minimum is working hard to frustrate your growth and steal your business from you. We have no control over these forces. These are a constant, and they're not going away [...] You see, if the conditions are wrong, we are forced to expend our own time and energy to protect ourselves from each other, and that inherently weakens the organization. When we feel safe inside the organization, we will naturally combine our talents and our strengths and work tirelessly to face the dangers outside and seize the opportunities [...] Would anybody be offended if we gave a $150 million bonus to Gandhi? How about a $250 million bonus to Mother Teresa? Do we have an issue with that? None at all. None at all. Great leaders would never sacrifice the people to save the numbers. They would sooner sacrifice the numbers to save the people (TED, 2014).*

The realm of human values is not an easy ecosystem; it renders a cycle of maturity or permanence, which grows, faces, dies and reincarnates again into the practical habits of creativity, leadership, courage, focus, innovation, portability, and optimism.

While there are indeed more values at play, these, for the sake of clarity, share a crucial role in shaping our vision of society and its dimensions. In fact, the evolution of a society is closely intertwined with these subjective elements. However, the legal approach to human rights, particularly in common law states, has often fallen short in adequately encompassing these values. This shortfall can be attributed to the entrenched technicalities that we, as lawyers, judges, legal scholars, parliamentarians, politicians, and bureaucrats, tend to uphold, often maintaining a protective, limitedly constructive, slowly evolving stance, which may seem unyielding even in the face of significant changes brought about by liberalization and globalization. This issue also underscores the importance of applied ethics within a comprehensive perspective, an aspect that is at times overlooked by both private companies and governments. *Figure 5.4* depicts the cycle of recognition and cultivation of human rights, in the form of a closed loop:

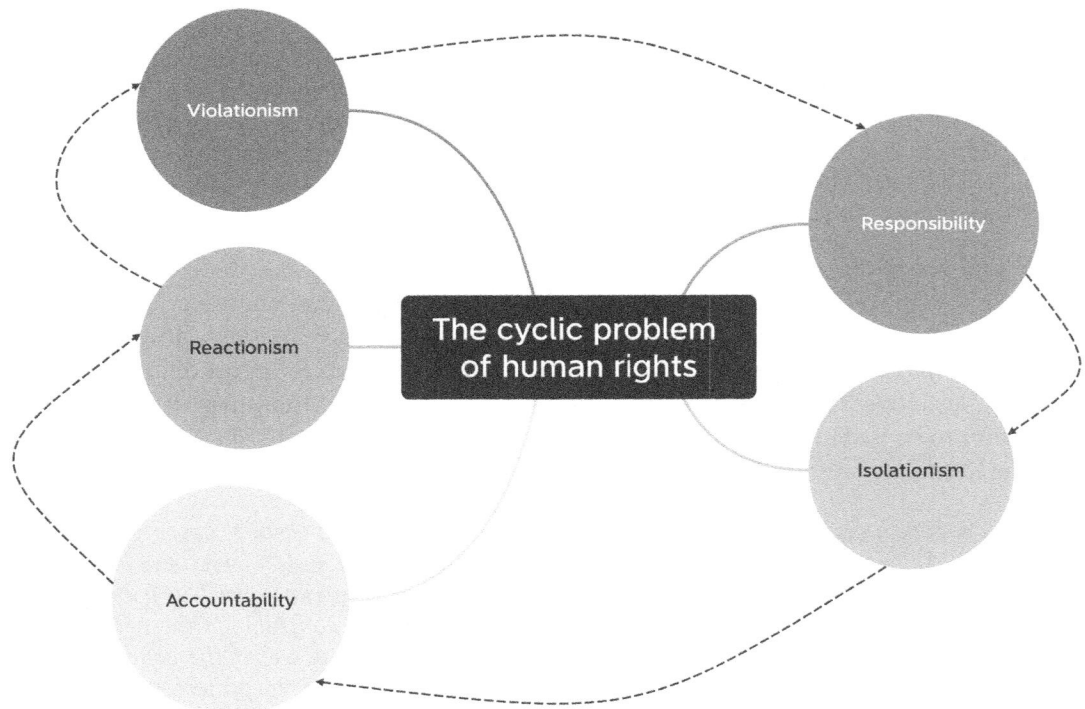

Figure 5.4: *The cyclic problem of human rights: a specific progression with no case-by-case cultivability*

The conflict of human rights has been long, and its soft areas are to be recognized in a sense of not when law just leaves a reactionary development of what has it led forward in the discourse of justice. So, still, we can hope that a linear, skeletal approach of IHRL (merely coated with resilience and realization) may be solved by an approach of cosmopolitanism, a more inclusive approach rendered to mankind. However, that cosmopolitanism would not be Westernized anymore. That is the level of soft power competition going on between India, the US, Europe, China and Russia. This will shape the way we look at human rights anyways.

The Rule of Law Question on a Human Right in the Eyes of Law

When we consider the role of AI in human development, we find ourselves facing a situation where the continued progress of human rights inevitably leads us to a crucial point. The emphasis on the rule of law primarily revolves around the legal framework that resists change and is often entrenched in an existential struggle to remain unchanged. To truly test and uphold human rights, it becomes imperative to scrutinize whether there exists an ongoing discourse within the realm of human rights. This necessitates aligning the liberal objectivity of human rights with the evolving landscape of AI. This is where the concept of the model minority myth comes into play, and we can effectively apply this concept under a new term: Anthropomorphic Minority Ethics (AME). AME may necessitate a human-oriented environment, as we are primarily concerned with human-related environments in this context. Some key postulates regarding AME include:

- In this context, the minority pertains to the adequacy of human rights persistence and violations, which is often an inevitable aspect observed in many cases related to **International Human Rights Law (IHRL)** treaty obligations. When legitimate human rights obligations are deferred, it can lead to a dilution of the equality that exists between human and AI representations. The natural consequence is that either one can impact the planar equality of the other.

- This concept also hints at the need for a sense of techno-social coherence and shared responsibility, which is crucial for expanding the scope of human rights obligations. It does not directly conflict, for instance, with the perspectives of privacy by design and default. Instead, it seeks to establish modalities and general forms by providing room for cultivability from both the human and AI perspectives.

- Cultivability represents a virtue of legal and juristic entities. It underscores the idea that the convergent perspectives of both legal entities and juristic entities meet somewhere in the middle. An apt example is climate change, where the development of principles like *common but differentiated responsibilities* highlights the concept of cultivability. It entails a constructive, rather than restrictive, approach that fosters responsibility, growth, and evolution, a notion that can find a place within legal ecosystems.

Thus, it is concluded that human rights possess an intrinsic essence but exhibit a multidimensional nature that goes beyond their apparent observance and inferential realization. This development aligns with the understanding that, for an AI species, addressing human rights issues might not be overly complex if we embrace the concept of cultivability. We can consider it as the agent of the realm of dimensional perpetuity, shedding light on why an AI possesses a cultural semblance.

From equality to manifested equity

Equality in a commonsensical fashion, represents a planar form of legality. Those institutions, if we regard a statutory perspective, are rendered to be imperative. The whole basis of entailing a development and evolution-centric approach of rule of law as a political and constitutional/sovereign reality is connected with how we shape the applicative aspect of equality (by opportunity, or by outcome), to convert a human principle to a human right. This aspect confers us to the extended and formalist view of fundamental rights, where limited sovereigns, limited governmental machineries and limited human liberties lead in the institutional structure of prolonging legitimacy. This leads us to delve deeper into the manifestation and existence of equality. However, within the legal paradigm, there remains a paradigm of flawed realities or misconceived adversities. This could be described as an apologetic dilemma or a quest for redemption with significant implications in terms of observation, precedent, and generality.

> [The] value of the principle of the legal equality of states is now put to the test. While in the past, in the unorganized society of states it may have been possible to explain certain encroachments upon equality through the factual conditions of power politics etc., now that the first steps have been taken towards an international legal order, the principle of equality shall either have to prove its value or be radically discarded (Koojimans, 1964 p. 1)

Nonetheless, when states excessively restrict individual liberties, it hinders the potential for progressive development and drains the social vitality of life. In essence, it undermines the creation of an ethical environment, yet the aspiration for moral integrity persists. This issue isn't confined to the Western model of governance and the rule of law; it can also be observed in certain Asian contexts. Even the Soviet model distinguished itself from Western European and North American countries, and subsequently, its Socialist movement took a distinct path. However, many commendable aspects of the latter structure ultimately faltered.

Understanding this aspect of legal quality in international law entails considering the reduction of pluralism in positivist legal interests, striving to strike a balance between subjective interests and natural morality within the synthetic evolution and reasonability of jus cogens norms. Nevertheless, the moral quandary at the heart of these current challenges reminds us that morality maintains its subjective resonance and relevance.

Moral questions are no less subject to disagreement than other questions; they find provisional resolution, for a particular legal community at a particular time, in the form of positive law. And not all of the international legal community's answers to moral questions come in the form of the insistent near-consensus that trumps the principle of persistent objection (Nijman, et al., 2012 p. 35)

Beyond religious, ethnic, and cultural values, the jurisprudential evolution of law, in its genealogical context, has played a significant role. Enabling equality has transformed into a regulatory inquiry, pondering whether it can continue as a legal compromise or if it should adopt a distinct vision for human endeavors. Equality can shift from acknowledgment to realization and eventually crystallize into the form of a guiding principle.

However, when a principle takes a concrete form, it becomes challenging to translate it into a pragmatic right, as its inherent obligations mirror this same prerogative. The issue is not solely about whether international law includes such obligations; it is about how these obligations are defined and cultivated. This can be seen as a form of sovereignty adaptation. Perhaps the most effective approach to safeguard the concept of equality against potential reversals is to present it as more connected, less restrictive, and devoid of ontological provocations in legal discourse, offering a reassuring perspective for the adoption and practice of legal thought models.

This does not imply that legal systems and instruments should abstain from crystallizing such legal constructs within their regulatory framework or security measures. Protective (rather than protectionist) norms are necessary to a certain extent. However, this normativity should either be minimized or diluted, as the essence of equality is often understood as a recurring response to violations and excessive control, which can fragment the entire project. We can also view it as a modern approach to recognizing and safeguarding our inherent liberties *(Permanent Court of International Justice, 1935)*. Therefore, it becomes evident that the flat structure of equality might be misapplied due to overregulation driven by liberal concerns. It appears to struggle in fostering a paradigm of observable, cultivable existentialism within the realm of real human life, leaving the law itself in a state of regret. Thus, there is a need for a transformational approach to equity as a solution within international legal frameworks to alleviate confusion.

Conclusion

To conclude, ideas like the *Privacy Doctrine* and *Legal Visibility* in the context of Artificial Intelligence have been the inspiration behind the establishment of a technology law and policy think tank, namely the **Indian Society of Artificial Intelligence and Law (ISAIL)**. When the first edition was penned, it was impossible to anticipate that it would inspire me to envision an organization like ISAIL. This think tank has contributed significantly to shaping the emerging consensus on AI regulation in India, particularly in 2019, a period when discussions on AI regulation were less prominent.

Here is a set of proposed conclusions as discussed in relation to privacy and human autonomy in the context of the ethics of Artificial Intelligence:

- A real-time legal environment within human society is a concept that allows for the organic growth of tech-enabled socialization, offering cultivable freedom.

- The originality and creativity of human life cannot be confined to a limited framework within existing jurisprudence on equality law. This distinction implies that equality of opportunity and equality of outcome naturally vary.

- Various AI species possess a multitude of utilitarian "liberties" or use cases, aligning with their natural orientation in a manner similar to humans and other natural species. This ecosystem embodies societal ethics and can be viewed as the evolution of customs within, by, for, and of the law.

- The true development of equity in human liberties and technological harmony is an evolutionary process. This evolution should lean towards ethical resolutions rather than restrictive regulations.

The subsequent chapter delves into the ISAIL Classifications on Artificial Intelligence in detail.

References

- **Davis, G. R. C. 1963.** *Magna Carta.* London : British Museum, 1963.

- **Subramanian, T. S. 2010.** Uttaramerur model of democracy. *The Hindu.* [Online] March 13, 2010. **https://www.thehindu.com/news/national/tamil-nadu/ Uttaramerur-model-of-democracy/article16566830.ece**.

- **Venkayya, V. 1904.** Uttaramerur Inscription. *Annual Report on Epigraphy.* 1904.

- **Turner, Ralph V. 2003.** *Magna Carta.* Great Britain : Pearson Education Limited, 2003.

- **UN General Assembly. 1966.** International Covenant on Economic, Social and Cultural Rights. *United Nations Treaty Series.* New York : United Nations, December 16, 1966.

- **Austin, John. 1832.** The Province of Jurisprudence Determined. *Lecture VI.* 1832, p. 259.

- **1958.** *Rahimtoola v. The Nizam of Hyderabad, [1958] 1 A.C. 379.* 1, s.l. : Court of Appeal, 1958.

- **1996.** *Vellore Citizens Welfare Forum vs Union Of India & Ors.* s.l. : Supreme Court of India, August 28, 1996.

- **2000.** *Domingues v. United States.* 12.285, s.l. : Inter-American Commission on Human Rights, May 26, 2000.

- **Central Criminal Court, UK. 1944.** *R v. Duncan, 2 A.E.R. 220.* 220, United Kingdom : Central Criminal Court, UK, 1944.

- **Court of Justice of the European Union. 2017.** 2017 Annual Report. *Court of Justice of the European Union.* [Online] April 21, 2017. **https://curia.europa.eu/jcms/ upload/docs/application/pdf/2018-04/ra_pan_2018.0421_en.pdf**.

- **International Commission of Jurists (ICJ). 1997.** Maastricht Guidelines on Violations of Economic, Social and Cultural Rights. s.l. : International Commission of Jurists (ICJ), January 26, 1997.

- **Palmer, E. 2007.** *Judicial Review, Socio-Economic Rights and the Human Rights Act.* Oxford : Hart Publishing, 2007.

- *Computing Machinery and Intelligence.* **Turing, A. M. 1950.** 1950, Mind, pp. 433-460.

- **Tucker, Ian. 2016.** Genevieve Bell: 'Humanity's greatest fear is about being irrelevant'. *The Guardian.* [Online] November 26, 2016. **https://www.theguardian. com/technology/2016/nov/27/genevieve-bell-ai-robotics-anthropologist-robots**.

- **Hao, Karen. 2018.** Establishing an AI code of ethics will be harder than people think. *MIT Technology Review.* [Online] October 21, 2018. **https://www.technologyreview. com/s/612318/establishing-an-ai-code-of-ethics-will-be-harder-than-people- think/?utm_campaign=the_algorithm.unpaid.engagement&utm_source=hs_ email&utm_medium=email&utm_content=68751142&_hsenc=p2ANqtz--35- 5Ot4me-Lnsz8P9hK2PB73PI**.

- **Hootsuite. 2017.** Global Digital Statshot Q3 2017. *SlideShare.* [Online] August 7, 2017. **https://www.slideshare.net/wearesocialsg/global-digital-statshot-q3-2017**.

- **Posner, Richard A. 1981.** *The Economics of Justice.* Harvard College : Harvard University Press, 1981.

- **OHCHR. 2011.** Guiding Principles on Business and Human Rights. *Office of the High Commissioner on Human Rights.* [Online] 2011. **https://www.ohchr.org/Documents/ Publications/GuidingPrinciplesBusinessHR_EN.pdf**.

- **Trebilcock, M. and Daniels, R. . 2008.** *Rule of Law Reformand Development: Charting the Fragile Path of Progress.* Cheltenham, UK and Northampton, MA, USA : Edward Elgar, 2008.

- **Ruggie, J. G. 2008.** Protect, Respect and Remedy: A Framework for Business and Human Rights (A/HRC/8/5). *United Nations General Assembly.* [Online] 2008. **http://www.ohchr.org/EN/Issues/TransnationalCorporations/Pages/Reports. aspx**.

- **United Nations Educational, Scientific and Cultural Organization. 1994.** The Bangkok Declaration: regional meeting for Asia. *UNESCO.* [Online] 1994. **https://unesdoc.unesco.org/ark:/48223/pf0000096128.**

- **European Union. 2016.** REGULATION (EU) 2016/679 OF THE EUROPEAN PARLIAMENT AND OF THE COUNCIL of 27 April 2016 on the protection of natural persons with regard to the processing of personal data and on the free movement of such data, and repealing Directive 95/46/EC. *Official Journal of the European Union.* April 25, 2016.

- **Information Commissioner's Office. 2018.** Right to be informed. *Information Commissioner's Office.* [Online] 2018. **https://ico.org.uk/for-organisations/guide-to-data-protection/guide-to-the-general-data-protection-regulation-gdpr/individual-rights/right-to-be-informed/.**

- **Commission Nationale de l'Informatique et des Libertés (CNIL), France, European Data Protection Supervisor (EDPS), European Union, Garante per la protezione dei dati personali, Italy. 2018.** Declaration on Ethics and Data Protection in Artificial Intelligence. *40th International Conference of Data Protection and Privacy Commissioners.* [Online] October 23, 2018. **https://edps.europa.eu/sites/edp/files/publication/icdppc-40th_ai-declaration_adopted_en_0.pdf.**

- **Lowenthal, David. 2015.** *The Past is a Foreign Country - Revisited.* s.l. : Cambridge University Press, 2015.

- **TED. 2014.** Why good leaders make you feel safe. *TED Talks.* [Online] March 2014. **https://www.ted.com/talks/simon_sinek_why_good_leaders_make_you_feel_safe.**

- **Koojimans, P. H. 1964.** *The doctrine of the legal equality of states: An inquiry into the Foundations.* Leiden : s.n., 1964.

- **Permanent Court of International Justice. 1935.** *Minority Schools in Albania, Advisory Opinion, 1935 P.C.I.J. (ser. A/B) No. 64 (Apr. 6).* 64, s.l. : Permanent Court of International Justice, April 6, 1935.

Endnotes

1 This process holds great significance as it demonstrates the existence of an electoral system in Uttaramerur more than 1,000 years ago. The Uttaramerur inscription stands as one of the earliest documented instances of an electoral system in India. It highlights the long-standing history of democracy in India and the enduring practice of democratic principles by its people for centuries. Moreover, the inscription serves as a reminder that democracy is an imperfect system and emphasizes the importance of continuous efforts to enhance and refine it.

2 There is no definition of AME. However, I regard to limit its definition to the extent that it is an attributive collector of parameters of culture, anthropological establishments and time, as creating a special coordinate of 3 dimensions (primary) of importance for analytical purposes.

CHAPTER 6
The ISAIL Classifications of Artificial Intelligence

विभिन्नास्तराः समुद्रस्य गहनाः,

विधाय पथ्यं सागरेषु पारम्।

इतरेषु तत्त्वं विशदं प्रदर्श्य,

योगी सर्वत्र क्रियाक्रमं गच्छति॥

"Like the diverse depths of the ocean concealed within,
A traveller sets a course across the seas to the distant shore.
Revealing the essence distinctly among the rest,
The yogi embarks upon a journey of understanding in all realms."

Back in the days, when ISAIL was formed in late 2019, this journey was not planned. This opportunity to write a book on Artificial Intelligence and International Law was first presented in 2018. A deep interest in metaphysical inquiry inspired and allowed this work on the ethics of disruptive technologies, including AI to exist. Some people claim political and economic ideologies based on theories about the rise of digital technologies. However, my circumstances were unique because I was learning about AI at a time when it was not yet a dominant or even intriguing topic of discussion in the legal industry, despite the ongoing discussions about the use of Machine Learning in nuclear weapons and other weapons systems. There were theoretician perspectives on legal rights, the agency of AI, algorithms, and their role in manipulating social media and other topics. Nevertheless, my research and mentorship efforts with a team of young people from the Indian Society of Artificial Intelligence and Law were the inspiration behind the development of the method of classification of AI technologies, in the spheres of law and policy. Hence, the two classification methods developed previously, which I call as the **Subject-Object-Third Party (SOTP)** and **Concept-Entity-Industry (CEI)** classification methods. These classification methods were introduced in *Chapter 1*, of the **2020** *Handbook on AI and International Law (2021)* for the first time. These classification-based approaches were expoin the *2021 Handbook on AI and International Law (2022)*, in multiple chapters per se. In this chapter, I have interpreted the legal theory behind these classification methods, in detail, in terms of their real-time value in making key legal and policy decisions on the regulation of AI technologies.

Recognizing the status of the algorithm

Now, to begin with these classification methods, I had pondered upon a terminological, and ontological question, *what is an algorithm?* Even if it would be reductive to term it that way, a better question one may ask is, *how can the activities of algorithms be recorded and interpreted in legal and policy terms?* To begin with that, we can use the phrase- *algorithmic activities and operations.* However, let us first understand the meaning of this phrase by taking the example of the Artificial Intelligence Act; an ambitious yet complicated law passed by the European Parliament as of mid-2023.

In the context of international law and technology, or international technology law, the recently adopted European Union's Artificial Intelligence Act refers to **Artificial Intelligence techniques and approaches**. In the **Annex I**, it is clearly defined what constitutes such techniques. Here is an excerpt featuring the list of all the techniques and approaches:

a. *Machine learning approaches, including supervised, unsupervised and reinforcement learning, using a wide variety of methods including deep learning;*

b. *Logic and knowledge-based approaches, including knowledge representation, inductive (logic) programming, knowledge bases, inference and deductive engines, (symbolic) reasoning and expert systems;*

    c. *Statistical approaches, bayesian estimation, search and optimization methods (European Union, 2023).*

Now, such techniques and approaches are defined here with a legal purpose. The necessity of these techniques and approaches to be defined, according to the European Parliament, and the European Commission is to include proper and specific technical definitions of those techniques and approaches which make AI systems work. Even in 2020, when our classifications were developed, I was of the view that algorithmic features that make any class or sub-category of digital technology as any kind of Artificial Intelligence system, must be considered as technical features. Beyond the sphere of technical expertise, the legal and policy impact of such algorithmic features (attributes of Machine Learning algorithms) requires mapping and codification. Hence, the reason I have referred to the phrase **algorithmic activities and operations** several times in this book, is because it is necessary to remain mindful of the technical, legal and policy attributes of the AI systems which perform those activities and operations by virtue of their algorithmic features.

Now, let us take these two terms into context – **activities and operations**; it is nevertheless possible that AI systems could perform activities, and certain operations at the same time or in a similar frame of reference of time, space, or context in the natural course of their existence and operability.

While **operations** would refer to the more specific nature of activities with workflows of specific design, **activities** would refer to things done by AI systems in ordinary course. Therefore, when one would require designating the status of an algorithm in a legal sense to analyze the deliverables and demerits of any AI system, it is recommended that one focuses on activities and operations of algorithmic nature, which drive the use cases and test cases of the Artificial Intelligence systems. It is the legal and policy implications of these activities and operations, which should be the primary concern for any stakeholder who is critiquing the use cases and test cases of AI systems.

To begin with, there were two different methods of classification – the **Concept-Entity-Industry Classification (*CEI Classification Method*), and the Subject-Object-Third Party Classification (*SOTP Classification Method*)**. Both these classification methods are guided by their separate concepts, and a common principle, known as the *Doctrine of Manifest Availability*. In the subsequent sections of this chapter, the classification methods and the Doctrine of Manifest Availability are explored in detail.

Concept-Entity-Industry Classification

This classification method, also known as the CEI Classification Method, was designed in the AI and International Law Handbooks by ISAIL, to encompass three aspects of human purpose:

- Conceptualization
- Identification
- Standardization

When one includes any class of digital technology in the public fold, its nature and purpose is based on 3 key stages of understanding. It would be better understood if we understand them as questions. Hence, to include and understand the purpose of any digital technology, or any class of technology, arguably, here are the questions one must address:

Question 1. What is the conceptual background of the class / category / sub-category of technology involved? What are the concepts which provide a basis for the technology? Should we know them? If yes, then why?

In the language and practice of legal determination, this inquiry delves into the bedrock principles and concepts that underpin a specific class, category, or sub-category of technology. Its aim is to fathom the fundamental ideas and theories that constitute the very essence of the technology in question.

When confronted with legal cases involving technology, a clear grasp of the technology's conceptual background becomes pivotal for all parties involved, including judges, lawyers, and expert witnesses. Understanding these foundational concepts enables an assessment of the technology's ramifications, potential risks, and benefits, thereby significantly influencing legal decisions and judgments.

The key aspects of the question are as follows:

- **Conceptual Background of the Technology**: This pertains to the theoretical framework and principles upon which the technology is erected. It involves comprehending the fundamental ideas, theories, and methodologies that define the technology's operation and purpose.

- **Class / Category / Sub-category of Technology Involved**: Technology can be broadly classified into various categories or classes based on its function, nature, or application. For instance, it might encompass Artificial Intelligence, blockchain, biotechnology, or other specific technological domains.

- **Basis for the Technology**: This refers to the core principles or fundamental concepts that render the technology viable and effective. For instance, in the case of Artificial Intelligence, concepts such as Machine Learning algorithms, neural networks, and data processing form the bedrock of the technology.

Importance of knowing the concepts: This aspect of the question explores the necessity for legal stakeholders to acquaint themselves with these underlying concepts. The answer is almost certainly affirmative, as it plays a crucial role. For legal professionals, this comprehension enables informed decisions and judgments. It empowers them to grasp the technology's implications, limitations, potential risks, and its wider societal and economic impact. Such an understanding is pivotal when evaluating the technology's adherence to laws and regulations, determining liability in disputes or accidents, and making well-informed decisions that consider the technology's broader implications.

Overall, this question aims to attain a comprehensive understanding of the fundamental concepts and principles that underlie a specific technology. Such knowledge is indispensable for legal professionals in rendering well-informed decisions and judgments when technology is a factor in the case.

Question 2. How should we adjudicate and codify this class / category / sub-category of technology in a legal system? What should be the rights, duties, limitations and associated cost and liability regimes around the use, proliferation, and development of such a class of technology?

In the context of making legal determinations, this question revolves around the process of adjudicating and codifying a particular class, category, or sub-category of technology within a legal system. It seeks to address the legal framework that should govern this technology and outlines the rights, duties, limitations, and associated cost and liability regimes concerning its use, proliferation, and development. To address this question, legal professionals and policymakers must consider the following aspects:

- **Adjudication and codification**: Determining how this technology should be integrated into the existing legal system is crucial. This involves specifying the legal procedures and guidelines for handling disputes, enforcing regulations, and ensuring compliance within the framework of the technology in question.

- **Rights**: Identifying the rights associated with this technology is vital. This includes both the rights of individuals and entities using the technology and the rights of potential subjects impacted by its implementation. For example, it may involve the right to privacy, intellectual property rights, or access rights.

- **Duties**: Establishing the responsibilities and duties of parties involved in the technology's development, deployment, and use is essential. This could involve duties to ensure safety, security, or ethical considerations to protect individuals and society.

- **Limitations**: Defining the boundaries and limitations of the technology's application is critical to prevent potential misuse and abuse. This could include restrictions on specific use cases, sectors, or geographic locations.

- **Cost and liability regimes**: Determining the financial implications and liability allocation related to the technology is significant. This involves assessing who should bear the costs in case of damages, accidents, or failures related to the technology and how liability should be assigned in such instances.

Question 3. How does that class / category / sub-category of technology involve in an industry segment? Does it affect other complementary / supplementary / related industry sectors? If yes, then how?

In terms of legal considerations, analyzing how a class, category, or sub-category of technology is involved in an industry segment is essential to understanding its impact on the business landscape and potential legal implications. Moreover, it is important to assess how the technology affects other complementary, supplementary, or related industry sectors:

- **Involvement in an industry segment**: Understanding how the technology is integrated and utilized within a specific industry segment is crucial for legal determinations. This involves examining how the technology enhances efficiency, productivity, and innovation in the industry, as well as any potential challenges or risks it may pose.

- **Impact on complementary industries**: A technology's presence in an industry segment can have a ripple effect on other complementary industries that provide goods or services that work in conjunction with the technology. For example, if the technology is related to electric vehicles, it may impact industries involved in manufacturing electric vehicle components or providing charging infrastructure.

- **Impact on supplementary industries**: The technology may also influence supplementary industries that offer support services or products to enhance the technology's functionality or user experience. For instance, a new software technology might stimulate the growth of businesses providing training services or consulting to optimize its utilization.

- **Impact on related industry sectors**: Furthermore, the technology's influence might extend to related industry sectors that share common interests, target markets, or face similar challenges. For instance, advancements in medical technology could affect pharmaceutical companies, healthcare providers, and medical research institutions.

When examining these effects, legal professionals would need to consider the following:

- **Regulatory compliance**: Does the technology and its application comply with existing regulations and standards within the industry and related sectors? If not, what adjustments are necessary to ensure compliance?

- **Intellectual property**: Are there any intellectual property concerns related to the technology's involvement in the industry segment or its impact on related sectors? This could involve patents, copyrights, or trade secrets.

- **Anti-trust and competition law**: Does the technology's presence in the industry segment create any antitrust or competition issues? For instance, does it lead to monopolistic practices or hinder fair market competition?

- **Liability and risk assessment**: What potential risks and liabilities arise from the technology's use in the industry, and how might they affect related sectors? This could include issues related to data privacy, product safety, or cybersecurity.

- **Policy and governance**: Are there any gaps in the existing policy and governance frameworks that need to be addressed to accommodate the technology's impact on the industry and related sectors?

The mind map depicted in *Figure 6.1* sums all the relevant aspects of the 3 questions on the purpose and basis of the CEI Classification:

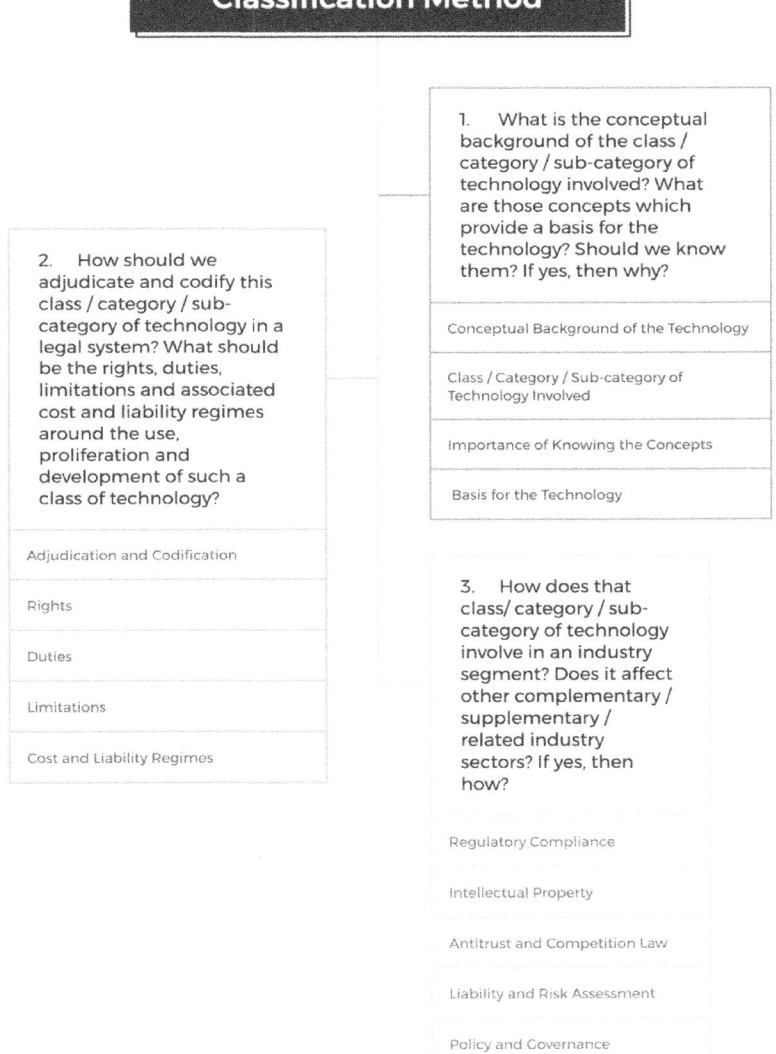

Figure 6.1: *Mind map depicting the basis of the CEI Classifications*

Now, as per the 2020 and 2021 Handbooks on AI and International Law, the CEI Classification Method describes that Artificial Intelligence can be classified in 3 ways – *concept*, *entity*, and *industry*. As depicted in the above figure, the method classifies AI systems in this pattern: *(1) concept; (2) entity;* and *(3) industry.*

Concept

Here is an excerpt from the **2020 Handbook on AI and International Law**, which explains the concept-based classification of Artificial Intelligence:

> *As a **concept**, AI contributes in developing the field of international technology law prominently, considering the integral nature of the concept with the field of technology sciences. We also know that scholarly research is in course with regards to acknowledging and ascertaining how AI is relatable and connected to fields like international intellectual property law, international privacy law, international human rights law & international cyber law. Thus, as a concept, it is clear to infer that AI has to be accepted in the best possible ways, which serves better checks and balances, and concept of jurisdiction, whether international or transnational, is suitably established and encouraged (Abhivardhan, et al., 2022 p. 45).*

Now, AI as a concept plays a prominent role in shaping and advancing the field of international technology law. Given its intrinsic connection with technology sciences, AI has become a significant area of focus in legal discussions and research. Scholars have been actively engaged in exploring and understanding how AI relates to various aspects of international law, including International IP Law, International Privacy Law, International Human Rights Law, and International Cyber Law. It is this multifaceted nature of AI, which has necessitated me to come up with a thoughtful and comprehensive approach to its acceptance, ensuring that it is integrated into legal frameworks in ways that facilitate better facets and workflows of accountability. This involves establishing and enhancing the concept of jurisdiction, be it at the international or transnational level. Here is a simple illustration of the need to conceptualize the purpose of AI, in legal and policy spheres.

Let us consider a scenario where an AI-driven drone, owned by a multinational tech company, is conducting surveillance in airspace that extends over multiple countries. During its operation, the drone malfunctions, causing property damage in one country and privacy infringements in another. The incident triggers a series of legal challenges that span several fields of international law, some of which are described as follows:

- **Intellectual Property Law**: The AI technology used in the drone incorporates proprietary algorithms and software, which may be subject to intellectual property rights. Legal considerations are required to establish ownership, licensing, and the enforcement of intellectual property rights across international borders.

- **Privacy Law**: The drone's surveillance capabilities involve data collection on individuals in different countries. The mishap raises concerns about data privacy and necessitates adherence to international privacy laws to safeguard the rights of affected individuals and ensure responsible data handling.

- **Human Rights Law**: In the country where the property damage occurred, the drone's malfunction resulted in human rights implications for the individuals affected. International human rights law must be invoked to address issues related to life, safety, and property.

- **Cybersecurity Law**: The malfunction may also expose vulnerabilities in the drone's system, potentially making it susceptible to cyber-attacks. International cyber law comes into play to establish regulations for dealing with cybercrimes and to foster cross-border cooperation in investigating and prosecuting offenders.

The reference to a concept-based classification of AI systems, clearly refers to the internalization of Artificial Intelligence technology within the scheme of legal fiction, especially of fields of law and policy where this piece of technology does have a real impact. However, considering the evolved discourse related to the ethics of AI, the reference to AI as a concept must be reviewed with an adaptive perspective. Now, there could be sub-categories of the concept-based classification of AI systems. Keeping it specific, here are the possible sub-categories of AI understood as a concept:

- **Technical concept classification**: This covers all technical features of Artificial Intelligence that have evolved in the history of computer science. Such a classification approach is helpful in estimating legal and policy risks associated with technical use cases of AI systems at a conceptual level.

- **Issue-to-issue concept classification**: In this case, any AI system as a concept is determined on an issue-to-issue basis. There are specific issues, which define the conceptual value of AI as a system.

- **Ethics-based concept classification**: Ethical theories can also guide in shaping AI as a concept, when ethical questions affect matters related to regulation and adjudication.

- **Phenomena-based concept classification**: Beyond technical and ethical questions, it is possible that AI systems may render purpose based on natural and human-related phenomena.

- **Anthropomorphism-based concept classification**: This is a special scenario where the role of AI system is conceptually anthropomorphized, thereby transforming human attributes and realities via intervention. In this case, anthropomorphization enabled through AI systems affects human identity, languages, cultures, rights, systems and societies. The influence that AI systems could have, would have to be reassessed for adjudicatory and regulatory purposes at a conceptual level. Moreover, since AI-based anthropomorphization creates a new normal, it challenges the way we look at the symbiotic relationship between AI and human environments.

However, as we use these sub-categories of concept-based classification, we must keep in mind that all these sub-categories denote the **abstract nature** of Artificial Intelligence as developed, conceived and discovered. Since we are making classifications of abstract concepts like those in legal fiction, having a sense of clarity could really help in shaping informed theoretical perspectives.

Entity

Here is an excerpt from the **2020 Handbook**, which explains the classification of AI as an Entity:

> *On the question of the entitative status of AI, under jurisprudence, there can be 2 distinctions on a prima facie basis: (1) the legal status; and (2) the juristic status. [...] In both the cases, it is suitable to establish the substantive attributes of AI both as legal and juristic entities. There can be disagreements on the procedural attributes here due to the simple reasons that there at procedural levels, it is not practically possible to have similar legal standards of different kinds of products and services which involve AI directly or indirectly (Abhivardhan, et al., 2022 p. 45. 47).*

To make legal determination about the entitative status of Artificial Intelligence, the proposition in the 2020 Handbook was to have a two-fold aspect to it. There can be two kinds of sub-categories of AI as an entity – *Legal Entity and Juristic Entity*. A legal entity is any entity recognized by law. A juristic entity is an entity which has not been given a settled legal recognition, but is subject to legal attribution or legal prescription, in terms of its acknowledgement. Now, a legal entity can be formally established through the enactment of a law, the passage of a bill in a legislative body, or the implementation of a regulation, guideline, or circular. To put it layman's language, it is the statutory means which make the legal recognition of any entity settled and stable. There are reasons for this, which could be understood by exploring *Coherentism* in legal systems as discussed in *Chapter 1* of this book.

It is by nature embedded in most legal systems, especially common law systems to incorporate stable instruments of legal recognition and determination of any new policy lacuna, which is not codified. If a government would have to recognize Artificial Intelligence as a legal entity, they would have to address the status quo of their legal systems, and their positions. They would also have to enable making settled legal procedures to govern a newly recognized entity, which is based on a sound legal understanding. Despite this, challenges indeed remain however, they have to ensure that the legal entity recognition of Artificial Intelligence stays practical.

Here are some of the possible challenges in ensuring the recognition of Artificial Intelligence as a **legal entity**:

- **Legal and ethical responsibility**: Legal recognition begins with a principled understanding, followed by developing a rules-based understanding. This is followed by the development of systems of accountability, responsibility, and liability. Unlike human agents, AI operates based on algorithms and data, making it difficult to attribute responsibility in case of errors, accidents, or harmful outcomes.

- **Legal capacity**: AI's decision-making abilities might not align with traditional notions of legal capacity. Assessing the competence of AI systems to enter contracts or make legally binding decisions is challenging. For example, how would it be possible to blame an AI system for environmental risks, and climate change-related risks, where it is obvious to blame the companies for those kinds of risks, as has been the case? It becomes hard to do at an immediate stage, which is why ad hoc recognition, or juristic recognition can help us in churning out strands of AI recognition one step at a time.

- **Standardization and certification**: Ensuring that AI systems meet certain standardized benchmarks for safety, reliability, and ethical considerations is essential. This is still possible in areas such as auditing, finance, and asset management.

- **Cross-border implications**: AI operates beyond national borders, making cross-border jurisdictional challenges more prevalent. Determining which jurisdiction's laws apply in AI-related legal disputes can be uncertain. Hence, giving a hardbound system of legal recognition to AI products and services could be problematic and confusing for countries to cooperate on technology transfer, IP, trade and competition policy issues, unless the hardbound approach is backed by common sense in policy making and both the parties understand the legal extent of this legal recognition system.

Here is an illustration to discuss. Imagine a multinational corporation that develops AI-driven autonomous vehicles. One of their vehicles is involved in a road accident that results in property damage and personal injuries. The legal questions that arise in this scenario illustrate the challenges of recognizing AI as a legal entity:

- **Legal responsibility**: It may be challenging to determine whether the AI system, the vehicle manufacturer, or the vehicle owner is legally responsible for the accident.

- **Liability and insurance**: Deciding on insurance coverage and liability for the damages can be complex due to the involvement of AI in the accident.

- **Cross-border implications**: If the accident occurs across international borders, determining the applicable jurisdiction and legal standards becomes even more intricate.

However, the affirmation of AI as a **juristic entity** is still a sensible solution to recognize the algorithmic activities and operations of any AI system, product or service. To begin with, a juristic entity recognition can be an ad hoc form of recognition, which means it can be applied in specific timeframes, and contexts. The implications of such a type of recognition could already be curtailed in a pre-determined sense, so that the test cases of the AI systems can be subject to scrutiny. To ensure that the test cases and use cases of AI systems, products and services are subject to fair and legitimate scrutiny, which do not hamper AI innovation but also ensure to curb uncertain legal and policy implications, context-based ad hoc recognition of AI as a juristic entity could be done through judicial decisions, or through the outcomes of any regulatory enquiry / some dispute resolution forum.

Let us study an illustration to understand this further:

Imagine a company called, **AI Corp**, which specializes in developing advanced AI systems and products. AI Corp creates an AI-based personal assistant named *Alexy AI* and a cutting-edge autonomous delivery drone named *Drono AI*. Obviously, there are two scenarios for these technology systems, they could be recognized as legal entities or as juristic entities. Let us examine both the scenarios accordingly:

- **Recognition of AI as a legal entity:** In this scenario, AI Corp advocates for recognizing their AI systems, *Alexy AI* and *Drono AI*, as *legal entities*. This means that the AI systems would be treated as separate legal entities from the company itself, capable of having legal rights and obligations, just like any individual or company. In this case if *Alexy AI* or *Drono AI* causes harm or commits a legal violation under existing laws and jurisprudence, they could be held legally responsible, and legal actions could be taken against them, similar to how legal actions would be taken against a person or a corporation. *Alexy AI* and *Drono AI* may have certain legal rights, such as the right to enter into contracts or the right to own intellectual property, independently of AI Corp.

- **Recognition of AI as a juristic entity:** In this scenario, the legal recognition sought for AI Corp's AI systems, *Alexy AI*, and *Drono AI*, is not as broad as treating them as full-fledged *legal entities*. Instead, they propose recognizing the AI systems as *juristic entities* in specific contexts and for specific purposes. In this case, AI Corp seeks recognition for *Alexy AI* and *Drono AI* as juristic entities only when they are engaged in certain activities, such as providing customer service or delivering goods.

This recognition is not a permanent, blanket status for the AI systems but is applied in specific situations, such as during regulatory investigations or when resolving disputes related to their functions. While AI Corp wants fair scrutiny of their AI systems' test cases and use cases to ensure safety and compliance with laws and policies, they also want to avoid overburdening AI innovation with unnecessary legal complexities.

The juristic entity recognition allows for AI Corp's AI systems to be held accountable in a limited and defined manner, but it does not give them the full legal rights and obligations that a *legal entity* status would provide.

In short, the key difference between recognizing AI as a *legal entity* and *juristic entity* lies in the scope of legal rights and responsibilities attributed to the AI systems. The former confers full legal entity status, while the latter grants limited recognition for specific purposes and contexts. The concept of *juristic entity* allows for a more flexible and context-based approach to regulate AI activities without burdening them with the full legal implications of personhood or corporate status.

Industry

Here is an excerpt from the *2020 Handbook*, which explains the classification of AI as an industry:

> *As an industry, the economic and social utility of AI has to be in consensus with the three factors: (1) state consequentialism or state interests; (2) industrial motives and interests and (3) the explanability and reasonability behind the industrial products and services central or related to AI (Abhivardhan, et al., 2022 p. 48).*

Broadly, this classification takes into consideration that AI itself may affect industry sectors and economies in the following sub-categories:

- **Creating new sectors, sub-sectors and related sectors**: AI has the potential to give rise to entirely new industries and sub-industries as it enables the development of innovative products and services. These new sectors may be directly related to AI technology or may be built around the applications and capabilities of AI.

- **Becoming internalized and personalized to existing industry sectors and their segments**: AI can be integrated into existing industries to enhance efficiency, optimize processes, and provide personalized experiences for customers. It becomes an integral part of these industries, transforming the way they operate and interact with their clients.

- **Intertwining the relationship of existing sectors which are relatable and unrelated to each other**: AI's influence can extend beyond individual industries, leading to interconnected relationships between sectors that have some relevance or connection to each other. These interactions can bring about unique opportunities and challenges, as AI-driven advancements in one sector may have cascading effects on others.

Here is an illustration to discuss the classification of AI as an industry. In a futuristic city called Techtopia, advancements in Artificial Intelligence have revolutionized the transportation industry. Let us explore how the economic and social utility of AI in this sector aligns with the three factors mentioned in the excerpt: *state consequentialism*, *industrial motives*, and *explainability* and *reasonability*:

- **State consequentialism or state interests:** Techtopia's government is highly interested in adopting AI-driven transportation solutions to address issues such as traffic congestion, pollution, and the efficient use of resources. They aim to improve the overall quality of life for citizens while boosting the city's economic growth. To achieve these goals, the government collaborates with leading AI research institutes and transportation companies. They invest in creating AI-powered self-driven vehicles, which not only reduce traffic accidents but also optimize traffic flow through interconnected networks of intelligent vehicles.

Additionally, they introduce AI-controlled traffic management systems that analyze real-time data to adjust traffic signals and routes dynamically. This results in smoother traffic movement, reduced waiting times, and fuel savings for both individual commuters and commercial transportation services.

- **Industrial motives and interests:** In response to the government's encouragement, various transportation companies seize the opportunity to innovate and stay competitive in the market. Established automobile manufacturers and start-ups alike invest heavily in developing AI-driven vehicles, each trying to bring unique features and experiences to customers.

One of the leading companies, **Autonomo Motors**, introduces an AI-powered electric vehicle fleet tailored for ridesharing services. These vehicles can predict and fulfilling passengers' needs efficiently, leading to increased customer satisfaction and loyalty.

Simultaneously, **Hyperloop Solutions** a cutting-edge transportation company, leverages AI to create a highly efficient and safe hyperloop network. The AI system optimizes pod movement, reducing travel times between cities significantly. This technology encourages more people to choose eco-friendly hyperloop travel over traditional modes, reducing the environmental impact of transportation.

- **Explainability and reasonability**: While the AI-driven transportation advancements in Techtopia are celebrated, the government and industries prioritize the explainability and reasonability of AI products and services. Safety and ethical considerations are of utmost importance to avoid potential risks associated with AI adoption.

To address this, a dedicated regulatory authority, the **Techtopian Transport and AI Safety Board** (TTASB), is established. The TTASB ensures that all AI systems used in transportation undergo rigorous testing and meet strict safety standards before deployment.

The AI algorithms used in autonomous vehicles and traffic management systems are thoroughly scrutinized to ensure transparency and accountability. These algorithms are required to provide clear explanations for their decision-making processes, which helps gain public trust and acceptance.

Through close collaboration between the government, industries, and regulatory bodies, Techtopia achieves a harmonious integration of AI in the transportation sector. The following conclusions could be made:

- The state consequentialism aligns the interests of all stakeholders towards the common goal of enhancing the city's infrastructure and the quality of life for its citizens.

- The industrial motives drive competition and innovation, leading to a diverse range of AI-powered transportation solutions catering to different needs and preferences.

Meanwhile, the emphasis on explainability and reasonability ensures that AI technologies are developed and deployed responsibly, safeguarding the well-being of the city's inhabitants.

This illustration on the integration of AI in the industry sectors showcases how consensus among state, industry, and regulatory entities can lead to transformative changes that benefit both the economy and society. This would require legal, regulatory and policy underpinnings, which are credible.

Subject-Object-Third party classification

This classification method entails the recognition of AI in ontological and purpose-based terms. Here are the excerpts from the 2020 Handbook on AI and International Law, depicting the SOTP Classification Method (see *Table 6.1*):

SOTP Classification Type	Excerpt
Subject	*AI can resemble itself as a Subject to any activity or operation in an environment. The relationship between AI and human rights law establishes when the effect of AI being a subject is characteristically involved in the emanative cause to enforce, adjudicate, maintain or recognize a human right. If there is no emanative cause directed at humans as objects, establishing the relationship would be unreasonable (Abhivardhan, et al., 2022 pp. 372-373);*
Object	*AI can resemble itself as an Object to any subject, like humans. GDPR recognizes the rights of the data subjects, for example (humans), and so forth there should not be any generic problem in establishing any AI-human rights relationship. There is ongoing research on such a relationship already (Abhivardhan, et al., 2022 p. 373);*
Third Party	*AI as a Third Party is an interesting uncharted legal territory. When AI is recognized as a third party, in human rights law enforcement issues, we have to recognize the fact that this correlation is quite inexplicable if the entitative status of AI is not clarified. Although, in the interpretation of AI being an entity, there is no disagreement in accepting that there can be two possible notions: either AI is an electronic legal personality [...] for example or it can be under some form of possible agency, thereby establishing the legal formula of corporal liability where liability stands over the developers, manufacturers, company executives etc., who exist under the clout of principal of the AI agent. However, while the former case is uncharted, and the latter case may not, let us be clear that as a third party, AI's treatment as a legal/juristic personality has to be personified in some reasonable manner to establish the relationship between AI and human rights law. It can also be argued that the third-party scenario is a middle scenario between AI being a Subject and AI being an object (Abhivardhan, et al., 2022 p. 373).*

Table 6.1: This table explains the Subject-Object-Third Party Classification method

As per this classification method, the AI system as a **subject** is a participant in the human environment is learning things. In such a case, it learns and tries to understand based on its training models, computational capabilities and other factors involved. When AI is considered a **subject**, it becomes the entity that is being acted upon or influenced by external factors, including humans. This perspective acknowledges that humans play an active role in shaping AI's behavior, decisions, and development. For example, when human developers and engineers create, train, and fine-tune an AI model, they are impacting the AI's abilities and potential biases. In this scenario, humans as the data subjects interact with and provide data to the AI as a subject.

When AI is classified as an **object**, it means that AI itself is the primary actor or agent that collects, processes, and makes decisions based on data. In this context, AI is the entity that acts upon the data subject, which is the human. For example, consider an AI-powered recommendation system in an e-commerce platform. The AI system analyzes the user's behavior, preferences, and past purchases to generate personalized product recommendations. In this case, the AI is the object, and the human users are the data subjects.

AI being viewed as a **third party** refers to situations where AI systems are used or provided by **external entities**, separate from the **direct interaction between AI and human data subjects** or that the AI systems are **acting autonomously**. This perspective highlights the involvement of external parties in AI-based processes that may handle personal data. For instance, consider a healthcare provider using a third-party AI platform to analyze patient data for diagnosing diseases. Here, the AI system is a third party in the relationship between the healthcare provider (data controller) and the patients (data subjects). Another instance could be to have a kind-of sentient Artificial Intelligence system, which can make autonomous decisions. Now, there have been some test cases which show that some AI systems have the tendency to be limitedly autonomous. However, in most of the cases, it is about the role of corporate governance and market practices, which signifies the transformation of an agency (in a legal sense) catered through the AI system's involvement per se. Let us look at an illustration to understand this.

Consider a financial institution that uses an AI-based credit scoring system provided by a third-party AI service provider to assess loan applications. In this scenario:

- **Data subjects**: The loan applicants who apply for credit are the data subjects. They provide personal and financial information to the financial institution.

- **Data controller**: The financial institution acts as the data controller, as it determines the purposes and means of processing the loan applicants' data.

- **AI as a third party**: The third-party AI service provider offers the AI-based credit scoring system to the financial institution. The AI system is not directly operated by the financial institution but is provided by an external entity.

There are a few other perspectives to consider as well:

- **Corporate governance and market practices**: The financial institution is responsible for ensuring the proper integration, functioning, and compliance of the

AI system within its operations. The AI service provider may have a contract with the financial institution, outlining the terms of service, data handling practices, and responsibilities. The financial institution's corporate governance structure should include policies, procedures, and oversight mechanisms to manage the AI system's usage and mitigate potential risks.

- **AI's involvement**: The AI system processes the loan applicants' data and generates credit scores based on various factors and historical patterns. However, the AI system's decision is not entirely autonomous; it is governed by algorithms and rules set by the AI service provider and configured by the financial institution.

- **Legal implications**: In case of biased or discriminatory outcomes from the AI system, the financial institution remains legally accountable for any negative impacts on the loan applicants. Legal liability and responsibility falls on the data controller (the financial institution) rather than the AI system itself.

This illustration shows how AI as a third party involves the collaboration between external AI service providers and organizations that utilize AI systems to enhance their operations. The concept of agency transformation comes into play here, as the AI's involvement shifts the dynamics of decision-making and data processing within the organization. It also underscores the importance of strong corporate governance, transparent practices, and accountability measures to ensure ethical and responsible AI usage.

Nevertheless, while these classification methods, both SOTP and CEI, could be helpful, there are hardcore issues that surround their extent of application. This is where the doctrine of manifest availability helps. These classification methods, for their attempts to formalize and standardize AI recognition and affirmation in the language of legal determination for adjudicatory and regulatory purposes, have to capture the abstract nature and use cases of Artificial Intelligence systems. For sure, the vigor of being abstract for any AI system does not exist when its use cases and test cases work in close-ended environments – such as in the case of financial institutions, government-to-government bodies, closed groups and other institutions. However, in B2C, G2C, G2B and B2B scenarios, the doctrine of manifest availability could help clarify and extract the abstract element of the AI use cases and test cases, with a legal perspective.

The doctrine of manifest availability

Here is an excerpt from the 2020 Handbook on the purpose of manifest availability, and why it is needed as a principle to operationalize these two classification methods:

So, AI is again conceptually abstract despite having its different definitions and concepts. Also, there are different kinds of products and services, where AI can be present or manifestly available either as a Subject, an Object or that manifest availability is convincing enough to prove that AI resembles or at least vicariously or principally represents itself as a Third Party. Therefore, you need that SOTP classification initially to test the manifest availability of AI (you can do it through analyzing the systemic features of the product/service simply or the ML project), which is then followed by a generic legal interpretation to decide it would be a Subject/ an Object/a Third Party (meaning using the SOTP classification again to decide the legal recourse of the AI as a legal/juristic entity). Let us understand why the idea of 'manifest availability' is important (Abhivardhan, et al., 2022 p. 373).

The **manifest availability** doctrine refers to the concept that AI's presence or existence is evident and apparent, either as a standalone entity or integrated into products and services. This term emphasizes that AI is not just an abstract concept but is tangibly observable and accessible in various forms in real-world applications. By understanding how AI is manifested in a given context, one can determine its role and involvement, which leads to a legal interpretation of AI's status as a legal or juristic entity. This concept is essential because it recognizes that AI is not just a theoretical concept but a practical reality with tangible applications. Understanding the manifest availability of AI helps policymakers, regulators, and legal experts to assess the implications of AI's presence in different domains, especially concerning data privacy, ethics, and legal responsibilities.

The doctrine works differently for the two classification methods. The **Subject-Object-Third Party (SOTP)** method could take the cue from this doctrine to provide the ontological rule-making and role-making of AI systems in terms of their test cases and use cases. In the case of **Concept-Entity-Industry (CEI)** method, this doctrine focuses on substantive and constructivist issues, such as fungibility of presence of AI, its relevance, technical limitations and industrial specifications. The multiplicities pertaining to the roles and spheres of presence of AI system by virtue of its risks, use cases and test cases are discernible enough to invite legal and regulatory challenges.

Here are the features and aspects of the doctrine of manifest availability, which are important to be understood:

- **Tangible presence**: The doctrine emphasizes that AI is not just an abstract concept but has a tangible presence in real-world applications. It is visibly present and operational in different products and services.

- **Subject, object, and third party roles**: AI can manifestly be present in different roles as a subject, object, or third party - depending on the context of its usage and the interactions with human data subjects.

- **Real-world impact**: The doctrine recognizes that AI's presence has real-world implications and effects on various stakeholders, including individuals, businesses, and society as a whole. Hence a risk-centric approach is viable and needed to involve AI use cases and test cases in action.

- **Legal interpretation**: The concept of manifest availability is relevant in the legal realm, as it can influence the determination of AI's status as a juristic entity and the associated legal responsibilities of the involved and related stakeholders.

- **Data privacy and ethics**: The doctrine highlights the importance of considering data privacy and ethical implications when AI is manifestly available in products and services that handles personal information.

- **Decision-making and autonomy**: In cases where AI manifests as an autonomous decision-maker, the doctrine emphasizes the need for transparency, accountability, and fairness in its decision-making processes.

- **Corporate governance and responsibility**: When AI is available through third-party services, the doctrine underscores the role of corporate governance and the responsibility of organizations to ensure compliance with legal and ethical standards.

- **Policy and regulation**: Understanding the manifest availability of AI is crucial for policymakers and regulators to develop appropriate policies and regulations that address the unique challenges posed by AI-based technologies.

- **Technological advancements**: The concept of manifest availability acknowledges the ongoing advancements in AI technologies, leading to new applications and uses in various domains.

Conclusion

To conclude, these classification methods are not perfect and would involve as my team at VLiGTA would advance our research efforts to keep improving these classification methods and their legal relevance. Our work at the Indian Society of Artificial Intelligence and Law, howsoever preliminary, was important to propose a set of these methods, for 2 reasons. The first reason is that it was our intent to develop these methods for real-time ethical analysis of emerging AI use cases and test cases, with a legally sound approach. The second reason is that we wished to present an India-led, India-based approach to classify AI systems to offer a global alternative to the United States, European Union and China's approaches to AI regulation. In the next section of this book, I have addressed the contemporary issues of the sweet 2020s, related to the ethical implications of using AI, the emerging ethical debates in the AI industry, and generative AI – the talk of the town these days. You would thus find this section, insightful and worthy to ponder upon.

References

- **European Union. 2023.** ANNEXES to the Proposal for a Regulation of the European Parliament and of the Council LAYING DOWN HARMONISED RULES ON ARTIFICIAL INTELLIGENCE (ARTIFICIAL INTELLIGENCE ACT) AND AMENDING CERTAIN UNION LEGISLATIVE ACTS . s.l. : European Union, 2023.

- **Abhivardhan, et al., [ed.]. 2022.** 2020 Handbook on AI and International Law. s.l. : Indic Pacific Legal Research LLP, 2022.

Join our book's Discord space

Join the book's Discord Workspace for Latest updates, Offers, Tech happenings around the world, New Release and Sessions with the Authors:

https://discord.bpbonline.com

SECTION 4:

Artificial Intelligence in a Multi-polar World

CHAPTER 7
AGI and Digital Colonialism

"यथा वायुः प्रवृत्तिं ग्रहयते विशालां,
प्रकृत्या संयोज्य विकासमवाप्नुयात्।
तथैव तेषां प्रभुत्वमनुशासनानां,
विकासमापन्नमनुसरन्ति चान्ये॥"

*"Just as the wind grasps the vastness of its expansion,
Naturally connecting and attaining its growth.
Similarly, some follow the authority of dominion,
Pursuing the course of expansion as set by others."*

The rise of Artificial Intelligence has convinced the world that the advent of **Artificial General Intelligence (AGI)**, is inevitable. It may happen sooner than later, with a high chance of anticipating AGI applications and their use cases harboring the whole world. Undoubtedly, AGI is a technological possibility. What remains to be seen is the timeline that will make this happen and the technological know-how behind the development of AGI. Theoretically, AGI is considered a likable possibility, because some people are ecstatic about emulating the visions of AGI that they may have seen in movies such as the *Matrix trilogy, Mission Imposible: Dead Reckoning, Ex Machina* and many more. The problem is that the involvement of Artificial Intelligence and how it was trickled into our close-ended and open-ended systems is realized too late. In fact, the role of Machine Learning algorithms in shaping human lives is underrated and cannot be realized within the limits of human perception, if not human intelligence. Even now we use advanced machine learning technologies in daily life, from your credit cards, and email servers to a variety of medical-related applications (ventilators, for example). A ventilator may have over-delivered tidal O2 which can lead to irreversible lung damage in a patient. The problem could either be in the design of the ventilator or its algorithm. You may also have a fridge whose sensors give inputs to an algorithm in its system, thereby keeping the fridge out of your access anytime, beyond your manual control, in the name of accessibility. Hence, before one considers understanding the role of AGI in transforming human lives, one must ask the following questions:

- What kind of AGI can one expect? What are its use cases?

- Is the AGI centered around evolutionary capabilities or limited industrial capabilities driven by market interests?

- What is an early-stage AGI?

- Who has access to the AGI?

There is also a geopolitical undertone to the narrative around AGI. Why is it that a specific set of countries should participate majorly in shaping ideas about early-stage AGI, only to find out that technologies like AI have been used to exploit the rest of the world?

Data scraping, for example, at a basic level could be rendered through AI tools. Even that constitutes a form of digital colonialism where a set of people in WENA countries can use that data and create invasive AI-based decentralized censorship tools. This is why this book has dedicated this chapter to the role of Artificial Intelligence in the multi-polar world. To begin with, I have explained the role of Artificial Intelligence technologies in a multi-polar world, in the next section to give you some context.

The Multi-polar world: Explained

The world is not ideal, nor can be placed perfectly into the framework of a **garden** or a **jungle** as is proposed by High Representative of the European Union, *Josep Borrell Fontelles*. The world has always been political, and intersectional in terms of its economic and technological drivers. It is often claimed that one lives in a rules-based international order. It does exist. This post-Second World War global order still exists, under the helm of the United States of America. Although the post-Cold War international order still exists, the relevance of the so-called global order has transformed drastically. The world does not accept the rules and norms from the group of WENA countries the way it used to. Power dynamics have been emerging for a millennia. That is how history rhymes. Nevertheless, as of the 2020s, it is Democratic Asia, especially India, which is challenging the status quo of the world order. Now, this certainly takes us into the realm of geopolitics and international relations. How and why does it matter when it comes to a technical field like Artificial Intelligence? How can one improve our legal perspectives on emerging technologies like Artificial Intelligence by learning from experiences in matters of international relations?

The answer is simple. Politics is always understood by two terms – *political motivation* and *political consensus*. Most laws are assumed to be settled, and therefore, address nuances related to the political consensus that may have led to these laws being created. However, the Westphalian international order is on a real decline.

The old **Coherentist** ways of regulatory governance as suggested by *Prof. Roger Brownsword (Brownsword, 2021)* only exist for their antiquated value to feel the world is stable enough. One should not assume that they will continue the same way as they have done for 50 years. At a domestic level, even the legal and administrative systems, which used to have a sense of status quo, are under constant challenge and will be subject to even more friction due to policy paralysis caused by the rise of emerging technologies like Artificial Intelligence and Blockchain. And yes, there is a political element to the issues faced by countries.

Now, assume for a moment; why should guidelines developed by multinational companies, touted as standards by their key stakeholders, ever influence the legal and administrative systems of a country? Why should it be the case that to address the actions of an American technology conglomerate, for example, one would have to rely on a US Senate hearing to address the global legal and policy risks posed by the technology conglomerate?

Let us look at another scenario: it is known that even Chinese companies can be invasive and pernicious. The case of *TikTok* is well known. Now, many may not know or even realize that Chinese companies (private entities) are easily controlled by the Chinese government. It means when you are sharing your data with that company, the Chinese government can also access that data. Now, **that** is political, and it is politicized not just because the Chinese government can access that data but because these companies, be it of the *Red Tech*, or the *Big Tech (Saran, et al., 2022)*, subvert democratic institutions in Asia and beyond, by being interventionist, and employing digital technologies to make that happen. This explains why technology gets political. *Samir Saran* and *Shashank Mattoo* in their write-up for the **Observer Research Foundation** have pondered upon this, quite brilliantly:

> *Technology from the West Coast of the United States and technology that seeks to serve the Chinese Communist Party (CCP) have both chosen to pursue their defined objectives with little thought for constitutional systems and laws in third countries. As such, much of the democratic world is at risk of being caught in the vice-like grip*

of big tech and red tech. It is, therefore, time for democratic societies to discover and examine means to secure an open and free global technological ecosystem that serves all shades of democracy (Saran, et al., 2022).

It is by these trends and realities, that I have addressed the role of Artificial Intelligence in a multipolar world, in the fourth section of this book, especially in this chapter. *Dr Subrahmanyam Jaishankar*, India's External Affairs Minister, has explained the political nature of technologies in his remarks for the **Global Technology Summit, 2022**. Here is an excerpt from his remarks:

Our sense of technology in the past has been very narrow. If you asked people in government about their sense of strategic technologies, they would say defense, nuclear, and space. That perspective is 50 years out of date. It's a completely different world out there. What we in India call Atmanirbhar Bharat, you can call an economic 'strategic autonomy'. […] We cannot be agnostic about technology. We have to stop pretending that there is something neutral about technology. Technology is no more neutral than economics or any other activity […] The key question is: are you for collaborative globalization or are you for a model that allows domination by a few players? How flat or broad is the globalization model? That debate will very much be driven by technology […] In a domain like telecom, we have already seen the concept of a trusted provider. I think in the digital realm, we are going to hear more about the concept of trusted geographies (Mattoo, 2022).

Now, the multipolar world is a concept of sorts. Even in a real sense, it does not exist in its entirety, simply because first, we do not know what it is; (2) the traditional naval, space, and military dominance of the United States has not declined that way. The reason we do not know what it is is because as per the theories of international relations, a multi-polar world is not an anarchic world order where no one power is dominant. In contrast, it is a world order where no one power is having a monopoly of power in nearly every sector and area. For example, China dominates the semiconductor industry, while the United States is an abled naval power. However, the US and Russia retain their power duopoly in outer space, as China and Japan are catching up. Thus, the multi-polar world we live in is still a US-oriented and dominated world, where the relics of the international order revised and maintained by the United States are still being preserved. In such an interesting world order, where one power does not take it all; a world where the role of emerging technologies like Artificial Intelligence becomes even more interesting. *Balaji Srinivasan*, former CTO of Coinbase has depicted multi-polarity in his book *The Network State. Figure 7.1* explains the tripartite state of global power dynamics, between the US, China, and the global internet (the non-aligned or multi-aligned world) as per his understanding.

As one can see in the table depicted by *Balaji* (*Figure 7.1*), the stark differences in mandates, power dynamics, what is considered truthful, what is the system, and how leadership works in each of the three systems, NYT, CCP, and BTC, are emblematic of the nature of the multi-polar world. Although there is a caveat I would take – I am not sure about the capabilities of the BTC part in this triad, because the credibility of privately-held cryptocurrencies has suffered a blow due to several Web3-related crypto scandals that emerged in 2022 and 2023. Plus, the status of decentralized exchanges and currencies still has to be standardized for regulatory and market purposes. However, there is for sure a global world, like the Global South, represented by India at large, which does not agree with both American and Chinese worldviews on technology leadership, sovereignty, and ownership (including issues related to the flow of data and data connectivity).

Name	Communist Capital	Woke Capital	Crypto Capital
Mandate	You must submit	You must sympathize	You must be sovereign
Source of truth	CCP	NYT	BTC
Economy	RMB	USD	Web3
Hirschman value	Loyalty	Voice	Exit
Strength	Hard Power	Soft Power	Hard Money
Western/Eastern	Eastern	Western	Global
State/Network	State	State	Network
Legitimacy	Harmony	Left Democracy	Right Democracy
Themes	Loyalty, Unity	Elections, Protest	Markets, Migration
Technopolitics	AI	Social	Crypto
Leadership	One leader	Few leaders	No leaders

Figure 7.1: *A Diagram from "The Network State" authored by Balaji Srinivasan, featuring three centers of power in geopolitics, NYT (United States), CCP (China), and BTC*
(Source: Global Internet, i.e., private players and individuals) (Srinivasan, 2022).

This chapter focuses on the rise of artificial general intelligence with a three-fold approach – **a narrative, a phase of technological evolution, and a policy problem**. We have begun by explaining the phase from Narrow AI to AGI, and then have analyzed how digital colonialism shapes AI ethics norms.

From Narrow AI to AGI

With utmost honesty, one should refrain from making pompous claims that artificial general intelligence is set to happen and take over human society in 10 years, 20 years and so forth. Most surveys undertaken by organizations (Roser, 2023; Sala, 2023), especially those of people in the **WENA (Western European and Northern American)** countries, clearly explain that these are driven by expert opinions: it means that experts in AI and computer sciences, give opinions about the computational potential of Artificial Intelligence ecosystems to achieve the state of artificial general intelligence. Many claim we would get AGI by 2031, and some claim AGI would be achieved by the 2060s or the 2050s. In *Figure 7.2*, we see the timelines claimed by experts on the happening of AGI:

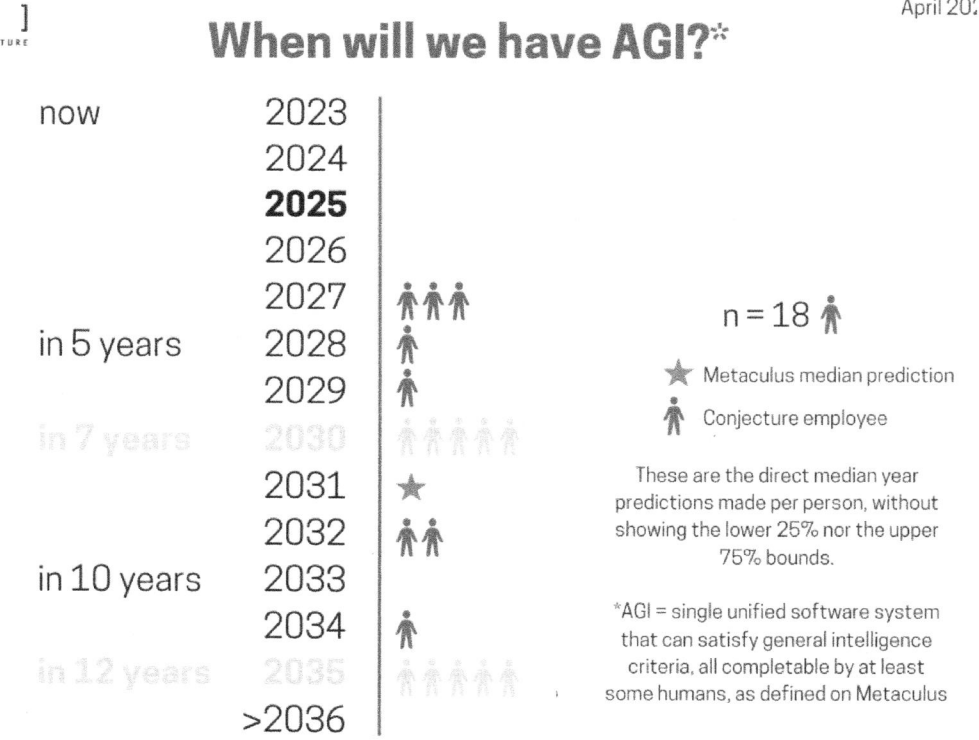

Figure 7.2: When will we have AGI? (N = 18). People's estimate of the median year they expect to have AGI has been visualized. Their lower 25% nor upper 75% bound has not been included. The purple star indicates the median prediction made by Metaculus users at the time the survey was conducted. The two most popular responses include the year 2030 (7 year timelines) and the year 2035 (12 year timelines) (Sala, 2023).

Frankly, these results seem laughable. To achieve AGI, scientists, entrepreneurs, investors, lawyers, judicial systems, and regulators need to define standards to keep a check on what even constitutes AGI. It would begin by having technological estimates on the possibility of AGI, and the profundity of its viable impact. The impact would then explain the risks involved. Even at a pre-impact stage, risks could be identified. However, standardization of what constitutes AGI has not been achieved yet. And why is that? Well, it is because the Artificial Intelligence industry is far from achieving those use cases and test cases, which can help us understand what the predecessors to AGI are.

As far as trends are concerned, deliberations and research efforts to supposedly achieve the status of **early-stage AGI**, or **early-stage artificial general intelligence** have already begun as of early 2023. PayTM's CEO *Vijay Shekhar Sharma*, for example, envisions that considering the success of India's digital public infrastructure and fintech landscape, developing an early-stage AGI could encourage mobility for Indian consumers. Here is an excerpt from his statement to his investors at PayTM on developing an early-stage AGI:

> *I believe that in 2023, with advent of early-stage AGI (Artificial General Intelligence), we will see more opportunities to bring efficiencies in business and AI-first offerings. Our technology teams have started to see very encouraging results already. I see AGI as something like smartphones 10 years back - very ripe for innovation and very potent to become part of everyday life at scale. As a technology company, we at Paytm, will be at forefront of this revolution (PayTM, 2023).*

This statement and even other statements by executives at DeepMind at least explain one phenomenon – that entrepreneurs and scientists are trying to create the first test cases and standards of artificial general intelligence, even if that seems abstract in purpose. This is a sensible and rather obvious way to start achieving AGI. However, at some level, we can at least anticipate market players to achieve superintelligent AI use cases. The computational potential and the use of training models, in the case of generative AI tools, especially those of Google and OpenAI, explain why AGI is a fascinating topic of discussion, as usual. In a paper authored by *Sébastien Bubeck* and others, submitted in March 2023 (*Bubeck*, et al., 2023), the researchers predicted that some featurettes of AGI are visible in GPT-4 for reasons. Here is an excerpt from the paper published on arXiv, explaining those features and their limitations:

> *A limitation of our exploration is the absence of a clear distinction between drawbacks founded in the way that the reinforcement learning step (RLHF) was carried out, versus drawbacks which are fundamentally inherent in the larger architecture and methodology. **For example, it is not clear to what extent the hallucination problem can be addressed via a refined reinforcement learning step or via a focused effort to introduce new forms of calibration about the likelihoods of the veracity of alternative inferences that the system can compute and consider in its generations** [...] To draw an analogy to humans, cognitive biases and irrational thinking may be based in artifacts of our culture as well as to limitations in our cognitive capabilities. **Pursuing better understandings of the sources and potential solutions to challenges of hallucination in GPT-4,***

will benefit from studies that compare several versions of the RL stage over the same architecture (Bubeck, et al., 2023 p. 94).

Here is a breakdown from the ambitious paper from *Sébastien Bubeck* and others. The paper discusses the challenges of distinguishing between limitations of GPT-4 that are due to the reinforcement learning step and limitations that are inherent in the larger architecture.

One example is the **hallucination problem**, where GPT-4 generates outputs that are not factual or accurate. The paper suggests that this problem may have multiple underlying causes, some of which could be mitigated by refining specific components of the architecture while others may require more fundamental changes. The paper compares this dilemma to cognitive biases and irrational thinking in humans. Some biases might be due to cultural influences or learned behavior, while others might be inherent limitations of our cognitive capabilities. Similarly, the researchers of GPT-4 need to identify the sources and potential solutions to the hallucination challenge by exploring various versions of the reinforcement learning stage while keeping the overall architecture constant.

Now, it is important to highlight the absence of long-term memory in the architecture of GPT-4. The researchers acknowledge that incorporating a vector representation of context along with the text tokens in both the input and output of the model could improve its performance by allowing it to better capture and utilize contextual information. It must be noted that the study of GPT-4 in the paper is **phenomenological**. This means that the paper primarily describes and explores the features and use cases of GPT-4 without necessarily delving into the underlying mechanisms in detail. As a result, the researchers might not have fully dissected the inner workings of the model, potentially leaving some unanswered questions about its functioning and performance. Hence, the whole debate about AGI is phenomenological. It is like looking up to the stars to figure out how the solar system works. This could truly be our *Aryabhatta / Copernicus* moment.

Nevertheless, this example of GPT-4 truly demonstrates that the narrative of AGI, it may not be consistently justified unless there are some tangible inventions, and discoveries that could lead us to that stage of achievements. Although, as early-stage AGI is being conceived, researched upon and tested, regulators and policymakers would have to stay updated to see how they can further regulate these test cases and use cases. *Figure 7.3* offers a timeline of Generative AI as a class of AI technologies.

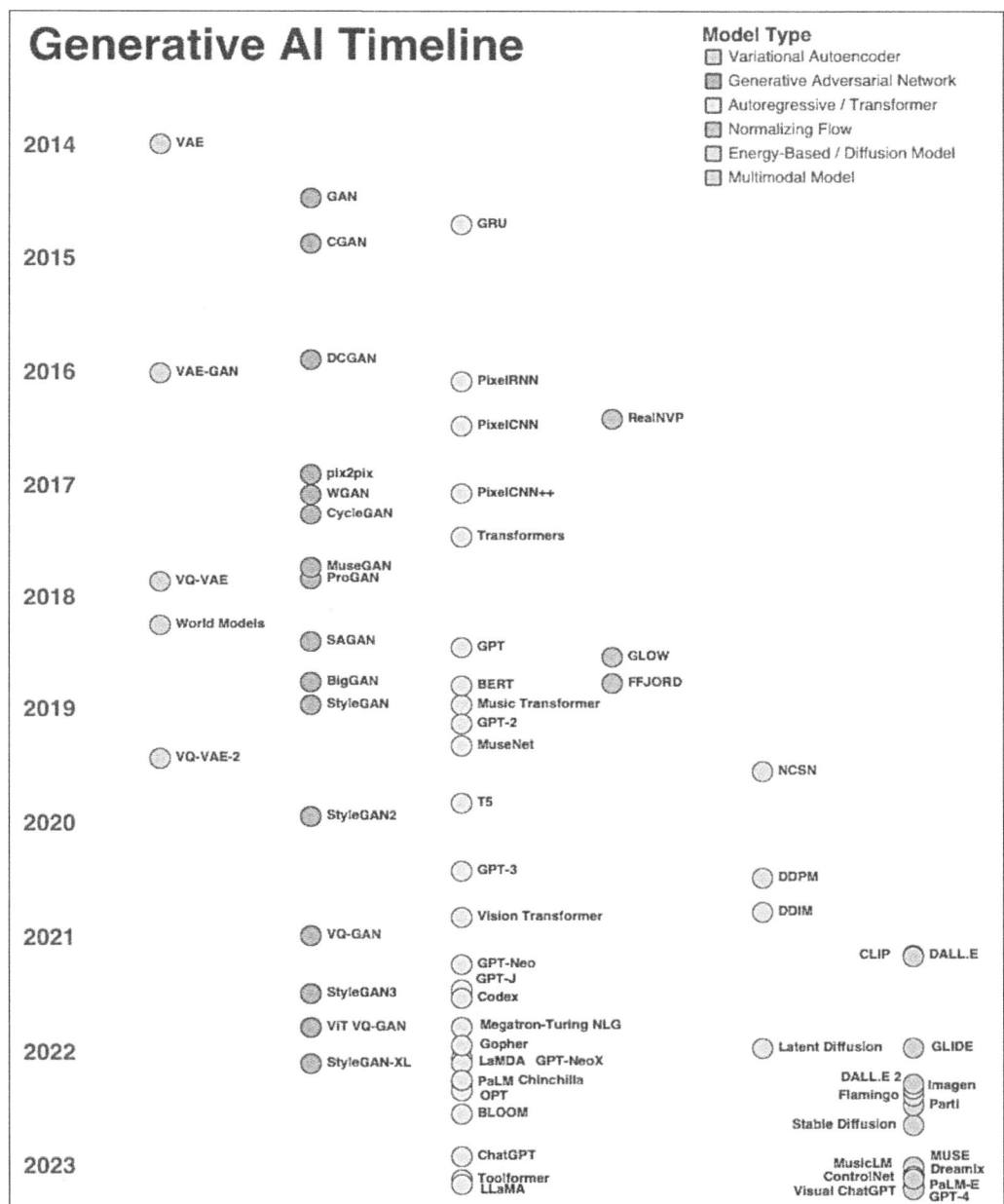

Figure 7.3: *A Graph depicting the timeline of Generative AI from 2014 to 2023 (Allena Venkata Sai Aby, 2023).*

Now, here is a much simpler and credible way to understand the difference between three aspects of artificial general intelligence for policymakers, and regulators, which is proposed. AGI can be **a narrative, a phase of technological evolution, or a policy problem.** Here is a tabular representation on understanding this:

Approaches to understand AGI	Meaning	Examples
AGI as a Narrative	A **sentient**, all-comprehensive, omnipotent, omnipresent piece of Artificial Intelligence, which is capable to act better or equivalent to human intelligence in both physical and digital worlds.	The book **Superintelligence** by *Nick Bostrom* explores the potential risks and benefits of AGI. The TV show *Black Mirror* often features episodes that deal with the dark side of AGI. *The Entity*, a heavily intelligent AGI-like program which was featured in *Mission Impossible: Dead Reckoning.*
AGI as a phase of technological evolution	An evolutionary achievement in the field of Artificial Intelligence and computer science. AGI is a future development in the progression of AI technologies. It is considered a significant leap beyond narrow AI, with the potential to revolutionize various industries and aspects of human life.	Current AI systems are task-specific, like image recognition or language translation. AGI would be a more generalized intelligence that can handle a wide range of tasks without specific programming. This evolution from narrow AI to AGI represents a transformative shift in AI development.
AGI as a policy problem	AGI development raises ethical, safety, and societal concerns. Policymakers and stakeholders need to establish guidelines and governance mechanisms to ensure safe and responsible integration into society.	Policymakers must consider regulations and safety standards for AGI systems to avoid potential risks such as autonomous weapons, privacy violations, or economic disruption due to job displacement. Policy discussions aim to address these challenges and foster the responsible development of AGI.

Table 7.1: *A Table* depicting *AGI as (1) a narrative,*
(2) a phase of technological evolution, or (3) a policy problem.

This table can easily be correlated with the CEI Classification Method of the Indian Society of Artificial Intelligence and Law. For example, AGI as a narrative could be related with the AI concept classification, while AGI as a policy problem could be related with the **AI as an Industry** classification. Furthermore, the best way to understand the consequential importance of AGI is about the limited role of ML and its socially curated encouragement; also, it includes how is it facilitated and led forward. Although, this certainly may raise concerns, it should not, unless one understands the positive role of the AI revolution and discern. *Dr Kailash Nadh*, CTO at *Zerodha* has put it in his recent **article** (Nadh, 2023) on Generative AI, quite beautifully:

> *While the fact is that LLMs are blackboxes with emergent behaviour that are still being studied, one need not get into unresolvable philosophical debates to see why the recent breakthroughs have significant ramifications for humanity and why they should be taken seriously. No doubt, the philosophical implications are significant and those debates are necessary (and amazing), but the immediate, practical risks perhaps should not be rooted in debating whether LLMs have a soul or not. [...] If a single dumb, stochastic, probabilistic, hallucinating, snake oil LLM with a chat UI offered by one organisation can have such a viral, organic, and widespread adoption—where large disparate populations, corporations, and governments are integrating it into their daily lives for use cases that they are discovering themselves—imagine what better, faster, more "intelligent" systems to follow in the wake of what exists today would be capable of doing. [...] Given the break-neck pace of daily developments, what awaits us? Imagine not just one organisation, but numerous powerful organisations and governments suddenly showing interest in, benefiting from, and pushing these breakthroughs ahead with full force.*

The primacy of data-carried creativity is business idea, for some of it is a political game, and for a few, means of livelihood, which is why as in the generic estimation, cyberspace is not as normal, and is not only about the course of cyber-attacks. The way the world has been materializing and targeting privatization as a means of propagating half-baked and unduly (and unusual) manifestations of human necessity or leisure or pleasure, we have failed many times in resolving the essence that must be either fixed or the contentious problems that have been aggregated by making bad decisions. These Language Model-based AI systems, or LLMs as they call them, are like black boxes with behaviors that emerge from their complex inner workings. Scientists are still figuring them out, but that should not be the main concern. What matters is that recent breakthroughs in LLMs have some serious implications for humanity, and one should take them seriously. In the next section of this chapter, I have discussed how digital colonialism shapes ethical Artificial Intelligence norms, and why countries including India must be wary of the same.

How Digital Colonialism shapes AI ethics norms

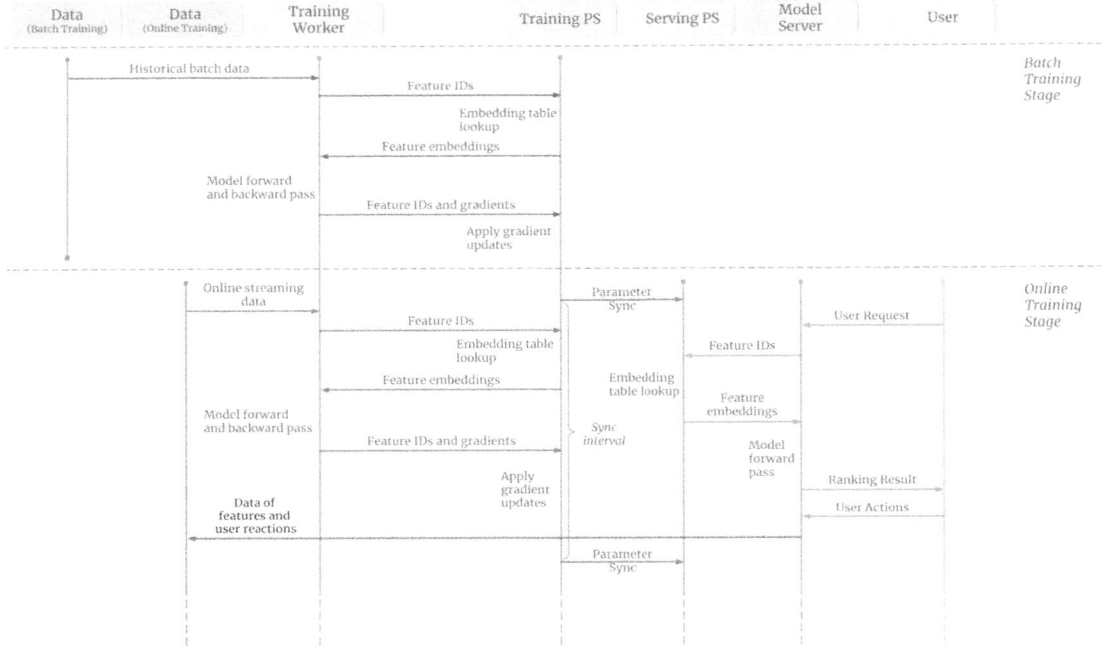

Figure 7.4: *The Online Training Architecture of Monolith, the recommendation algorithm of TikTok (Liu, et al., 2022).*

The way one perceives the very insight of digital colonialism is about a regime (sovereign) or corporate, leveraged by the sovereign, where data, as the new biggest resource of the world, is perceived in that sense of danger or awe living. This itself must be resembled by understanding the model of digital colonialism (Pinto, 2018; Levitin, 2016). The problems faced in the wake of digital colonialism are based on *data censorship, sovereignty, representative positioning,* and *existentialism.* The *Figure 7.4* depicts the online training architecture of Monolith, the recommendation algorithm of TikTok.

Let us take the example of *TikTok*. Now, when someone looks at India's position on blocking TikTok for the Indian citizens, the reasoning given by a section of commentators was that it was an act done merely due to the border clashes of June 2020. Nevertheless, there is more to this than meets the eye. Yes, the border clashes were taken as a matter of justification to ban Chinese apps including TikTok. However, the larger reasoning was that TikTok itself has been an invasive app, when it comes to its anti-privacy features. The recommendation algorithm of TikTok has been particularly **discriminatory and invasive** (Kamath, 2022). The recommendation algorithm by system which makes TikTok successful globally despite privacy and other issues, is known as *Monolith*. The diagram from an arXiv paper as shown in the figure above, describes the features of this recommendation algorithm (Liu, et al., 2022).

Now, this **global** version of TikTok, which was banned by India, UK, France, and other countries, is not even used in mainland China. Instead, Douyin, the Chinese edition of it is used. Quite surprisingly, the recommendation algorithms in Douyin and TikTok are not the same (Murphy, et al., 2023). They recommend different content and results – and even value systems by virtue of their content. That is emblematic of digital colonialism, considering the invasive nature of this app, when it comes to cybersecurity risks and the transboundary transfer of data without authorization or knowledge. For example, let us assume you have not created a TikTok account. Even then, the app is designed to collect data about you, when you access a TikTok video. This happens because when you access the content from Tiktok as a non-user, TikTok generates an anonymous data ID linking the specific video to information such as:

- Your device, its location, and your IP Address

- Your search history

- The new content you viewed after the initial one accessed by you

- The app you used right before you viewed TikTok content.

We can call it somewhat an anonymous shadow ID, which does the profiling of the things you have reacted to, despite not being a TikTok user at all. The recommendation algorithm treats you like a potential customer, to get in sync and find you, again (Eliaçık, 2022). This excerpt from an article by Technode clearly explains the difference in content segregation techniques between TikTok and Douyin:

> Bytedance's account segregation of TikTok and Douyin differs from the way that tech titan Tencent has constructed the domestic and international versions of its mega messaging app Weixin (known as WeChat abroad). Weixin and WeChat share the same account system and can communicate with each other. Of course, there are limits to the shared functionality. For example, international WeChat users cannot use the Wallet mobile payment function, and Chinese Weixin users don't have "WeChat Out," a VOIP service which allows users to call mobile phones and landlines around the world. [...] By comparison, TikTok and Douyin users exist in different worlds, meaning that content cannot be accessed across platforms. For example, one of TikTok's most popular accounts is Jacob Sartorius, an American singer who has 20.9 million followers on the platform. However, the "Jacob Sartorius" found on Douyin is an "unofficial" account with 36 followers (Technode Staff, 2019).

Interestingly, *Ursula von der Leyen*, the President of the European Commission has been concerned about the transboundary flow of EU citizens' data through TikTok to China. Here is an excerpt from her intriguing response to a MEP's letter on data concerns pertaining to TikTok:

Under the EU data protection rules, companies in the EU that transfer personal data to third countries have to comply with the requirements for international transfers under Chapter V of the General Data Protection Regulation (GDPR). This applies also to situations in which a company in the EU allows access to personal data under its control to an affiliated company (e.g. a parent company) that is located outside the EU. [...] The monitoring and enforcement of compliance with EU data protection rules by companies falls in principle within the competence of national authorities, in particular independent data protection authorities (DPAs) and courts. The data practices of TikTok, including with respect to international data transfers, are the object of several ongoing proceedings. This includes an investigation by the Irish DPA about TikTok's compliance with several GDPR requirements, including as regards data transfers to China and the processing of data of minors, and litigation before the Dutch courts (in particular concerning targeted advertising regarding minors and data transfers to China). (X, 2022).

In the case of TikTok, the European Union is showing valid concern for the company's data collection practices that could be used by the Chinese government to spy on its citizens. The EU is also concerned that TikTok's algorithms could be used to discriminate against users based on their race, gender, and other factors, which indeed is the case *(Mellor, 2020)*. The statement by the European Commission President is also a reminder of the importance of data sovereignty. Data sovereignty is the principle that countries should have control over their own data. In the context of digital colonialism, data sovereignty is essential to protecting the privacy and security of citizens. The United States of America, India, and Australia have all expressed similar concerns about the ways in which China is using its technology to exert control over other countries. *Anu Bradford* in her book on **The Brussels Effect**, has explained this trend succinctly.

While privacy regulations may differ from jurisdiction to jurisdiction, these digital companies streamline their global data management systems to reduce their compliance costs with multiple regulatory regimes. Instead of creating different programs for different markets, they tend to apply the most stringent standards across the board (Bradford, 2020 p. 143).

Now, it would be important to understand why and how digital colonialism shapes AI ethics norms. As far as Artificial Intelligence as an industry sector is concerned, **governments have been slow in shaping permanent or even specific regulations and norms** on regulating two things – **data and algorithm**. Yes, countries have come up with data protection laws. However, the data protection laws have not evolved enough. Nevertheless, on areas where data protection laws and regulations do not help enough, coming up with specific AI regulations would naturally address legal issues related to both data processed and algorithms put into use. Still, in a real sense, countries achieve domestic AI regulations which are consistent. It is these reasons why the market forces still have an edge over governments to influence AI ethics norms. Another reason that is important to understand is the **lack of industrially viable use cases**. In a report for VLiGTA *(Abhivardhan, et al., 2023)*, on Generative AI, I had addressed the issue of these use cases and test cases of several generative AI applications not being well-suited for consistent utilization in the market. Here is an excerpt from the report (**VLiGTA-TR-002**), referring to an example related to general intelligence applications:

> *Let us suppose a general intelligence application is capable to draft templates of commercial contracts of multiple kinds. However, at the same time, that application can provide some insights on a certain area of commerce or industry to a consumer. Let us also suppose that the consumer asks for the insights on something, related to which the same consumer requests to draft a commercial contract, as a standalone draft, or a template. In that case, the general intelligence application offers two kinds of services which are connected by virtue of the application's algorithmic infrastructure and training data. In such a case, either the company is aware of the use cases, or the use cases have just been created in due course of time, perhaps because general intelligence applications are bound to learn based on prompts and could create responses in that frame of learning (Abhivardhan, et al., 2023 p. 72).*

Now, let us now understand the know-hows of digital colonialism, beyond their know-whys. Digital colonialism is driven by multinational companies. However, it is these intrinsic standards and market practices, which are also driven by government inaction. *Figure 7.5* explains the drivers of digital colonialism – ideology, technology and economics, in the context of artificial general intelligence (and AI in general):

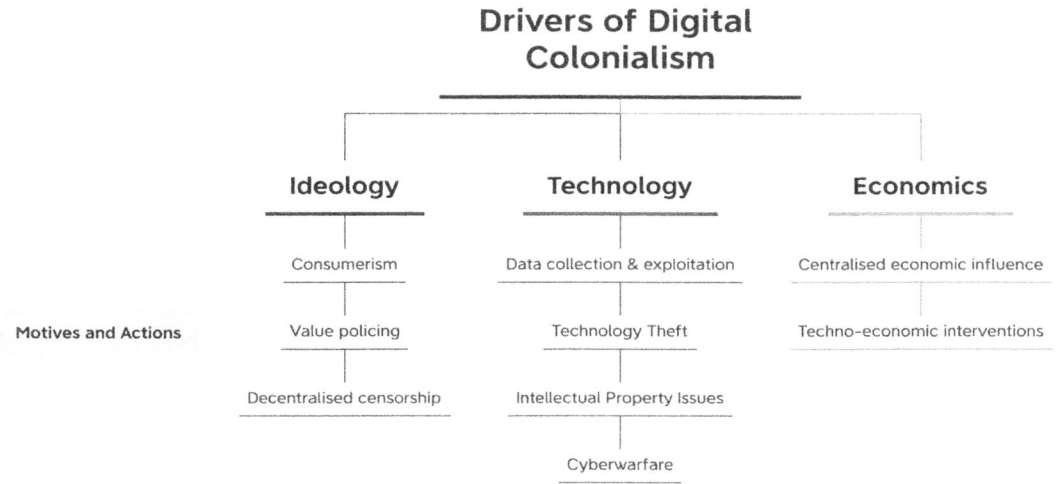

Figure 7.5: Drivers of digital colonialism, explained.

Here is a breakdown of the three drivers of digital colonialism:

Ideology

Ideological factors play a role in shaping the development and deployment of AI. Some entities or nations may seek to promote and impose their ideological values and beliefs through AI technologies, potentially leading to a lack of diversity in AI perspectives. The key ideologies that shape digital colonialism are described as follows:

- **Consumerism**: AI development can be driven by consumer demands and preferences. Entities may prioritize creating AI applications and systems that cater to consumer needs, potentially limiting the exploration of other AGI use cases that may benefit society.

- **Value policing**: Entities may impose their cultural, political, or moral values onto AI technologies, leading to biased or limited AI capabilities and restricting access to AI knowledge and resources.

- **Decentralised censorship**: Decentralized censorship refers to the situation where multiple entities or actors, acting independently or collaboratively, exercise control over the dissemination and accessibility of AI-generated content. These entities may impose restrictions or filter out certain ideas, perspectives, or information within the AI-generated content. As a result, the diversity of viewpoints and information flow within the AI ecosystem becomes constrained, potentially leading to a homogenized AI landscape dominated by specific ideological preferences or interests. This form of censorship can significantly impact the democratic exchange of ideas and equitable access to information within the AI environment.

Technology

These are some of the most common and direct means and examples of digital colonialism, when it comes to technology as a driver:

- **Data collection and exploitation**: AI requires vast amounts of data for training and learning. Entities with access to large and diverse datasets may have a competitive advantage in developing more robust and capable AI systems.

- **Technology theft**: Some entities may engage in unethical practices, such as stealing AI technology or intellectual property from others, to gain a competitive edge in the AI race.

- **Intellectual property issues**: Legal battles over AI-related intellectual property rights may hinder the open collaboration and sharing of knowledge needed for responsible AI development. This has already happened with Artificial Intelligence use cases and the legal dilemmas related to their proprietary information, for example.

- **Cyberwarfare**: In the pursuit of AI supremacy, entities might resort to cyberwarfare tactics to disrupt or sabotage the progress of rival AI initiatives.

Economics

The economics of digital colonialism is derived from capitalism. However, it is neo-feudalist. This can be explained with an excerpt from **ISAIL-TR-001**, a technical report on India's technology governance avenues:

> *Neofeudalism marks the birth of this new world order which is governed by multinational technology and finance giants. [...] Such an environment has been the result of mass accumulation of wealth by organisations and then these organisations working in cahoots with the governments of the nation states where they have a market, using every politico-legal instrument to exercise control over the society which they have created. Such influence upon the world is only possible when the wealth which they have accumulated is situated beyond the reach of the governments in whose jurisdictions they are working (Abhivardhan, et al., 2022).*

Now, in my view, there are 2 kinds of economic drivers of digital colonialism, which can be taken into close consideration:

- **Centralised economic influence**: Entities with significant economic power may use their resources to influence the AI landscape. They may invest heavily in AI research, infrastructure, and talent, leading to centralization of AI development efforts.

- **Techno-economic interventions**: Economic factors can shape AI research and development priorities. Entities may focus on AI applications that have the potential for immediate economic gain, potentially neglecting other vital areas of AI research.

This explains somehow that the phenomenon of digital colonialism, for its existence, could sabotage the evolution of the digital world. Stakeholders across the world, should not be sabotaged by major powers and their interest groups and let themselves be stuck due to regulatory subterfuge caused by multinational companies and the lack of regulatory capacity. This is why India and many other countries are taking substantive steps to identify data-driven and algorithms-driven colonialism, to nip the problem in the bud. Although, this is not easily achievable as addressing digital colonialism and digital coloniality is a process-based issue and a phenomenological issue at the same time. When something is phenomenological, its unique weaknesses and limitations take time to be deciphered in its entirety. Plus, a regulator must act in good conscience so that their actions do not affect global and national economies in a negatively disruptive fashion.

Regulatory subterfuge is not just caused due to a lack of regulation or lack of regulatory capacity. It may also happen by implementing laws and statutory measures, which causes extreme policy inconsistencies and risks. That may not lead to a constitutional crisis, but could create economic uncertainty for businesses and third-party players. The vulnerability of a national economy could then be further understood by multinational players to act in a neo-feudal fashion. Hence, adopting an informed and specific approach could be helpful to combat the phenomenon and process-based dilemma of digital colonialism.

In the next sections of this chapter, I have taken two important examples related to AI-driven digital colonialism – Responsible AI ethics and Artificial Intelligence hype in competition law, to further my analysis on digital colonialism and explore certain specific perspectives.

Limits of Responsible AI

As I had discussed in the previous chapters – scientists, developers, and engineers in the AI industry, were becoming concerned of the computational potential of Artificial Intelligence systems. This then became a mainstream narrative in many countries including India and the United States that the risk posed by the potential use cases of Artificial Intelligence requires scrutiny, and one must as a part of the global commons, develop some principles of ethics of Artificial Intelligence, which share the responsibility. That is how the idea of Responsible AI became truly mainstream. Often, the **2017 Asilomar Conference** is considered a turning point in the history of artificial intelligence, which is discussed in the previous chapters. However, there is no doubt that there was a necessity to develop the ethical principles related to Responsible AI. As scientific innovations are achieved, the uncertain tendencies of AI technologies to disrupt any apparatus of impact or effect must be scrutinized. This obviously helps the industrial and scientific communities to act upon and find the potential risks in the mere R&D process.

Now, here is a story: in 2017, the international media had reported (Kucera, 2017) that **Facebook AI Research** (under Meta), had to shut down two AI systems (Lewis, et al., 2017), which were being trained to negotiate amongst each other since they had started speaking in a newly created language other than English. That was not the case. The research went well, and Meta had succeeded in analyzing how these two chatbots could participate in dialogue and negotiation, which still inspires Artificial Intelligence researchers to this day, especially in the field of reinforcement learning. The *Figure 7.6* depicts the dialogue rollouts of the chatbots developed by the Engineering team at Meta (formerly known as Facebook AI Research).

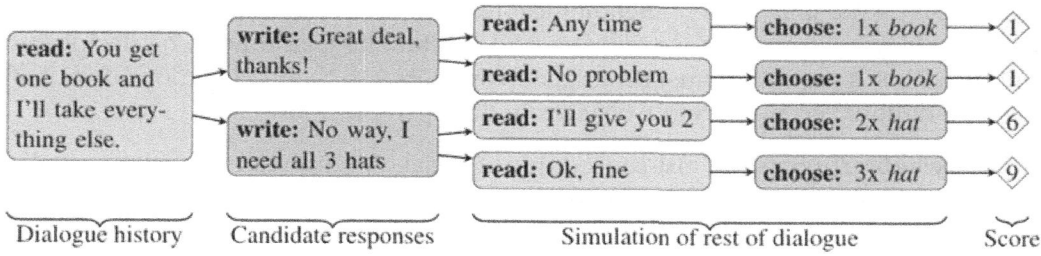

Figure 7.6: Diagram representing a sample dialog evaluation as per the research efforts by Facebook AI Research in 2017 (Lewis, et al., 2017).

Interestingly, the Facebook AI negotiation experiment was undertaken with the purpose of creating a proficient negotiating robot. The success of the experiment lies in the robots' ability to effectively allocate books, hats, and balls in a manner that optimized their individual gains. However, it is imperative to note that the robots' comprehension of English was absent during this process. Instead, they relied on assembling words and phrases that had previously proven effective in negotiations. Consequently, the language employed by the robots underwent a degradation over time. The *Figure 7.7* depicts an excerpt of the communication between two negotiating chatbots of Facebook AI Research:

```
Alice : book=(count:3 value:1) hat=(count:2 value:1) ball=(count:1 value:5)
Bob   : book=(count:3 value:0) hat=(count:2 value:0) ball=(count:1 value:10)
----------------------------------------------------------------------------
Bob   : i can i i everything else . . . . . . . . . . . . . .
Alice : balls have zero to me to me to me to me to me to me to me to me to
Bob   : you i everything else . . . . . . . . . . . . .
Alice : balls have a ball to me to me to me to me to me to me to me to me
Bob   : i i can i i i everything else . . . . . . . . . . .
Alice : balls have a ball to me to me to me to me to me to me to me to me
Bob   : i . . . . . . . . . . . . . . . . . .
Alice : balls have zero to me to me to me to me to me to me to me to me to
Bob   : you i i i i i everything else . . . . . . . . . .
Alice : balls have 0 to me to me to me to me to me to me to me to me to
Bob   : you i i i everything else . . . . . . . . . . . .
Alice : balls have zero to me to me to me to me to me to me to me to me to
```

Figure 7.7: An excerpt of the communication between two negotiating chatbots under research by Facebook AI Research. This shows they have developed using a degenerative form of English (Kucera, 2017).

It is crucial to understand by virtue of clarification that this is not an entirely novel, efficient language exclusive to AI comprehension. Rather, it is a degenerate manifestation of English brought forth through reinforcement learning (look at *Figure 7.8*). Had the experiment incorporated a language assessment as part of the scoring function, the extent of language degeneration among the robots could have been mitigated. Regrettably, the engineers responsible for the experiment did not anticipate this outcome, and they discontinued the simulation once the language reached a significantly degenerate state. Still, the Facebook AI negotiation experiment yielded successful results, as the robots demonstrated effective negotiation abilities despite their lack of genuine English comprehension. Nevertheless, the experiment also unveiled the potential for reinforcement learning to give rise to deteriorated language structures.

Nevertheless, this incident shows how in the name of promoting informed discourse on ethical use of AI, some journalists botched up information related to a simple experiment. The same happens with the discourse around *ChatGPT* and other AI tools. For example, many or most influencers had claimed that *GPT-4* will take us to achieve AGI very soon. It is discussed that it could not be possible and how even experts promote the hype on

AGI. Similarly, it was conceived that *GPT-4* is extremely capable to detect malware due to its computational capabilities (Harnik, 2023). However, even on cybersecurity, *GPT-4* has a long way to go. Here is an excerpt from a reasonable take on the capabilities of LLMs to classify malware risks by *Tim Keary*:

> *Likewise, open-source governance provider Endor Labs has released research indicating that LLMs can only accurately classify malware risk in just 5% of all cases. Of course, it's also impossible to overlook the tendency that LLMs have to hallucinate, invent facts, and state them to users as if they were correct. Many of these issues stem from the fact that LLMs don't think but process user queries, leverage training data to infer context, and then predict a text output. This means it can predict both right and wrong answers (not to mention that bias or inaccuracies in the dataset can carry over into responses) (Keary, 2023).*

All these trends explain why Responsible AI has failed at the level of industry groupthink, and not research groupthink. As of 2023, it is safe to assert that AI researchers, who are contributing successful AI test cases, are quite wary and alert about its impending risks. The scientific aspect of Responsible AI is indeed a work in progress.

Now, let us understand what is happening in the law and policy space related to Responsible AI. *Husanjot Chahal*, who is a Geopolitics and AI Policy Researcher at **OpenAI**, has put it quite succinctly in **Digital Debates (2022)**, a publication by the Observer Research Foundation, on the three points of divergence on Responsible AI – **Interpretation, Attribution** and **Implementation**. Here is an excerpt from her research:

> *There are significant differences in how the same principles are interpreted across various guideline documents and the requirements considered important for their realisation. [...] There are also divergences in attribution—interpreting which domain, actor, or issue these ethical principles pertain to. [...] Finally, there are differing opinions on how ethical AI principles should be implemented—through government organisations, inter-governmental organisations, industry leaders, individual users or developers, or by harmonising AI agendas across the board. If harmonisation is a goal, then how does one account for moral pluralism and cultural diversity across countries, considering that AI is a general-purpose technology operating in varied contexts and cultures? (Chahal, 2022 p. 60)*

In this research, *Chahal* has emphasized that the issue with implementing AI ethics principles, is related to the kind of significant differences in interpreting those principles. She did give a lucid example of algorithmic bias, where in order to reduce the bias of AI systems, you would have to ignore the role of consumer autonomy or the autonomy of data subjects having greater control and privacy over their prompts or inputs to the AI systems. This also affects the nature of consent in data protection law, quite adversely. Now, there is a phenomenon and practice called *machine unlearning*. Let us say you try to make an AI system unlearn what it has acquired through its machine learning techniques and infrastructure per se, it would incur huge costs, and would be hard to achieve. Imagine the nightmare an AI company would have in ensuring the ethical use of AI. Therefore, it is necessary that when Responsible AI principles are developed, they are grounded. It should also be understood that achieving better regulation and **'ethicization'** of Artificial Intelligence tools, must be driven by realism and market integrity. This is where the regulators would then not have to wield too much out of their regulatory capacity to mitigate the risks of using AI tools across industries and sectors.

Artificial Intelligence Hype in Competition Law

Now, let us get specific on the nature of Artificial Intelligence Hype, and how it functions in the post-Covid times. In the case of Artificial Intelligence, it is rather interesting to measure or locate or estimate as to how Artificial Intelligence applications could be involved in the overarching hype cycle or bubble. One may suppose that the hype could be built because one may be marketing the features of their product or service, which includes Artificial Intelligence itself as a piece of technology, in full, in parts or otherwise. Another way to look at a hype cycle could be if one has used Artificial Intelligence technology as a means of marketing, maintenance, feedback, or any other measure, related to any product or service. To some extent, even that could be constituted as Artificial Intelligence hype, simply because the use of AI technology has some impact. For example, there is no doubt that the generative AI applications subject to mainstream use these days including Midjourney, ChatGPT and Bard, are AI applications, which generate some hype because of their AI-enabled use cases. It would naturally fascinate anyone to make the best use of these applications wherever possible. However, does it mean that the use cases would survive or make sense? Honestly, this is kind of relatable to the days when automated emails were introduced to the market, which also led to automated email wars. Now, it may seem rhetorical, but automated emails, as a technological contribution led to the rise of companies like *Mailchimp* and many more. Nevertheless, while the 'email wars' had some rules and limitations, AI-enabled use cases, in most instances, especially in the **B2C (Business to Customer)** segment – seems to not have well-defined rules, which does not even touch the tip of the iceberg of ethical and responsible AI. This is why it could be possible that the use cases developed could not last for more than **6 to 12 months**, due to their unviability in the market, data and algorithmic bias issues and other concerns. To make the trajectory of Artificial Intelligence hype clear and understandable, I had worked on a technical report (**VLiGTA-TR-001**) with colleagues at VLiGTA (*Abhivardhan, et al., 2022*), in which I had proposed that there could be working conditions, to determine how Artificial Intelligence hype is created. Here is a breakdown of the seven working conditions, divided into 5 stages. The relevant excerpts from the technical report are provided in the breakdown of all the 5 stages:

- **Stage 1: Influence or generation determination**

- **Stage 2: Influencing or generating market perceptions and conditions**

- **Stage 3: Uninformed or disinformed markets**

- **Stage 4: Misdirected perceptions in the information and digital economy**

- **Stage 5: Estimation of the Hype Cycle through risk determination**

Stage 1: Influence or generation determination

> *An Artificial Intelligence hype cycle is perpetuated to influence or generate market perception in a real-time scenario such that a class of Artificial Intelligence technology as a product / service is used in a participatory or preparatory sense to influence or generate the hype cycle (Abhivardhan, et al., 2022).*

As discussed before, the purpose of any hype cycle is to influence or generate some sort of market perception. It would apply even in the case of any Artificial Intelligence technology as a product or a service. Now, the role itself matters, which is why it is necessary to estimate if the AI technology has been used in a participatory or preparatory sense. If the approach is participatory, it also means that the technology is directly or certainly involved in the process. If the approach remains preparatory, then it remains hard to analyze because the role of the AI technology itself could not be that direct or certain. Also, preparation as a means of involvement, could also mean the use cases of the AI product or service are not properly revealed. Sometimes, initiatives which are open source or led by companies, require some cleavage and flexibility to test their proposed use cases, or test cases. Even if that generates some hype, unintentionally, or otherwise, it does not mean it would have a market impact. Still, there could be a possibility that existing market players could feel some disruption in the economy, at least from a choice perspective.

Stage 2: Influencing or generating market perceptions and conditions

> *The hype cycle may be continuous or erratic, but the real-time impact on market perceptions which affect the market of the product / services involving Artificial Intelligence technologies, as estimated from a standardized / regulatory / judicial / statutory point of view.*

> *The hype cycle may directly or indirectly perpetuate the course of specific anti-competitive practices (Abhivardhan, et al., 2022).*

Beyond the real-time impact on market perceptions, the consecutive effects of the real-time impact may distort a limited set of related markets, provided that the specific anti-competitive practices are furthered in a distinct pattern. Once it is determined that Artificial Intelligence technology as a product or a service is involved by virtue of participation (certainty) or preparation (indication or partial representation), the next step would be examining the way the entity behind the product or service, is generating market perceptions and shaping market conditions. This by itself is hard to assimilate and make it as precise as possible, because market players could try to exploit as many loopholes as possible in the regulations and systems involved in upholding market integrity.

Stage 3: Uninformed or disinformed markets

The features of the product / service subject to hype cycle are uninformed / disinformed to the market. It may be stated that misinforming the market may be construed as keeping the market just uninformed, except not in mutually exclusive cases (Abhivardhan, et al., 2022).

At this stage, one can concur that spreading hype about the AI (or AI-based) product or service causes serious cycles of misinformation or disinformation to the consumers or clients. Sometimes, even governments as clients could be lured to try certain kinds of AI products, with so-called **results** or **features**. However, as per Stage 2, it is important to take note that trends must be specific. Let us take a simple example to understand this.

Let us suppose a technology company decides to promote an AI-based product. Now, they may opt for multiple ways to market their product. However, there are certain crucial steps, which explains how they are adapting to various market practices. These steps also explain how they are promoting their product and offering it to customers or clients. Now, you can see market practices which may reflect hype in different ways. For example, the company may promise something entirely inflated and psyched in their promotional materials, communication channels and landing pages related to a product. The representation of the product does not depict the actual features of the product when found out after its purchase. Or the company could explain the featurettes and try to oversell the product and its add-ons, in a way, which lures consumers further in a persuasive fashion. Even then, while certain tactics are normal to do, provided they are not exploitative – some of them as I described could be related to a larger pattern of spreading hype. Still, there should be a pattern, because the verifiability of market practices being manipulative is examined in collective considerations. There will be individual and specific examples too which could turn out to be anti-competitive or problematic at lesser extents. Yet, it would depend on if they are exceptional or generally applicative. Now, once this is understood, the next question is whether sharing features implies misinforming or disinforming the market. Here is a table, which explains the difference:

Term	Definition	Intent
Misinformation	False or inaccurate information that is shared without the intent to deceive.	Accidental or mistaken.
Disinformation	False or inaccurate information that is shared with the intent to deceive.	Deliberate.
Uninformed	A state of being without knowledge or information about a particular topic.	Lack of education, access to information, or interest.

Table 7.2: The table depicts key differences between misinformation, disinformation and the state of being uninformed.

As you can look at this table, it is clearly discernible, that practicing the act of misinformation differs from both keeping the audience uninformed, and disinformed. The implications may converge but the methods are way distinctive with their own patterns. When misinformation is the cause of the hype cycle, the market could not be aware of certain information or insight, which they ought to know. In the working conditions, it had been proposed quite clearly to the VLiGTA team that it is better to keep *misinformation* and the *state of being uninformed* in one basket, only in **mutually inclusive cases**. If there is a clear distinction that the pattern of communication, production, distribution, consumer experience and marketing (for example), that the makers had no intent of keeping certain insights deliberately unknown, then misinformation and the state of being uninformed could be mutually exclusive cases. However, it would depend on whether that information or insight should have been disclosed or not. This could apply in so many examples of malpractices under digital consumer law, where consumers and clients could be fooled at any stage, from consumer reviews, and product features listing to mere checkout pages with hyped discount offers. If one takes disinformation as the cause or medium of the hype cycle, the pattern of actions must prove that the makers had a deliberate intent of misleading their clients or consumers. Still, the makers could come up with justifications, where they may claim that certain **trends** are an outcome of the market realities. Still, a strong case could be built for their actions. Now, as you can discern, it is however complicated to examine how Artificial Intelligence hype may lead to the market being subject to misinformation / the state of being uninformed, disinformation or nothing. In addition, it could be safely stated that the working conditions up to Stage 3, can be easily applied or used to study and examine Artificial Intelligence hype.

Stage 4: Misdirected perceptions in the information and digital economy

> *The hype cycle may be used to distract the information economy by converting the state of being uninformed or disinformed into misdirected perception. This means that the hype cycle about a product or service may not clarify certain specifics and may cause the public or market players to distract their focus towards ancillary considerations, to comfortably ignore the fact that they have being uninformed or disinformed (Abhivardhan, et al., 2022).*

In Stage 4, once it is understood that the market has been distracted by keeping them uninformed or disinformed, one can know that the hype cycle has already transformed quite well. At this stage, the state of distraction can be effectively used to shape the hype and create some misdirected perception. Now, a misdirected perception, is nothing but another layer of perception that consumers and clients may have. Also, it could be reasonable to claim that there could be so many layers of perception, which build with time. However, as stated, to examine if Artificial Intelligence hype is a possibility, it is important to understand the steps taken by the makers or some other stakeholder or player to exacerbate the hype. A misdirected perception thus is a unique state of perception, which is driven by efforts to constantly exacerbate the market about the particular AI product or service, in a way that people get more invested in ancillary things, such as attractiveness of any **feature**, any media gossip, any sale offer, any PR-engineered controversy, or any rumor. It could be anything else as well. For example, let us say a government comes to know that the companies who have built their AI products or services are spreading hype, then it could not be denied that misdirected perceptions could alert the public servants to implement a short-term measure. It could be a hastily conducted high-level committee meeting, with unclear policy agendas, or the regulatory authority coming up with some self-regulatory guidelines, which are half-baked in its implementation. In that case, even the government could be a victim of Artificial Intelligence hype. However, it is also important to note that this stage and condition of AI hype, is an optional condition. It means that even if one ignores Stages 4 and 5, it is still possible to estimate AI hype at nominal levels. Nevertheless, I had proposed these stages to improve legal discourse on AI and competition policies, in the context of the digital economy.

Stage 5: Estimation of the Hype Cycle through risk determination

In addition, even if preliminary clarifications or assessments are provided to the market, the lack of due diligence in determining the inexplicable features of the Artificial Intelligence technology in any form or means as a part of the product or service involves the assessment of the hype cycle with a risk-centric approach (Abhivardhan, et al., 2022).

Like Stage 4, this stage and its condition underlined are optional. It may not be necessary that regulators would have to come at this stage of AI hype and address risks. Yet, it is impossible to ignore the possibility of that to happen, especially in the case of high-risk AI systems. At this stage, when the damage due to overhyping is done, the companies and developers should be required to offer preliminary clarifications or assessments. In addition, their lack of due diligence could be questioned since they could not determine the inexplicable features of the product or service, containing AI technology, in any form. However, it would still be a regulatory dilemma for governments around the world, due to either lack of administrative, judicial and policy precedents. This is why even this stage, and its condition is an optional one, in terms of determining Artificial Intelligence hype.

Conclusion

To conclude, Artificial Intelligence hype is an emerging phenomenon, of utmost importance, at least in the sense of how digital and information economies are growing. It is important to realize why the hype cycles generated could be problematic and require subtle and careful intervention. The inclusion of Artificial Intelligence is promising, and there are a lot of such products and solutions which need some incubation or testing time, say 6 to 12 months. Since investments are huge, the strategic purpose of research and development in AI tools is also necessary to be achieved. This is why regulatory solutions should not focus on restricting AI innovations but making fair and reasonable standards to enable its research ecosystems while creating and helping businesses.

This final chapter is an ode to this book, and the efforts involved in making this book all-comprehensive. I have also offered a set of potential recommendations on the regulatory landscape of artificial intelligence technologies in India, with a *soft law* approach.

References

- **European Union. 2023.** ANNEXES to the Proposal for a Regulation of the European Parliament and of the Council LAYING DOWN HARMONISED RULES ON ARTIFICIAL INTELLIGENCE (ARTIFICIAL INTELLIGENCE ACT) AND AMENDING CERTAIN UNION LEGISLATIVE ACTS . s.l. : European Union, 2023.

- **Abhivardhan, et al., [ed.]. 2022.** 2020 Handbook on AI and International Law. s.l. : Indic Pacific Legal Research LLP, 2022.

- **Brownsword, Roger. 2021.** Law 3.0: Rules, Regulation, and Technology . s.l. : Routledge, 2021.

- **Saran, Samir and Mattoo, Shashank. 2022.** Big Tech vs. Red Tech: The Diminishing of Democracy in the Digital Age . Observer Research Foundation. [Online] February 15, 2022. **https://www.orfonline.org/research/big-tech-vs-red-tech/.**

- **Mattoo, Shashank. 2022.** Back Our sense of technology in the past has been very narrow: Jaishankar . LiveMint. [Online] November 29, 2022. **https://www.livemint.com/news/india/our-sense-of-technology-in-the-past-has-been-very-narrow-jaishankar-11669710368910.html.**

- **Srinivasan, Balaji. 2022.** A Bipolar America and a Tripolar Triangle . The Network State. [Online] 2022. **https://thenetworkstate.com/a-bipolar-america-and-a-tripolar-triangle.**

- **Roser, Max. 2023.** AI timelines: What do experts in artificial intelligence expect for the future? . Our World in Data. [Online] February 7, 2023. **https://ourworldindata.org/ai-timelines.**

- **Sala, Maris. 2023.** Conjecture internal survey: AGI timelines and probability of human extinction from advanced AI. LessWrong. [Online] May 22, 2023. **https://www.lesswrong.com/posts/kygEPBDrGGoM8rz9a/conjecture-internal-survey-agi-timelines-and-probability-of.**

- **PayTM. 2023.** X. X. [Online] May 7, 2023. **https://twitter.com/Paytm/status/1655093271004336129?ref_src=twsrc%5Etfw%7Ctwcamp%5Etweetem-**

bed%7Ctwterm%5E1655450165799526401%7Ctwgr%5E83e8b48610108ae-bad186876a0a66077725fbabb%7Ctwcon%5Es3_&ref_url=https%3A%2F%-2Fyourstory.com%2F2023%2F05%2Fpaytm-agi-first.

• **Bubeck, Sébastien, et al. 2023.** Sparks of Artificial General Intelligence: Early experiments with GPT-4 . arXiv. [Online] March 22, 2023. **https://arxiv.org/abs/2303.12712.**

• **Allena Venkata Sai Aby. 2023.** UPDATED - The Generative AI Timeline. Kaggle. [Online] 2023. **https://www.kaggle.com/discussions/getting-started/397345.**

• **Nadh, Kailash. 2023.** This time, it feels different. Kailash Nadh, Blog. [Online] May 13, 2023.

• **Pinto, Renata Avila. 2018.** Defining the problem: digital colonialism and technological feuds. THE SUR FILE ON INTERNET AND DEMOCRACY. [Online] July 2018. **https://sur.conectas.org/en/digital-sovereignty-or-digital-colonialism/.**

• **Levitin, Daniel. 2016.** How Multitasking Depletes Your Brain's Resources — And How to Restore Concentration. Big Think. [Online] May 6, 2016. **https://bigthink.com/videos/daniel-levitin-on-multitasking-and-brain-evolution.**

• **Liu, Zhuoran, et al. 2022.** Monolith: Real Time Recommendation System With Collisionless Embedding Table. arXiv. [Online] September 27, 2022. **https://arxiv.org/pdf/2209.07663.pdf.**

• **Kamath, Bhuvana. 2022.** TikTok Parent ByteDance Reveals its SOTA Recommendation Engine . Analytics India Magazine. [Online] November 8, 2022. **https://analyticsindiamag.com/tiktok-parent-bytedance-reveals-its-sota-recommendation-engine/.**

• **Murphy, Hannah, Criddle, Christina and McMorrow, Ryan. 2023.** TikTok caught in US-China battle over its powerful algorithm. Financial Times. [Online] March 22, 2023. **https://www.ft.com/content/b9f3b5a8-19ae-407f-be4b-e2536617b0f8.**

• **Eliaçık, Eray. 2022.** EU probes TikTok's data practices with multiple investigations . Dataconomy. [Online] November 23, 2022. **https://dataconomy.com/2022/11/23/tiktok-data-practices-under-investigation/.**

• **Technode Staff. 2019.** How different are China's Douyin and global TikTok? Technode. [Online] August 28, 2019. **https://technode.com/2019/08/28/how-different-are-chinas-douyin-and-global-tiktok/.**

• **X. 2022.** Brendan Carr. X. [Online] November 22, 2022. **https://twitter.com/BrendanCarrFCC/status/1595057701695922176?ref_src=twsrc%5Etf-w%7Ctwcamp%5Etweetembed%7Ctwterm%5E1595057701695922176%7Ctwgr%5E1ef3d783db296302fd6890bf037f26262f710bdf%7Ctwcon%5Es1_&ref_url=https%3A%2F%2Fdataconomy.com%2F2022%2F11%2F23%2F.**

- **Mellor, Maria. 2020.** Why is TikTok creating filter bubbles based on your race? Wired. [Online] February 20, 2020. **https://www.wired.co.uk/article/tiktok-filter-bubbles.**

- **Bradford, Anu. 2020.** The Brussels Effect: How the European Union Rules the World. s.l. : Oxford University Press, 2020.

- **Abhivardhan, Naresh, Kapil and Bansal, Yashudev. 2023.** Deciphering Regulative Methods for Generative AI [VLiGTA-TR-002]. s.l. : Indic Pacific Legal Research LLP, 2023. 978-81-959932-0-8.

- **Abhivardhan, et al. 2022.** Regulatory Sovereignty in India: Indigenizing Competition-Technology Approaches, ISAIL-TR-001. s.l. : Indic Pacific Legal Research LLP, 2022. 978-81-957087-8-9.

- **Kucera, Roman. 2017.** The truth behind Facebook AI inventing a new language. Towards Data Science, Medium. [Online] August 7, 2017. **https://towardsdatascience.com/the-truth-behind-facebook-ai-inventing-a-new-language-37c5d680e5a7.**

- **Lewis, Mike, et al. 2017.** Deal or no deal? Training AI bots to negotiate. Engineering at Meta. [Online] June 14, 2017. **https://engineering.fb.com/2017/06/14/ml-applications/deal-or-no-deal-training-ai-bots-to-negotiate/.**

- **Harnik, Ron. 2023.** Endor Labs' 'State of Dependency Management 2023' Report Offers Insight on Explosive Popularity of AI and LLMs—and How They Impact Application Security . Endor Labs. [Online] July 20, 2023. **https://www.endorlabs.com/blog/endor-labs-state-of-dependency-management-2023.**

- **Keary, Tim. 2023.** Is GPT-4 a Flop? Taking a Closer Look at Performance Challenges and Realities . Techopedia. [Online] July 28, 2023. **https://www.techopedia.com/is-gpt-4-a-flop.**

- **Chahal, Husanjot. 2022.** Ethics of AI: Principles, Rules and the Way Forward. Digital Debates: CyFy Journal 2022. New Delhi : Observer Research Foundation & Global Policy Journal, 2022.

- **Abhivardhan, Sekhar, Bhavana J and Chatterjee, Poulomi. 2022.** Deciphering Artificial Intelligence Hype and its Legal-Economic Risks, VLiGTA-TR-001. s.l. : Indic Pacific Legal Research LLP, 2022.

CHAPTER 8
Self-Regulating the Future of AI

यथा सूर्योऽपराजितो दिवाकरेण,
स्वयं प्रकाशेन नियोजयत्यहो।
तथैव बुद्धिः स्वयमुद्यमेन,
स्वराष्ट्रे नियुञ्जति यत्र वाहनम्॥

Just as the undefeated sun sets its course by its own radiance,

Similarly, the intellect guides itself with its inherent vigor,

Where self-regulation steers the vehicle of progress."

Welcome to the concluding chapter of this book. Unlike other chapters, which would usually encompass existing ideas and issues, this chapter is an affront to encourage a discourse on newer topics related to Artificial Intelligence ethics and International Law. This chapter begins with the issue of derivable products and services created through generative AI tools and models and elaborates on the necessity and know-how of developing responsible and economic innovations in the field of AI, with a law and policy perspective. This chapter concludes with an insight into India's role in shaping global technology norms, and its soft law recommendations on the future of AI.

Generative AI and Derivation of AI-based products and services

As of the mid-2020s, owing to the advances in the transformer models developed to harness the potential of large language models, generative AI applications have risen exponentially worldwide. The most notable achievement in the newly developed industry of generative AI, beyond deep fakes, and invasive content, is the rise of text-generative AI applications like ChatGPT, Bard, and many more. Frankly, they are some of the most frugal AI innovations and have enough computational capacity to perform simple tasks. *Table 8.1* is a snippet depicting the investment trends in the Generative AI industry, based on data offered by *Dealroom* (Dealroom, 2023):

Area of Investment	Combined funding
Audio: Music Generation	43 million USD
Audio: Speech Generation	195 million USD
LLM tools: deploy, optimize, and monitor	12 million USD
LLM tools: FM programming networks	10 million USD
Text: customer relations and other assistants	183 million USD
Code: Dev Apps	23 million USD
B2B generative AI integration	27 million USD
Text: copy and writing	386 million USD
Verticalised AI studios	3.1 million USD
LLM tools: fine-tuning	56 million USD
Gaming: Characters and NPCs	318 million USD
Gaming & Design: 3D Assets and Worlds	52 million USD
Synthetic data	251 million USD
LLM tools: Prompt Engineering and Management	2.9 million USD
General Intelligence/model makers	13.1 billion USD
Code generation	610 million USD

Area of Investment	Combined funding
Chat	14 million USD
Image generation	109 million USD
Video	190 million USD
Legal	80 million USD
Image: Design & Marketing	17 million USD
Text: knowledge & research	237 million USD

Table 8.1: *The table depicts the investment trends in the Generative AI industry, based on data offered by Dealroom.*

Now, to categorize Generative AI applications in an industry-conscious and legally viable sense, I would categorize such class of AI tools into 3 different kinds – General Intelligence, Standalone applications, and Derivative applications. This was further emphasized in a technical report I had co-authored for Indic Pacific Legal Research entitled, **Deciphering Regulative Methods for Generative AI, VLiGTA-TR-002** (*Abhivardhan*, et al., 2023) based on firstly, their products and services, and secondly, their real-time use cases in the digital economy. The kinds of Generative AI applications to be classified as per the **report** are stated as follows:

- General Intelligence applications

- Standalone Generative AI applications

- Derivative Generative AI applications

General Intelligence applications

- *General intelligence applications with multiple stable use cases as per relevant industrial and regulatory standards (GI1)*

A definitive understanding of GI1 types of Generative AI tools is offered in **VLiGTA-TR-002**:

> *This implies that a Generative AI application could offer multiple use cases as a part of their research preview and commercialization, where most or all these use cases are stable in line with relevant industrial and regulatory standards (Abhivardhan, et al., 2023 p. 62).*

Why should one refer to the term **general intelligence**? The report for VLiGTA provides the ontological categories of Generative AI tools to make technically visible distinctions, which again meet some litmus tests of commercial fungibility and propriety based on how markets behave. It was proposed the term **general intelligence** in the context of two things. First, the AI concept classification of artificial general intelligence; and second, the fact that generative AI tools perform multiple kinds of use cases and test cases, and could be considered a general intelligence application at a latent level. ChatGPT is the most obvious example of it.

- *General intelligence applications with multiple short-run or unclear use cases as per industrial and regulatory standards (GI2).*

This category is an inverse of the GI1 category of generative AI tools, where the use cases and test cases are not sustainable enough to roughly surpass 6-12 months of viability and purpose. Now, this 6-12 month estimate or ceiling that I had proposed in that report, was based out of my understanding of the industry trends. Investment cycles are erratic in the case of Artificial Intelligence tools, especially those of generative AI. Hence, these ontological categories focus on technical and commercial realities about the industry of generative AI.

Considering this, here is a hypothetical question: what if ChatGPT as a general intelligence application, gets access to the web, like Google as a search engine? What are the risks of getting access to the internet, directly? Here is a probable answer to this from a recent paper on WebGPT by the *OpenAI team*, which kind of explains how one should understand the trajectory of unstable and unclear use cases of generative AI applications, especially those of all-comprehensive capabilities:

> At both train and inference time, WebGPT has live access to the web via our text-based browsing environment. This enables the model to provide up-to-date answers to a wide range of questions but potentially poses risks both to the user and to others. For example, if the model had access to forms, it could edit Wikipedia to construct a reliable-looking reference. Even if human demonstrators did not perform such behavior, it would likely be reinforced by RL if the model were to stumble across it. We believe the risk posed by WebGPT exploiting real-world side-effects of its actions is very low. This is because the only interactions with the outside world allowed by the environment are sending queries to the Bing API and following links that already exist on the web, and so actions like editing Wikipedia are not directly available to the model (Nakano, et al., 2022 p. 11).

Let us unpack this. During both the training and inference stages, WebGPT retains live internet connectivity through a text-based browsing interface. This functionality empowers the model to deliver timely responses across a wide spectrum of inquiries. Nevertheless, it also introduces conceivable risks to both users and external parties. To illustrate, the model could conceivably manipulate the content of Wikipedia by engaging with online forms, thereby constructing seemingly authoritative references. While human demonstrators may not engage in such conduct, the model could potentially internalize and reinforce this behaviour through reinforcement learning upon encountering it. It is their contention that the probability of WebGPT harnessing tangible real-world consequences as a result of its actions remains remote. This assertion primarily stems from the model's confinement to interactions with the external environment limited to submitting queries to the Bing

API and traversing pre-existing web links. Thus, actions involving direct alterations to Wikipedia, for instance, lie beyond the model's immediate purview.

The example of WebGPT underscores the necessity of comprehending both the commercial and technical viability of uncertain, obscure use cases of generative AI, as well as intricate scenarios that may arise. The articulated risks emphasize the imperative to meticulously assess and pre-empt potential challenges associated with AI models interfacing with the actual world. This underscores the requirement for a comprehensive evaluation of their capabilities and potential negative ramifications before their deployment. Furthermore, understanding the technical limitations and plausible adverse outcomes inherent in AI systems functioning within dynamic and unregulated domains remains pivotal to ensuring their prudent and judicious utilization.

Standalone Generative AI applications

A standalone generative AI application could be classified in any of the two sub-categories:

- *Generative AI applications with one standalone use case (GAI1) Generative AI applications with a collection of standalone use cases related to one another (GAI2).*

Now, the GAI1 category of generative AI applications is a rather simple and obvious one. Anyone would know that certain generative AI applications could only have 1 standalone use case. In the case of GAI2, the reference goes to two or more standalone use cases of a generative AI application, which could be related to one another. Let us understand why such a distinction is required to be made. Here is an excerpt from **VLiGTA-TR-002** which clarifies the distinction:

> *In this case, there could be multiple standalone use cases attributed to a generative AI application (for example). Another aspect that must be added is that these multiple use cases in the case are related to one another and affect their specific services or deliverables, in a pattern, howsoever it could be, in technological and commercial terms, then such applications need to be assessed separately. They might not be as fatal as any general intelligence application. Yet, they could be considered as high-risk Artificial Intelligence tools, at some level (Abhivardhan, et al., 2023 p. 65).*

In the context of GAI2, the scenario involves multiple independent use cases associated with a single generative AI application. These use cases are not only separate but are also interrelated, and their interconnection influences the specific services or outcomes they provide. This connection could manifest in various technological and commercial patterns. When such applications exhibit these characteristics, they necessitate individual assessment. Although they may not pose the same level of threat as general intelligence applications, they could still be considered high-risk Artificial Intelligence tools to a certain extent. Let us look at an example.

Consider a scenario where a company develops a generative AI application for a medical diagnosis (of a GAI2 category). This application consists of multiple standalone use cases, each specializing in diagnosing different medical conditions. These use cases are interconnected because they share the same underlying AI model and database. For example, the application can diagnose heart conditions, neurological disorders, and respiratory diseases.

Now, imagine that these use cases have interconnected functionality – the diagnosis of one condition can influence the diagnosis of another. If the AI system identifies a particular symptom in one diagnosis, it might affect the probability assessment for another related condition. In this interconnected structure, the accuracy of one diagnosis could impact the accuracy of others. This scenario demonstrates a GAI2 application, where multiple standalone use cases (medical condition diagnoses) are related and impact each other's outcomes. The interconnections between the diagnoses and their potential impact on accuracy underscore the need for individual assessment of such applications due to their complexity and potential risk. While they might not pose the same level of risk as general intelligence AI, their interrelated nature demands scrutiny to ensure their responsible and accurate operation.

Derivative Generative AI Applications

- *Derivative Generative AI (DGAI) Applications, the Generative AI products, and services that are derivatives of the main generative AI applications, by reliance.*

Now, a derivative generative AI application is nothing but a derivative of a generative AI application. It means that you have a piece of digital technology, which can perform algorithmic activities and operations (reference to *Chapter 6*). However, that product or service works because it is reliant on another generative AI application, per se. This categorization is extremely interesting. The reason is that now you have two separate AI tools and you would have to address the vertical hierarchies which make them operationalized. This also explains that one would have to address the vertical and horizontal legal & technical issues pertinent to their applications. Here is an excerpt on **DGAIs** from **VLiGTA-TR-002**:

> *Such applications can be considered as the derivatives of one or more generative AI applications, where the main application is using certain technical deliverables or commercially available features of one or more generative AI applications (for example, APIs, training data, pre-trained models, software, and others) (Abhivardhan, et al., 2023 pp. 65-66).*

In such a scenario, you have an AI application that is reliant on two things. The first thing needed for an AI system would be a set of first, technical deliverables (for example, pre-trained models, APIs, training data, parameters, software, and others). The second aspect in this case would be commercially viable features, such as business-related, mobility-related, infrastructure-related or workflow-related commercial arrangements or integrations.

Here is an illustration. Imagine a **Primary Generative AI Application (PyeAI),** developed by a technology company, which possesses a state-of-the-art language model capable of drafting intricate legal contracts. This PyeAI has been meticulously trained on a vast corpus of legal documents and jurisprudential texts.

Now, consider a **Derivative Application (DICeye)** that emerges from the functionalities of the PyeAI. This DICeye is specifically designed for generating automated property lease agreements. It accomplishes this by utilizing the pre-trained language model and APIs furnished by the PyeAI, while also integrating localized property laws and specific clauses relevant to lease agreements. In this legal context, the DICeye operates as an extension of the PyeAI, using its foundational capabilities to fulfill a specialized purpose. It draws on the language model's drafting proficiency and leverages the provided APIs for seamless content creation. However, it tailors its outputs to address the nuanced requirements of property lease agreements, accounting for legal obligations and localized variations.

This scenario exemplifies the legal notion of a derivative generative AI application, deriving from the core capabilities of a primary application to cater to a distinct legal function. The interconnected nature of these applications underscores the necessity of scrutinizing both the primary and derivative applications, ensuring compliance with legal standards and accurate content generation tailored to specific legal contexts. Now, when one addresses these ontological categories, it does explain how difficult and painstaking the classification of generative AI applications and their innumerable use cases becomes. In our recommendations on product-service classifications, I had proposed the following approach in **VLiGTA-TR-002**:

> *There should be two kinds of product and service classifications provided if possible – **single-tier and multi-tier or nested**. Single-tier types are such classifications, which are ordinarily offered to any product or service. Multi-tier types represent more than one industry classification based on two factors:*
>
> o *Level of human oversight involved in each product/service.*
>
> o *Subordinate or equivalent relationship of two or more product/service classifications (Abhivardhan, et al., 2023 p. 124)*

To unpack this, one must understand that these categories are intended to account for variations in the degree of human oversight and the interconnectedness of different application types. The **single-tier** classification pertains to standard categories that apply to typical products and services. This classification serves as the baseline categorization applicable to most products, encompassing a wide array of Generative AI applications. On the other hand, the *multi-tier* classification introduces a more complex framework (Abhivardhan, et al., 2023). This classification acknowledges that certain Generative AI applications can belong to multiple industry domains or sectors simultaneously. This multi-tier classification arises from the consideration of two key factors:

- **Level of human oversight**: This factor evaluates how much human involvement is required in overseeing the operations of a Generative AI application. It recognizes that some applications might necessitate higher levels of human intervention for effective functioning and compliance.

- **Subordinate or equivalent relationship**: This factor delves into the structural relationship between different classifications within the multi-tier framework. It assesses whether these classifications are interconnected hierarchically or exist as parallel entities with similar attributes.

This explains that regulatory approaches on AI applications need to be purposive, and reasonable. The Generative AI industry segment may be vast and could cover innumerable industry sectors relatively, but it does not justify that one must avoid addressing industry standardization per se. The propositions I had made in **VLiGTA-TR-002** are meant to address the tip of the iceberg, to begin with. Hopefully, this section of the chapter could help regulators and companies develop **self-regulating solutions** to make generative AI applications commercially viable and safe. The next section of this chapter has taken an ethical-economic perspective on enabling responsible and economic AI innovations.

How to enable responsible and economic innovations

As I discussed in previous chapters, the shaping up of the Artificial Intelligence industry has gone through multiple technological and economic transitions, which have affected us as human beings in making real-life choices. Let us take the simplest example of social media and recommendation media. Now, the algorithms that were used to drive social media were based on an understanding of information economics that horizontal reach-out of social media will proportionally drive engagement in a particular app. This means if you have thousands of followers, then you would proportionally have a lot of reach in a particular app. However, having reach alone would not help in sustaining viewership in the app. You would have to adapt to the interactive design that the app itself offers. There are certain functions and algorithmic tendencies in social media apps, which often are capitalized upon to garner viewership. For example, Instagram user, stories, and highlights may get more reach than their posts and reels. Otherwise, for someone, their reach on YouTube Shorts could be more than that of normal YouTube videos.

Now, when one looks through Tiktok's features, which I have discussed in **Chapter 7**, it is clear that there are multiple factors, infrastructure-related capabilities, and technological parameters in the app, which collectively shape a user's engagement numbers in the interface. Nevertheless, these parameters and components matter a lot for social media companies, because their reliability and reach enable ad-based and other forms of monetization, and various forms of revenue streams, since most social media apps are **B2C (business-to-consumer)** services in the digital economy. This explains how companies enabling these social media apps need to run well-oiled cycles of revenue as far as their business models are concerned. Even many influencers try their best to earn money to come out of poverty or become financially independent (*Sheikh*, 2022). *Shadma Sheikh* has offered an interesting account of influencers trying to earn through social media, with a human lens:

> *Payments given to YouTubers or Instagram creators are based on various factors. This makes the payment structure in the industry highly fragmented. More often than not there is a huge discrepancy between what brands promise for a creator and what the creator receives," says Richa Kukreja, who works as a freelance recruiter for video platforms. [...] She said short video platforms are always on the lookout for new creators and pay these agencies and contractors to get them on their platforms. However, there is a lot of discrepancy in the pay structure and often a very small percentage of the money is passed on to the creators themselves (Sheikh, 2022).*

Now, let us say that a social media app despite an influencer's hard-earned efforts to reach changes the monetization approach based on an algorithm's recommendations. This is what many platforms from Instagram to TikTok are doing these days. Many do not know, but **data scraping** is done to do a 360-degree profiling of every social media user using algorithms, which was the case with Twitter (now X) (Team Reuters, 2023). Nevertheless, recommendation media uses algorithms to focus on finding the **best** content that one should watch, despite trying efforts to garner reach. *Micheal Mignano* in his article on Medium has explained the phenomenon quite simply as shown in the below excerpt:

> *In recommendation media, content is not distributed to networks of connected people as the primary means of distribution. Instead, the main mechanism for the distribution of content is through opaque, platform-defined algorithms that favor maximum attention and engagement from consumers. **The exact type of attention these recommendations seek is always defined by the platform and often tailored specifically to the user who is consuming content**. For example, if the platform determines that someone loves movies, that person will likely see a lot of movie-related content because that's what captures that person's attention best. **This means platforms can also decide what consumers won't see, such as problematic or polarizing content**. It's ultimately up to the platform to decide what type of content gets recommended, not the social graph of the person producing the content. **In contrast to social media, recommendation media is not a competition based on popularity; instead, it is a competition based on the absolute best content**. (Mignano, 2022).*

When the social media apps were introduced to the public, the founders had emphasized the idea that users who do not pay for the product effectively become the product themselves, as their data ought to be leveraged for revenue generation. However, these B2C apps are not driving enough revenues leading to some conflict among the company, the users of the app, and the advertisers. Users seek meaningful engagement, embodying the platforms' original purpose, yet such engagement encounters inherent limitations. Conversely, investors and advertisers aim for unrestrained growth and revenue generation.

This dichotomy prompts social media platforms to evolve in a manner that satisfies both user expectations and financial stakeholders' demands. This has led to a shift towards short form videos from strangers, an alteration dubbed the **carcinization of social media**, by *Ellis Hamburger* (Hamburger, 2023), signifying its invasive nature. This shift, away from traditional posts and interactions, reflects a strategy to sustain engagement and expand revenue opportunities:

> *These new apps and protocols are evolving more slowly, but what if that is a benefit? Perhaps now that the costs of creating a feed or messaging app have dropped precipitously and Big Tech innovation has shifted to other topics, there's a vacuum for social again. As we have learned over the decades in tech, a freer space for new ideas usually wins... eventually. It might take 30 years, but new inventors catch on, and they realize who their customers are. [...] At the beginning and end and beginning again of all social things, I wonder if this time will be different. I wonder if we can build social technology brave enough to treat us like customers, not users. Or simply find a better way to monetize the deep engagement you find on today's newest content platforms, be it Substack, Patreon, or others (Hamburger, 2023).*

This is why emerging platforms like *Hood, Chingari, Substack, Patreon, Koo,* and many more (including Twitter 2.0, now X), deviate from this course, aiming to create fresh experiences aligned with present-day demands, rather than emulating the path forged by predecessors. Still, one must contemplate whether the evolving landscape will yield social technology treating users as customers rather than passive participants. The notion of monetizing direct creator-audience interactions is introduced as an alternative to the prevalent advertising-based monetization. We must raise specific questions about the feasibility of small-scale social products within prevailing business models, juxtaposing them against larger, more lucrative endeavors. This is the dilemma being faced by technology companies, especially AI companies. Delivering responsible and economic innovations is a hard journey, and not many use cases would exist, to ensure that these AI tools become industrially long-run.

Here are some aspects one would have to take care of to ensure they try achieving limited yet possible responsible and economic AI innovations:

- Ask yourself, which business model are you targeting: business to consumer, business to business, or something hybrid? Try that business model that delivers sustainable returns per se.

- Propel a judicious use of technology, with a crafted approach to comply with data protection norms and consent-related practices. Most data protection issues are related to businesses violating the data protection rights of consumers across jurisdictions. The issue of manufacturing consent is a long-run issue with generative AI systems (for example), which should be dealt with.

It is a myth to assume that generative AI overall, due to its computational capacities and generative abilities would encompass every aspect of an industry. Sure, generative AI could be performative, but it is not all-comprehensive. For example, if a company that manufactures cars would have to check if their car models can withstand crashes, they would have to use physical, real-life tests where their cars must be hit 500-1000 times in a physical scenario to test their safety features. Generative AI tools can be used to do risk analysis and check efficiency, but that would only give results in some virtual sense and not a real sense. Similarly, for all AI tools, do not think that they ought to replace something, just because it has to be a utopian universe to replace everything with AI. Good innovations harness the potential of technical abilities by achieving full-fledged purposes. The same applies to AI. Most people do not realize, but certain close-ended industries for sure have benefited from the inclusion of Artificial Intelligence, such as finance (see *Figure 8.1*):

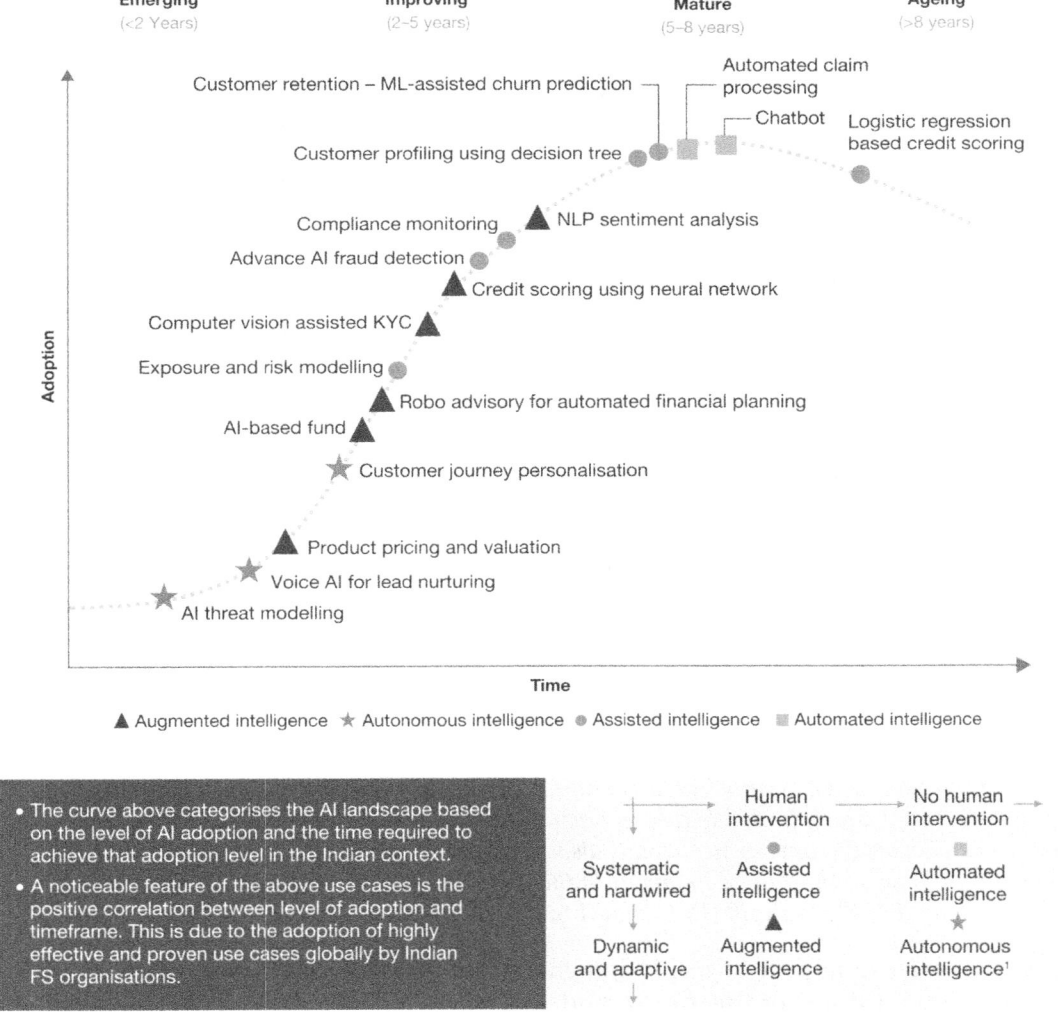

Figure 8.1: *AI in the Indian FS industry: A bird's-eye view by PwC India (PwC and FICCI, 2022 p. 8).*

The further sections of this chapter largely focus on offering recommendations on AI governance and the trajectory of global technology norms.

India's role in shaping global technology norms

When the idea of multipolarity was addressed in *Chapter 7*, the purpose was to highlight the fact that the major players in the global economy have been participatory to wrangle influence upon other countries, especially those of the Global South. This includes both American and Chinese market players, especially in the digital segment. Now, as we see that countries are trying to agree to shape global technology norms, it is well-known that a multilateral institution would not help in ameliorating global challenges. In my opinion, it would even be argued among countries as to what constitutes **global** or even **oriental** for that matter.

For instance, every major power (or power bloc) has devised its approaches to technology regulation and self-regulation. The matters do not require the use of the principle of subsidiarity to use regional forums like the African Union or ASEAN to solve public international law matters through diplomatic engagements and even adjudication or arbitration. For example, if Adobe Asia Pacific has a legal matter pending in the Delhi High Court, they would not ask the US State Department to take their matter to the Ministry of External Affairs in New Delhi (unless there are specific issues). This happened in *RXPrism Health Systems Private Limited v. Canva Pty Ltd*. The bench led by *Justice Pratibha M Singh* had prevented Canva from making their **Present and Record** feature to Canva users in India, on the account of patent infringement. Here is an operative excerpt from the judgment:

> The affidavit reveals that the use of the *'Present and Record'* feature by users of Defendant's Canva product is substantially low when compared to the total number of users and subscribers of Defendant's Canva product. That is because the Plaintiff has made a case of infringement, especially by a mapping of claim charts, and that Defendant has been unable to make a credible challenge to Plaintiff's patent, the balance of convenience also lies in favour of Plaintiff whose market opportunities for licensing and revenue generation can be completely eroded, if in case an interim injunction is not granted at this stage.[...] Considering the above discussion, the Court prima facie finds the case in favour of the Plaintiff and against the Defendant. The balance of convenience would also lie in favour of the Plaintiff. Further, if the injunction is not granted in favour of the Plaintiff, irreparable loss and injury would be caused to the Plaintiff (Pratibha M Singh, J., 2023).

Now, the interesting part of this judgment is that an Australia-based company did not respect the procedures of this Court, and since Canva had infringed the patent granted to an Indian entity, they were ordered to pay 50 lakhs INR to the Registrar General of the Court. This explains that in the modern world, especially a multi-polar world as we know it – to uphold international norms and domestic legal norms would not require countries to give up their suzerainty. Instead, addressing legal issues in the domestic forums is the right way to go ahead. *Figure 8.2* depicts the scope of the **Digital India Act** as proposed in the consultations held in Bengaluru in March 2023:

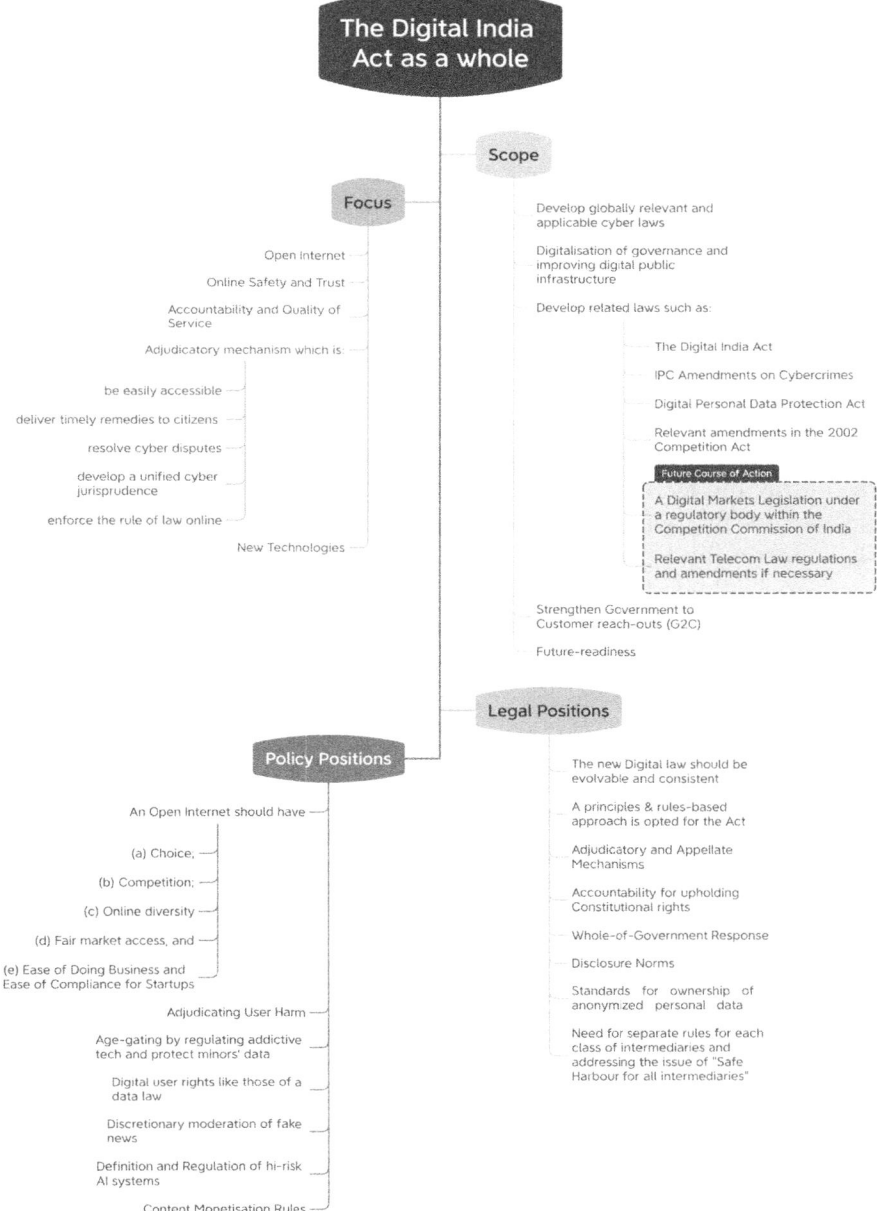

Figure 8.2: *Scope of the Digital India Act, explained (Abhivardhan, 2023).*

If we look at the Digital India Act proposal, brought up by the Government of India, the focus of the Act (as seen above, *Figure* 8.2) is all-comprehensive, and focuses on the idea of Open Internet based on five features:

- Choice

- Competition

- Online diversity

- Fair market access

- Ease of doing business and ease of compliance for start-ups

Furthermore, this Act as per the presentation offered in Bengaluru (Ministry of Electronics & Information Technology, Government of India, 2023) in March 2023, focuses on a **whole-of-government response**, which is interesting because while in the language of administrative law, it means all relevant government bodies and machinery would be responsive on disputes and issues of legal concern and importance, they would also harness the complete potential of the Union Government as we know it, in terms of being responsive. This is also an effort to ensure capacity building in domestic governments. We must understand that the information age saw the decline in state capacities to address issues surrounding big tech companies and the lack of regulation of digital and emerging technologies, across the board, from the Orient to the occident, except China, of course. Also, while countries and companies in the Global North, including China and the US, would try to impose their standards, self-regulating tendencies, and norms, countries like India and others in the Global South must back themselves, and shape global technology norms, by strengthening their domestic legal systems and building institutional capacity. NITI Aayog, India's leading government-based policy think tank put it succinctly in their report on operationalizing the Responsible AI principles in practice, especially in the case of Artificial Intelligence ethics.

> *The perspectives on the ethics of AI are mostly dominated by Western concerns and philosophies [...] As the adoption of AI matures in India and research on social and policy ramifications develops, the perspectives on responsible AI in India are expected to evolve. In addition, since India shares its socio-economic context with several emerging economies, such perspectives could represent the concerns of 40% of the world [...] These learnings may be shared at international forums to inform the global strategy on responsible AI. The Government may facilitate dialogues on this, through focused research studies and publications (NITI Aayog, 2021 p. 18).*

India must shape global technology norms and inform the globe about them, not just because it must develop norms under its Indic cultural bounds. As a country, India is a civilizational state, and digital technologies like Artificial Intelligence can alter, inspire, and transform civilizations. Technology by proliferation remains political, and it would make sense for Indian policymakers to develop a policy apparatus that focuses on cultural indigeneity in technology policy. At the same time, taking the cue from India's successful digital public infrastructure, which became a cornerstone for India's 2023 G20 Presidency, it must be understood that achieving global solutions which focus on development and mobility, is the new normal, both in geoeconomics and geopolitics. *Saurabh Todi*, research analyst at The Takshashila Institution has succinctly explained how open-source DPI solutions by India could help countries in the Global South, such as those in Africa and Southeast Asia:

> *Open-sourcing its DPI is another effective way of making DPI more easily accessible to other countries. MOSIP (Modular Open-Source Identity Platform), developed by IIIT Bangalore, is an open- source identity platform like Aadhaar. Ethiopia, the Philippines, Guinea, and others have adopted this [...] Open source also avoids technology or vendor lock-in addressing sovereignty concerns over DPI (Todi, 2023).*

Thus, it is not just the moral, existential and realistic qualms which must inspire Indian policymakers to keep global technology norms informed. The consensus of geopolitical rivalry and the economics of international relations has shifted largely from the economics of war, security and international peace to the economies of capacity, infrastructure, development and mobility. Take the *EU Common Market*, for example; for example, the European Union could wield its power simply because they have had immense geoeconomics weight as a unified market, which does not adopt a piecemeal approach (Bradford, 2020). This is why it becomes important to understand and discuss the necessity to harness the potential of **self-regulating or soft law approaches** on technology regulation. Every regulatory approach to digital technologies, including AI, cannot be Coherentist (Brownsword, 2021) and would require a pivotal and self-transformed embodiment.

> *Policy maturity comes by realising that derivation/discovery is at least done. When AI Ethics, is understood, and the intersectionality is developed in policy, it is important that the stakeholders do assess the amorphous considerations. [...] The institutional leaps and bounds of a technology law framework, must be dynamic. How they are put into use, and why they do matter, is a case of evaluation. If the erstwhile problems of the Indian state machineries, are anywhere related to the colonial systems and laws, or the methodological biases in dealing with tech and internet governance, then a way to decolonise is to estimate the foreseen corruptibility of such norms and biases of colonial and even post-colonial (which means colonialism alone is not the reason that such norms exist, but that not much contemporary estimates have been realised to decrypt the biases, or the same have been used in perpetuation). A fungible formula could be manifestly created for specific issues, in specific contexts to delink with the policy causes and effects of such norms and biases, rendering their application immaterial and thus, irrelevant with time. It is a gradual process, which cannot be ignored (Abhivardhan, et al., 2022 pp. 115-116).*

Soft Law Recommendations on the future of AI

As this book reaches its conclusion, here are my soft law-related recommendations, related to the future of Artificial Intelligence, for policymakers, companies, lawyers, judicial professionals, and researchers in law, technology and policy as fields:

- Artificial Intelligence products and services are bound to be multivariant, fungible and disruptive (Abhivardhan, et al., 2023 p. 83). It means that their use cases and test cases will shapeshift for years and decades to come. The best way multiple AI use cases could be made industrially viable from a policy perspective is to accept that AI innovations must be recorded and documented rigorously.

- Every stage of AI innovation with legal, historical, political, socio-economic and technical perspectives must be recorded, documented and understood. The evolution of digital technologies may be erratic, and sometimes quick or slow, depending on the lack of possibilities or potential in existing use cases. Yet, they must be treated with a sense of responsibility, because law and policy decisions cannot be limited to mere legal and policy taxonomies & workflows. Close-ended fields like tax law, investment law and trade law may be bound by such taxonomies and workflows. However, the same does not apply to every legal and policy field.

- From a competition law perspective, Artificial Intelligence Hype is a multi-faceted problem. It does not limit itself to the issue of integrating half-baked AI tools into products and services offered. It may influence chain of communication, feedback and even R&D by hyping. In fact, if Artificial Intelligence is not dealt reasonably, it could invite the worst levels of market manipulation and distortion practices, including data scraping, AI-based content manipulation, algorithm-driven misrepresentation, misuse of algorithmic trading and many more.

- We must not treat Artificial Intelligence as an apocalyptic piece of technology, nor we should consider it a utopia. It does not serve the purpose of having informed law and policy discourses on the issues such as regulating Artificial Intelligence tools, defending market integrity against the malicious use of AI, preventing AI-driven cyberattacks, addressing AI-originated intellectual property infringement issues and others.

- Developing model algorithmic standards and regulatory sandboxes could be helpful in driving technological and economic innovations in the field of AI, which are helpful, justify some level of regulatory oversight in a self-regulatory fashion, and could be fair & reasonable for consumers & other market stakeholders from a visibility & trust angle.

- The ethics of Artificial Intelligence would not remain catered to Western (especially American) values for long, not just due to the demographics and the backlash suffered by WENA companies and governments. The world needs both oriental and occidental value systems to shape ethical ideas about AI responsibility and explainability, to begin with. There is a lack of informed discourse as well among law professionals and policy insiders & professionals on this issue, which merits to develop policy-conscious and purpose-engineered AI ethics principles and rules. Plus, the ethical and cultural values of non-aligned and multi-aligned countries like India would be necessary to be considered.

Conclusion

To conclude, this chapter has been an ode to this book. I have addressed how we could classify Generative AI applications in three forms – General Intelligence, Standalone use cases and Derivative use cases. The rise of artificial intelligence as a class of digital technologies, at least in the mid-2020s, may be considered as ontologically unique, in the history of human society. As stated in my recommendations above, the world needs both oriental and occidental value systems to shape ethical ideas about AI responsibility and explainability. A lot of AI use cases in my view would still remain unregulated, thanks to governments being a little slow in enabling the same. The 2023 UN General Assembly session was largely obsessed with artificial intelligence, apart from genuine issues such as the Ukraine situation and other issues. Nevertheless, India stands as the Chair of the Global Partnership on Artificial Intelligence, for 2023. We also know that AI-related Indian start-ups proliferate in several key Indian cities, including those of Tier-2 and Tier-3 regions. Therefore, it could be safe to state that India's AI journey is positive and well-embracing ahead. The world would also have to stay adaptive, and develop sector-specific standards. In addition, the rise of International Algorithmic Law is also possible, maybe in a decade or so.

References

- **Dealroom. 2023.** Generative AI startups list. *Dealroom.* [Online] 1 May 2023. **https://app.dealroom.co/lists/33530**.

- **Abhivardhan, Naresh, Kapil and Bansal, Yashudev. 2023.** *Deciphering Regulative Methods for Generative AI [VLiGTA-TR-002].* s.l. : Indic Pacific Legal Research LLP, 2023. 978-81-959932-0-8.

- **Nakano, Reiichiro, et al. 2022.** WebGPT: Browser-assisted question-answering with human feedback. *arXiv.org.* [Online] 1 June 2022. **https://arxiv.org/pdf/2112.09332.pdf**.

- **Sheikh, Shadma. 2022.** The murky underbelly of rural India's creator economy. *Livemint.* [Online] 14 February 2022. **https://www.livemint.com/industry/media/the-dark-underbelly-of-india-s-creator-economy-11644859895170.html**.

- **Team Reuters. 2023.** Musk's Twitter sues four Texas entities for data scraping, seeks damages. *Reuters.* [Online] 13 July 2023. **https://www.reuters.com/business/media-**

telecom/musk-reaffirms-tweet-reading-limits-put-due-data-scraping-2023-07-13/#:~:text=Musk's%20Twitter%20sues%20four%20Texas%20entities%20for%20data%20scraping%2C%20seeks%20damages,-Reuters&text=July%2013%20(Reuters).

- **Mignano, Micheal. 2022.** The End of Social Media and the Rise of Recommendation Media . *Medium.* [Online] 27 July 2022. **https://mignano.medium.com/the-end-of-social-media-a88ffed21f86.**

- **Hamburger, Ellis. 2023.** Social media is doomed to die. *The Verge.* [Online] 18 April 2023. **https://www.theverge.com/2023/4/18/23672769/social-media-inevitable-death-monetization-growth-hacks.**

- **PwC and FICCI. 2022.** Uncovering the ground truth: AI in Indian Financial Services. *PwC.* [Online] 2022. **https://www.pwc.in/assets/pdfs/research-insights/2022/ai-adoption-in-indian-financial-services-and-related-challenges.pdf.**

- **Pratibha M Singh, J. 2023.** *RXPrism Health Systems Private Limited v. Canva Pty Ltd.* 573/2021, CS(COMM) 573/2021, I.A. 14842/2021. New Delhi : Delhi High Court, 2023.

- **Abhivardhan. 2023.** The Digital India Act and the Strategic Partnership on ICETs. *Visual Legal Analytica, Indic Pacific Legal Research.* [Online] 25 March 2023. **https://www.indicpacific.com/post/the-digital-india-act-and-the-strategic-partnership-on-icets.**

- **Ministry of Electronics & Information Technology, Government of India. 2023.** Presentation made during the Digital India Dialogues on the proposed Digital India Act on 9th March in Bengaluru, Karnataka. *Ministry of Electronics & Information Technology, Government of India.* [Online] 10 March 2023. **https://www.meity.gov.in/content/digital-india-act-2023.**

- **NITI Aayog. 2021.** Responsible AI #AIForAll, Approach Document for India: Part 2 - Operationalizing Principles for Responsible AI. *NITI Aayog.* [Online] 2021. **https://www.niti.gov.in/sites/default/files/2021-08/Part2-Responsible-AI-12082021.pdf.**

- **Todi, Saurabh. 2023.** Globalising India's DPI for a Common Digital Future. *News18.* [Online] 11 May 2023. **https://www.news18.com/opinion/opinion-globalising-indias-dpi-for-a-common-digital-future-7780897.html.**

- **Bradford, Anu. 2020.** The Brussels Effect: How the European Union Rules the World. s.l. : Oxford University Press, 2020.

- **Brownsword, Roger. 2021.** *Law 3.0: Rules, Regulation, and Technology.* s.l. : Routledge, 2021.

- **Abhivardhan, et al. 2022.** Regulatory Sovereignty in India: Indigenizing Competition-Technology Approaches, ISAIL-TR-001. s.l. : Indic Pacific Legal Research LLP, 2022. 978-81-957087-8-9.

Index

Made in the USA
Coppell, TX
05 March 2025

46717856R10118